The Climax of Liberal Politics

The Climax of Liberal Politics

British Liberalism in Theory and Practice 1868 – 1918

Michael Bentley

Senior Lecturer in History, University of Sheffield

Edward Arnold

© Michael Bentley 1987
First published in Great Britain 1987 by
Edward Arnold (Publishers) Ltd, 41 Bedford Square, London WC1B 3DQ

Edward Arnold (Australia) Pty Ltd, 80 Waverley Road, Caulfield East,
Victoria 3145, Australia

Edward Arnold, 3 East Read Street, Baltimore, Maryland 21202, USA

Bentley, Michael
 The climax of liberal politics: British liberalism in theory and practice, 1868–1918.
 1. Liberalism — Great Britain —
 History
 I. Title
 320.5′ 1′ 0941   JC599.G7
 ISBN 0-7131-6494-8

Text set in 10/11pt Plantin Compugraphic
by Colset Private Limited, Singapore
Made and printed in Great Britain
by Richard Clay plc, Bungay, Suffolk

Contents

List of Figures

List of Maps

Preface

Several streams in the author's experience find their confluence in this short examination of Liberal history. The need to fill an obvious hole in the literature about the subject supplied one disreputable stimulus. A sense of difficulty voiced by students trying to form a picture of Liberal history across a longer time-span than they usually encounter in studies of the Liberal party provided a second. Yet neither would have contributed more than a puddle in the absence of a third. For without my commission from the publisher to write an analytical survey of this kind, the book would never have begun to happen; and without his encouragement and patience it would unquestionably have run into the sands somewhere along the way. That he has had to wait too long goes without saying in these years of the New Austerity; but his extensions of credit only enhance my gratitude. In acknowledging a debt to the writing of other historians as a starting-point for one's own thoughts, the recognition likewise seems insufficient when the obligations incurred by any general account of a period must manifestly be great. The debt owed to my family mounts meanwhile with its cheerful inevitability − an account beyond recognition and forever overdrawn.

Michael Bentley
Sheffield, February 1987

Introduction

A man or woman born in 1848 – the year of European revolution – would have reached the age of political awareness in time to watch Gladstone reshape the character of Liberal politics after 1868. Such a person might then have experienced the years of crisis and division – the split over Ireland in 1886, the years of desperate survival through the 1890s – and still not have reached retirement when the Liberal party won its most resounding popular acclaim in the general election of 1906. Old age would then, however, have brought more head-shaking and regret than mere passage of time usually brings. Ideals and opinions that had hardened over a lifetime suffered the stress of a world war; and old Liberals watched everything they had venerated and themselves tried to represent drain away in the Britain of Baldwin. Within the span of a single long life, or more typically within two generations of Liberal enthusiasm, the British Liberal party had congealed into a major political power, enjoyed a period of unparalleled success, plunged into crisis in the mid 1880s, resurged as though by mass affirmation in 1906 and then broken into pieces at the hands of Falkenhayn, Hindenburg and Lloyd George. The doctrines that accompanied its career had also changed in trying to cope with various versions of modernity: socialism, empire, nationalism, depression, competition, militarism. To attach the party to its doctrines seems sensible, therefore, in a history such as this that seeks an overview of the liberal past during its most critical years.

Twenty years ago the objective would have retained a becoming modesty. The Liberal party then simply 'embodied' doctrines in a fairly straightforward sense and to write the history of one produced *ipso facto* a history of the other. In the atmosphere of the 1950s and early 1960s, an author could describe a 'Liberal tradition'[1] and leave the reader comfortable: indeed, any need for a book like this one would not have arisen. The situation changed markedly in 1966 when Liberal historians received simultaneous news of their subject's birth and death. For with the appearance of John Vincent's *The Formation of the Liberal Party 1857–68* and Trevor Wilson's *The Downfall of the Liberal party 1914–35*, two new polés of argument established them-

---

[1] Alan Bullock and Maurice Shock, *The Liberal Tradition from Fox to Keynes* (1956) is typical of the *genre*. Cf. S. Maccoby, *English Radicalism* (5 vols., 1955–61) and John Derry, *The Radical Tradition: Tom Paine to Lloyd George* (1967).

selves in the discussion of 'historic' Liberalism. Since then the period within and between the compass of those books has turned into a quagmire, deepest when viewed from the 1970s but still regularly churned in the eighties and particularly so in the years following the formation of the Social Democratic party. From a period of paucity punctuated by undemanding accounts, the postwar history of the years of Liberal supremacy and crisis between the ascendency of Gladstone and the coming of the First World War has evolved into a battle-ground for testing the mettle of a wide range of propositions, not merely about the nature of Liberalism but more fundamentally about the functioning of the British political system.

This revolution has brought in its train some unpleasant consequences for the general reader interested in politics or the serious student anxious to learn about Liberal history but unfamiliar with the period. An explosion in the volume of litera-ture now leaves the mind befuddled; and with the possible exception of British foreign policy in the 1930s, Liberalism in the late nineteenth and early twentieth centuries has occupied more space in academic books, articles and dissertations than any other subject in recent British history. Not only does the amount of material cause difficulty, moreover, but its conceptual level and technical sophistication also prove highly intimidating to those approaching accounts of the subject for the first time. Part of the purpose of this brief book lies, therefore, precisely in making the territory more accessible and signposting some of its more congested corners. Doing this in a white-coated way sounds attractive: many students would like nothing better than a clinical inspection of the material followed by a report on its lowest common factor. But the request confuses all that can be confused in historical discussion. We do not begin with 'the facts' because the facts are not there until somebody decides that they are; and the reason historians decide in the way they do depends in turn on the questions they have asked and their intelligence in trying to acquire evidence that answers them. Attempting a 'synthesis' of the positions taken by various schools of thought that have commented on the history of Liberalism makes no more sense than seeking an accommodation between the practices of a Baptist chapel and a Buddhist temple. Nothing less than a world-view comprises the frame in which images of Liberalism are set; nothing less than an acknowledgement of plurality will come close to an understanding of how the history of British Liberalism has reached paper.

The final chapter of this book will examine parts of that process in some detail, but pointing to some of its frictions may establish the width of the argument at the outset. To sketch the starting-points of very divergent arguments raises problems, admittedly, in leading the reader away from an interest in Liberals and Liberalism towards more abstract concerns raised by political history as an intellectual dis-cipline. Those interested in the story of Liberal politics could, therefore, proceed immediately to chapter one without pausing over the following impressions of half-a-dozen ways in which the project might be understood. Serious students and readers with an interest in the basis of disagreement about so much Liberal history may, on the other hand, find it helpful to consider for a moment the styles of argument to which the subject has in recent years tended to give rise, if only to sense the degree to which Liberal history has dimensions beneath its surface. Perhaps the complication comes out best in a few cameos of how the portrait often seems mounted.

The pietistic frame

In its simpler forms this amounts to little more than nostalgia for a great Liberal age when morals were Morals and men were Men. It suggests that individuals of the luminosity of Gladstone, Campbell-Bannerman and Asquith gave the age its special flavour and brought to Liberalism a distinction never achieved since. It sees in the Liberalism that they in their various ways practised a form of higher truth that has since been dragged down by the pressures of a less-worthy political environment. Naturally this frame of reference comprises an important element in modern Liberal self-imagery and plays some role in the history that party activists tend to write. Only a year before the publication of this book, the veteran Liberal politician Mr Jo Grimond asked modern Liberals to consider how 'disappointed' would have been the great classical Liberal thinkers – Mill, Acton, Dicey, Marshall, Keynes, Beveridge – with the present state of Liberal party policy; he looked back to 'the happy position of the party before the First World War when most people knew roughly what it stood for'; he looked to someone who could 'inject into politics something of Gladstone's fervour, humanity and breadth of vision', or at least the prudence of Lord Melbourne, 'another great Liberal'.[2] This is Sunday-school Liberalism and no more harmful than Conservative assumptions that the modern party bears some resemblance to that of Sir Robert Peel or Labour activists' attempts to demonstrate that they stand in the tradition of Keir Hardie.

Academics sometimes colour this view in a more subtle pastel wash. The reader may easily miss it altogether by not knowing in advance that historians who write about Liberalism are themselves often Liberals. Humanities departments in the universities comprise in the 1980s a powerful energy-centre for the Liberal party or the more recent Alliance and it is possible to discover in accounts of historic Liberalism a search for evidence that the party of the future has secure roots in a successful section of the Liberal past. There exists, for example, an 'official' history of the party written by an erstwhile candidate with an introduction by a former leader of the party.[3] Elsewhere the mood receives less overt stress but is present none the less. This is not to imply the concoction of cheap propaganda, and most certainly not to question the integrity and professional skill of historians of Victorian and Edwardian politics who happen also to be Liberals, but rather to draw attention to the way in which this period presents a *locus classicus* for what Oakeshott calls a 'practical past'. Modern Liberals want to disclose an historical Liberal party that does well in its great period against the challenges posed by twentieth-century conditions before a less great period undermines it. There is nothing wrong with that conviction, indeed a considerable quantity of historical evidence can be made available for its support; but assumptions are better stated than implied. A further feature of pietism needs mention, moreover, in its judgemental aspect. Those who seek heroes often find villains; and an important facet of the pietistic mentality lies in its willingness to blame individuals for the failure of authentic Liberalism (somehow defined) to survive. There are a number of candidates: Gladstone would win a few votes, Joseph Chamberlain more. Both pale beside the weight of Liberal condemnation heaped on Lloyd George whom many modern Liberals are still happy to blame for most of the present century's misfortunes.

[2] 'Jo Grimond looks at the state of the party now in the light of its days of glory.' See feature article on 'Reasserting Liberals' true values', *The Times*, 24 September 1986 and my reply, *ibid.*, 29 September. Cf. Ian Bradley's judgement on the post-Gladstonians: 'Not even their most ardent admirers would claim . . . that this admittedly talented generation of Liberals had the same faith in the human spirit as the generation of Gladstone.' *The Optimists: themes and personalities in Victorian Liberalism* (1980), 260.

[3] Roy Douglas, *The History of the Liberal Party 1895–1970* (1971), with a foreword by Jeremy Thorpe. For a more recent example – dedicated to David Steel – see George Watson, *The Idea of Liberalism: studies for a new map of politics* (1986).

The comparative frame

This is pietism seen in negative. The distinctiveness of period and territory fades against a more spacious background as America and Europe come also into focus. Not that comparative historians of Liberalism would denigrate the period's achievements or its personalities. Rather, they would prefer to juxtapose the Liberalism current in Britain against variants current elsewhere; and the result (like the unspoken intention) of this procedure is to make European or global forces the central causal influences in what made British Liberalism take the form it did. The presupposition is that history has to be understood in the round: all great historical phenomena have origins and ramifications that run beyond the boundaries of states. It follows that a sensitive history of Liberalism will need to confront the possibility that British experience merely re-enacted or refracted that of other countries or regions. This position is worth taking seriously because it comments helpfully on certain historical developments that contain a clear sense of linearity, such as the development and maturing of a capitalist system of economic production. But the protagonists of comparative history seem often to possess an inner vision of continuity between divergent histories as part of a (literal) *Weltanschauung* built on hopes that nationalism is an aberration and that the future holds something better for us all. Its authors have no more time for great countries than they have for great men; their hearts often belong to the EEC, the Third World and a conception of global Reason.

The danger of this perspective lies in the willingness, often eagerness, of its users to reduce all forms of historical discussion to a consideration of direction and process and a blindness to the individuated, the unique and the counter-thematic: a province in which even the pious have one eye. Little more need be said about the comparative approach for the moment since the first chapter of this book will consider the illumination it offers to historians of British Liberalism. The conclusion will emerge that it throws some light, but not much.

The ideological frame

This borrows fragments from the foregoing images: from the heroic, it abstracts the notion of a 'tradition'; from the comparative, it appropriates the idea of continuity across territory. But it is distinctive rather in the stress placed on Liberalism conceived as a bundle of recognizable and persistent ideas that have prowled around the western hemisphere over the last century looking for and finding a variety of homes. This frame of reference remains indifferent to the party- or group-base to which the ideas are referred: the centre of attention fixes on the ideas themselves and turns only as a second level of enquiry to the organized bodies that embody or represent them. In speaking of an ideological frame one is not, therefore, identifying a position that employs ideology whereas others do not. All positions taken in the discussion of Liberal history must of their very nature presuppose ideological assumptions. What distinguishes this position is rather a temptation to see ideas in some disembodied sense as central to the discussion and invulnerable to an analysis that questions their point of origin or the purposes that may have lain behind their announcement or rehearsal. To this degree, argument about the effectiveness of such an approach reflects a concern long evident to political theorists in their internal dispute over the status of a 'history of ideas' and the possibility of framing an account of political positions without embedding them in a precise context of time, place and intention.[4]

The functions of an ideological understanding of Liberalism have been two: to supply a rhetorical language for defectors; and to contribute to the core of a social-science discipline.

One way in which to claim consistency in a world dominated by change lies, after all, in representing politics as a series of abstract doctrines that float above the party *mêlée*. Politicians uncomfortable with the company they keep and intellectuals concerned to justify positions that appear eccentric use their connexion with a set of leading ideas to insist that everyone else has deviated while they have retained the higher loyalty. Among British Liberals the technique became evident in the days before 'party' hardened into its modern channels. Just as that process began in the 1830s, for example, Sir James Graham explained his defection from the Whigs as a form of resistance to change rather than a capitulation to circumstance.

> I obtained the representation of my native county . . . as a member of the Old Whig party, pledged to Parliamentary Reform, but the avowed friend of the Protestant Church Establishment, and the enemy of Ballot, short Parliaments, and all the nostrums by which the regal and aristocratic power is assailed. It is needless to advert to my secession from the Whigs. They retain the name, but, as I contend, have changed their principles. I retain my principles and am indifferent to the name.[5]

A similar sense of purity underlay some of the Whig defections to the Conservative party in the 1870s and 80s; and it strongly flavoured the rationale of ex-Liberals who moved across to Labour after 1914. They had remained Liberals (the argument ran) but the truly liberal party now called itself the Labour party. Stephen Spender's *Forward From Liberalism* (1937) made the same claim for socialism as an intellectual identity and saw the stance assumed by many young men on the Left as a natural extension of liberal ideals. The point about these various arguments lies not in their speciousness as forms of *ex post facto* justification but in their common representation of Liberalism as a commitment to certain identifiable doctrines and values which can be held from many different locations without prejudice to their nature, rather in the way that one might pull a collection of balloons by their strings from one place to another.

Under the title 'political theory', 'political philosophy' or 'the history of political thought', social science has taken to studying the balloons rather than their holders or the places where they stand. The procedure brings with it a substantial validating literature and there seems little need here to question its purpose: it is no less 'correct' to arrange the material in this way than in some other. What is interesting to a student of Liberalism is the division of the subject by the British intelligentsia into two areas of attention — the history of Liberal parties and the history of liberal ideas — determined not so much by the nature of the material as by the education of those who make the division. The ideological frame of reference for a study of Liberalism is what a student is most likely to learn in a Politics, Philosophy or Social Studies

[4] The location of much of this argument has been early-modern in its period but nevertheless has clear implications for modern historians of political ideas. For an introduction to this important discussion, one might begin with 'Political Thought and Political Action: a symposium on Quentin Skinner', *Political Theory* 2 (1974), 251–303 and progress to Howard Warrender, 'Political Theory and Historiography: a reply to Professor Quentin Skinner on Hobbes', *Historical Journal*, XXII (1979), 931–40.
[5] Graham to Stanley, 24 November 1837, quoted in Norman Gash, *Reaction and Reconstruction in English Politics 1832–52* (Oxford, 1965), 159n.

department of a university or polytechnic in Britain. Liberalism under this light becomes a series of persuasions about certain categories that have acquired benchmark significance in the history of political ideas: authority, freedom, contract, sovereignty, natural law, natural rights, justice, obligation. The method consists principally of analysing celebrated 'texts' in order to determine the attitude of major thinkers to these concepts; and for British Liberalism in the nineteenth century the *dramatis personae* would normally amount to the Utilitarians (concentrating particularly on John Stuart Mill) followed by the Idealists and particularly T. H. Green.[6]

The approach followed in this book will occasionally reflect the concerns of the ideological frame of reference, especially in the stress it will place on the change of attitude to the question of political sovereignty among Liberal thinkers after 1870. But the ideas current among Liberals will be tied into the working of the party structure to a degree unusual (and unwelcome) among theorists of ideology.

The economistic frame

No balloons here: the metaphors all point to bedrock and subsoil. 'Economism' amounts to a dated form of marxism that speaks the language of 'base and superstructure' and sees the economic domain as the point of origin for all political change. Modern marxists have transcended it, not least through the criticism of Gramsci.[7] But in this period of Liberal history it retains an audience that extends far beyond marxists to embrace labour historians of various denominations and supply the presuppositions for a *soi-disant* radical social history of Liberalism.

Highest among possible promontories in this image of the period after 1868 stands neither the peak of electoral performance in 1906 nor the coming of the First World War in 1914, so much as the peaking of the economy around 1873 and the implications of the long decline that followed. Whatever the superficial successes of Liberalism after Gladstone's first government of 1868–74, for the economistic historian the writing is already on the wall for the Liberal party once this fundamental economic shift has occurred. Competition from America and Germany will reveal the inadequacy of Britain's industrial base and in turn stimulate the awareness of the industrial working class; that awareness will translate itself into the aggression of the New Unionism in the 1880s and 1890s; the Independent Labour party of 1893 and the Labour party of 1906 will therefore establish a power base that a social democratic party cannot hope to overturn; and by 1914 the status of Liberalism as the reflection of an outmoded class structure will become evident. The commentary supplied on Liberal history from this perspective takes the form of an evolutionary language implying the direction of certain tendencies within capitalism to which the Liberal party and its ideas fall victim. Always the expression of a particular system of economic relations (and of a Protestant ideology reinforcing their rationale), Liberalism finds itself going the way of other European liberal groups in having no answer to the arrival of class politics and the presence of political interest-groups designed expressly to minister to the working class.

The present writer finds the assumptions behind this mode of history philosophic-

---

[6] A recent exception to this narrow reading of the subject is Anthony Arblaster's *The Rise and Decline of Western Liberalism* (Oxford, 1984) which examines Liberal ideology through a body of material that includes novelists, E. M. Forster for instance, and the members of the Bloomsbury Group.

[7] See Roger Simon, *Gramsci's Political Thought* (1982) for an introduction to economism and Gramsci's position about it.

ally stultifying and the conclusions arising from them unintelligent in face of the counter-evidence available. Yet in rejecting economism as a doctrine, it cannot be gainsaid that the significance of a new economic environment after the 1870s demands a location in any convincing portrait of the Liberal future. It certainly will not be ignored in this book.

The sociological frame

An increasing interest among the present generation of historians in situating political subjects in a social location goes some way towards explaining the currency of sociological explanations of Liberalism. In one sense the thought says nothing at all: political arguments plainly take some of their nature from the society that they affect. But the social interpretation of Liberalism goes further to suggest ways in which British politics changed significantly in the late nineteenth and early twentieth centuries because the nature of British society underwent important modification. The emergence of social class plainly figures in this sense of change but it does not dominate it; nor does the economy function as a catch-all explanation for social behaviour. Expressed as a shift in sociological perspective, the focus moves from Marx to Weber.[8] The town certainly plays a major part in this recasting because new urbanism after 1860 lies behind some of the value-structures and social displacements that this model would want to highlight. The presence of an artisanate with its eye on a first house; the reshaping of the workplace into a less personal environment as industry moves into larger units; the arrival of a lower middle class feeding on London; the drift away from organized religious observance to what was probably an unorganized yet still highly-significant sense of social morality: such elements and the stimulus they may have provided towards revision of political ambitions and proposals, receive more stress within this understanding of change than do economic and electoral statistics. At the level of parliamentary politics, similarly, the agenda records new priorities. The social background of various political agents – ministers, MPs, constituency activists – come under closer scrutiny than the legislation they promoted or their election manifestoes. Their connexion with business or the professions, their clubs, congregations and marriage partners, receive a more urgent consideration than their constitutional function. In chapter two of this book we shall use some of these axes to present a picture of the Liberal party's social complexion.

A further consideration lends this view of the period particular support. It lies in the range of evidence among the writings of Liberal intellectuals and politicians suggesting that sociological investigation often lay at the centre of *contemporary* awareness. Mayhew, Booth, Rowntree, and the Webbs come to mind, perhaps, before the more overtly Liberal social analysts of the period; but the work of Bosanquet, Hobhouse, Hobson, Masterman, Chiozza Money and many less notable individuals contributed to a stream of social criticism that had its source in a certain conception of Liberal society and which arguably surged into central channels of party behaviour and strategy.[9] This aspect of Liberal identity will appear at a number

[8] This shift of focus finds some reflection in the prelude to Peter Clarke, *Lancashire and the New Liberalism* (Cambridge, 1971), 3–24.
[9] From among a large literature one might single out here Stephan Collini, *Liberalism and Sociology: political argument in England 1880–1914* (Cambridge, 1979) and Michael Freeden, *The New Liberalism: an ideology of social reform* (Oxford, 1977), for their analyses of ways in which a sociological concern manifested itself in Liberal thought.

of points in this book, especially in chapters three and five which examine trends in Liberal theory, and in chapter seven which brings together some strands of theory and practice in Edwardian Britain. In part that response follows from the obvious importance attaching to social limiting-factors in the development of a plausible view of politics. But it also depends to no small degree on this writer's commitment to presenting political history as an account of contemporary consciousness.

The perceptual frame

The purpose of inserting this lens stems from its authenticity. We have available for this period a documentation unique in the breadth of its survivals. The late nineteenth century is recent enough to promise preservation across a wide spectrum of sources and free, until around the turn of century, from the distortion of the dictated letter or, far worse, the coming of the telephone. To a degree envied by the medievalist or early modernist, the historian of modern politics can construct a picture of the past as it partially appeared to those for whom it was the present. Doing so presents obvious dangers: the temptation to concentrate on an élite because the survivals bequeathed by that sector tend to prove richer and less ambivalent than those of other social levels; the risk, more seriously, of missing deep structural elements in the situation by remarking only on those aspects that reached the consciousness of contemporaries. Searching for a sense of *Verstehen* in the mind of one age, we possibly lose the opportunity for *Besserverstehen* reserved to the perspective of a later one. Yet the virtues of proceeding in this light seem to transcend its limitations. For the method accomplishes three crucial objectives: it distinguishes between human and animal status and rejects the reduction of human consciousness to a series of patterned responses; it permits the actors an openness of future that other methods tend to prohibit; and it offers an instrument that Karl Popper rightly urged on all historians – a means of evaluating the claims of conflicting hypotheses. In all history these merits seem desirable. In the history of so controversial an area as the one discussed here, they demand respect.

Where this rather theoretical position will appear in this book is in the perfectly bland reporting of what certain categories of source seem capable of showing. In trying to create the thought-world of Liberal intellectuals from their books and papers we shall not assume that its reference points replicated those of cabinet ministers. Nor shall we decide that 'objective' forces explain why politicians did what they did until their relics compel us to think so. Leaving historical actors to think badly, act inappropriately, behave stupidly, plan unseeingly and see myopically may not strike the reader as much of a concession on the part of posterity, but it remains surprising how few historians of Liberal politics seem willing to grant their Liberals that meagre privilege. Above all, this book will want to insist that Victorian and Edwardian Liberals thought their thoughts and hatched their strategies from within a framework of perception that changed more slowly than ministries and legislation but which nevertheless has a history. A brief outline such as this study can only hint at its content but an awareness of its presence will at least help make these fascinating people a little more real.

Each of these images, taken alone, presents nothing better than caricature. But in practice those frames never appear alone. One image becomes superimposed on another; a view of the period from one angle is superseded by a perception from a different one. Sometimes it helps understanding to acknowledge this sense of *collage* but also to remain aware of the components out of which the picture takes its form; and it is in this spirit that these images of Liberalism have their purpose. This book will look at most of them during its course in order to silhouette a facet of the whole, but the reader is entitled to know that the sociological and perceptual lenses strike this writer as the most effective in bringing British Liberalism into definition. If the book has a starting-point then these viewpoints best suggest it.

This still leaves unresolved a pressing question about method. One of the most difficult problems facing any author who wishes to communicate a complicated texture of ideas to a readership new to the period and its problems concerns the level of prior knowledge one ought to assume and possible ways of structuring the argument to make it more accessible than that usually offered by an academic monograph. These considerations have governed the principles on which *The Climax of Liberal Politics* has been constructed. Chapters one and two concern themselves with comparative and global questions and a body of raw data about the British Liberal party. The point of proceeding in this way lies in the hope that it may prove possible to begin with the less contentious areas of the subject and delay the introduction of the more difficult sectors of discussion until later. Needless to say, the result will have no claim to an 'agreed' history; but the subject-matter may give a student looking for a foothold in the material rather more confidence than the historiographical review contained in the last chapter. Chapters three to seven then analyse the period in a mostly narrative fashion in order to suggest the flavour of change over time in Liberal politics between the Gladstonian period and the disaster of the First World War.

These chapters progress also in difficulty because the variables contributing to Liberalism by the Edwardian period are both wider in range and more imponderable in their force (granted present awareness) than those that governed the heyday of 'individualist' Liberalism in the 1860s and 70s. The treatment will oscillate between the provinces of theory and practice – a strategic decision that reflects some underlying assumptions about the tenuousness of their mutual relation. It will become clear that theory's impact on 'practical' politics will be taken in this study to have been partial, subtle, time-lagged, encoded and sometimes beyond recovery through documentary evidence. It suits the working out of this position to consider the twin domains under separate illumination, except for the decade or so before the First World War when a rather more positively-charged climate of opinion and writing makes the separation problematic in an introductory book of this kind. Between them, these chapters investigating the evolution (or degeneration) of Liberalism present enough of the story to make intelligible the final chapter which selects three major areas of dispute in current argumentation among historians and political scientists and subjects the various positions taken about them to critical scrutiny.

Because so much of the contemporary discussion of 'theory' in social science seeks points of contact between the individual and the social, between 'agency' and 'structure', the tone of this book may seem more negative than its author would want, in a different climate, to imply. But the idea that theory prescribes practice in some direct and causal way within the British political system has too much life left in it to licence a simple description of life's imitating art.[10] Neither, and in the same breath, do cardboard cut-outs calculating their next step in personal advancement suffice as models for politicians, who could not avoid mixing their profession with fearful

[10]See Michael Bentley, 'Party Doctrine and Thought', in M. Bentley and J. Stevenson (eds.), *High and Low Politics in Modern Britain: ten studies* (Oxford, 1983), 123–53.

asymmetries in their experience, temperament, talent and mission.[11] Bringing these perceptions together must, for all the complications that follow, make more sense than treating them as moments of impatient scepticism better forgotten at the study door. The objective behind this modest examination of Liberalism must therefore be that the reader will discover some perspectives about why the history of Liberalism has proved so fraught and come into contact with some of the many possible evaluations of the most powerful historic *bloc* to appear in Britain's political history before the coming of the Left as a central determinant of parliamentary politics. Both the perspectives and the evaluations demand from the reader a certain persistence; but then, beware the writer who makes this subject sound easy.

[11]J. P. Parry has, for example, recently argued for the reassertion of 'ideas' and 'prejudices' as keys to understanding Liberal politics: 'a closer attention to the intellectual setting in which political activity took place is a necessary precondition for an understanding of the interest which politics evoked, the anxieties which is aroused, and the consequences of those anxieties for future developments.' See J. P. Parry, *Democracy and Religion: Gladstone and the Liberal party 1867–75* (Cambridge, 1986), 3. Cf. the same author's review article, 'High and Low Politics in Britain', *Historical Journal*, XXIX (1986), 753–70.

1

The View from Mars

Historical writing should not – cannot – begin with 'the facts'. Assumptions and questions plainly come first: they construct the net that culls what seems relevant in the sources. But it seems persuasive nevertheless that some questions permit straightforward and widely agreed answers; and to this minimal extent, it may assist the clarity of this introduction to nineteenth-century Liberalism to begin with the uncontentious if only because, by the end of the book, doubts will germinate in the mind of the reader over the possibility of saying anything at all about the subject that does not provoke several kinds of challenge. To identify those parts of the discussion that may allow a smoother passage is far from easy, however, since the 'simple' questions frequently lead directly towards unexpected difficulty. 'What *was* Liberalism?', may strike someone new to the period as a reasonable question to ask at the outset. It is in fact an invitation to shoot Niagara. The answer to it will appear in this book only as a cumulative impression or encoded message throughout the text. 'How important was Gladstone?' 'Why did the Liberal party collapse?' These innocent queries conceal an evil worthy of Moriarty; they will come into focus only in the later chapters. It may prove possible, on the other hand, to consider immediately two perspectives that will help suggest a framework for discussion. One of them asks (as historians of British Liberalism rarely do) about the distinctiveness of Liberalism in the United Kingdom in the nineteenth century compared with the experience of the western world generally. The other draws attention to some accessible (and theoretically quantifiable) characteristics of the Liberal party during the years that will become our centre of concern. Little attempt will be made at this stage to develop these points because, in a very real sense, the rest of the book may be read as a gloss on them.

Standing as far away as Mars may seem extravagant. But the global embodiments and resonances of Liberalism need some acknowledgement, not least because comparative historians use the notion of process to *explain* British Liberalism as a function of others. It is often argued, for example, that the failure of continental countries to sustain their forms of liberal politics in itself provides evidence for the view that British Liberalism would also run into extreme difficulty because each 'liberalism' is depicted as the clone of a central evolutionary development. The thesis frequently has an economic dimension and argues that the industrial dislocations and initiatives of the late nineteenth century supply one common thread in the texture of all liberalisms. Each country produced a different history for its brand of liberalism to the extent that it needed to adapt its economic processes to the regime operating there.[1] Those regimes can themselves be seen as part of the common weave, more-over, as in Arno Mayer's theory of the pre-1914 *ancien régime*, which he portrays as 'a distinctly pan-European phenomenon'. Looking back from the First World War, Mayer discerns 'the first and protogenic phase of this general crisis [in] the latter-day remobilization of Europe's *anciens régimes*. Though losing ground to the forces of industrial capitalism, the forces of the old order were still sufficiently wilful and powerful to resist and slow down the course of history, if necessary by recourse to violence.'[2] In both these styles of discussion the history of British Liberalism becomes an aspect of European life-cycles.

Nor need the examination remain inside the bounds of Europe. The period examined in this book was one dominated by expansion into distant areas of the globe and by the consolidation of empires. In the New World, America demonstrated a liberalism of a kind, Canada a rather different one. Australia had many points of contact with British Liberalism while giving rise to a highly-distinctive political structure. It follows that any location of liberalism will prove partial unless it makes an effort to traverse the world. The complexity of liberalism means, furthermore, that the trip will be pointless if it proves no more than a travelogue: some delimitation of the field and separation of its elements seem advisable.

Judging from the tenor of modern political writing and debate, it appears that literate and politically aware Europeans carry in their mind some conception of Liberalism which at least enables the word to strike a chord of recognition. It remains the case that there are almost as many meanings as Liberals. Sharpening these many images for the purpose of celebration or exorcism has preoccupied historians, states-men and social theorists since the American and French revolutions of the late eighteenth century. And because radically diverse political parties, each arrogating to itself the Liberal virtues in essence if not in name, have entrenched themselves in the western democracies, so has the task deepened in its difficulty. After two centuries of 'Liberal' experience, indeed, the most that can be said about the various versions is that the observations on which their evocation depends usually reduce to one of three types of statement. The first of them assumes that liberalism has a small 'l' and draws attention to a supposed canon of political axioms and recommendations about (say) the protection of the liberty of the individual from the depredations of governments and other individuals, or the promotion of unhindered commerce and trade between nations, or the importance of equal opportunity within the social system. Statements that fall into this category survive all attempts to render them counterfeit. It is no use demonstrating that 'liberals' of one kind or another have disbelieved or infringed them at various points in space and time: these statements are not intended to report a state of affairs but rather to indicate how a liberal world might be made if everyone could be persuaded to behave rationally. The second connotation works in reverse fashion by beginning with the world and its institutions. Here the word starts with a capital letter and is a form of plural noun that suggests a shorthand description encompassing the activities and utterances of people who think of themselves as Liberals and support Liberal parties. Recalling Herbert Morrison's remark that

---

[1] Norman Stone, *Europe Transformed 1878–1919* (1983), 16 and *passim*. Professor Stone's striking and influential book may be read as an attempt to situate all European politics in a common evolutionary process.

[2] Arno J. Mayer, *The Persistence of the Ancien Régime: Europe to the Great War* (1981), 4.

socialism is what the Labour party does, 'Liberalism' is, on this reckoning, as Liberal does. Between and beyond these perceptions there lies, however, a third – one that contains most of the central resonances of modern Liberal discourse. It assumes that Liberalism is neither simply a doctrine nor a description of political behaviour but rather a way of expressing the relationship between great ideas and the attempts of individuals and institutions to embody and realize them. It is at once a description of the world and an identity that transcends it. Its theorists spend their lives in a confrontation with reality. Its practitioners cannot escape a conversation with eternity. This book will want to say something about both.

Democracy, nationalism, capitalism

The intellectual background of nineteenth-century confrontations and conversations rarely reached back more than a century. Of course, one can press the 'origins' of Liberalism backwards as far as any society that demonstrates a streak of values which Liberals deem civilized, or that individuated view of the world on which they normally rest. The Renaissance, the Reformation, the scientific revolution of the seventeenth century: there is no shortage of plausible catalysts. Certainly it makes sense to locate in some such way the preconditions for a style of social thought that wishes to conceive of 'society' as something less real than the units that comprise it. But the generation that came to maturity in the second half of the nineteenth century inevitably felt aware of more recent and spectacular reference-points of which at least two, the idea of democracy and the force of nationalism, had impinged on the most brackish consciousness. Both slogans had become shrill during the American revolution and the war of independence from Britain between 1776 and 1782. They had reappeared in an even more menacing or inspiring way in the cataclysm whose heat still impressed itself on writers a century later. For the French revolution of 1789 and the Napoleonic empire that followed became bench-marks for political discussion among the European intelligentsia until the First World War – a persistent reminder of the power of people who lack a voice, an indication of what must surely come to other countries unless their Liberals led them to safety.

Safety did not, for most Liberals, amount merely to capitulation in face of the mob. Indeed the diversion of democracy often preoccupied them more than its promotion. In the American case the problem had largely solved itself because a unique configuration of race, territory and class allowed the Founding Fathers a degree of liberal bravado which sympathizers in Europe could hardly emulate in the wake of Napoleon. 'The generation which commences a revolution,' Thomas Jefferson wrote to John Adams in 1823, 'rarely completes it'. He had Europe in mind and he had no doubt that the completion would come. 'Habituated from their infancy to passive simulation of body and mind to their kings and priests, they are not qualified when called on to think and provide for themselves . . . . But as a younger and more instructed race comes on, the sentiment becomes more and more intuitive . . . . In France, the first effort was defeated by Robespierre, the second by Bonaparte, the third by Louis XVIII and his holy allies: another is yet to come, and all Europe, Russia excepted, has caught the spirit; and all will attain representative government, more or less perfect . . . . To attain all this, however, rivers of blood must yet flow, and years of desolation.'[3] People living in the anticipated path of the rivers of blood

[3] Quoted in Saul K. Padover, *Thomas Jefferson on Democracy* (New York, 1939), 21.

naturally took a more circumspect view. Everyone could agree about castigating distant and detested Russia whose tsarist autocracy found few defenders among western Liberals. Yet Europe's most talented observer of American democracy in the nineteenth century turned out to be a Norman aristocrat who saw little to relish, either, in the onset of a revolutionary democracy. The point of Liberalism lay, for a man like Alexis de Tocqueville, not in imposing equality between individuals in a society but rather in maximizing the liberty, somehow defined, of each:

> There is certainly a virile and legitimate passion for equality which spurs every man to desire strength and esteem, which tends, indeed, to raise small men to the level of the great. But there is also to be met with in the human heart a depraved taste for equality, which induces the weak to desire to humble the strong, which brings men to prefer equality in slavery to inequality in freedom.[4]

Indeed, the spokesmen of European Liberalism, among whom the Frenchman de Tocqueville and the Englishman John Stuart Mill had acquired pre-eminence by mid century, valued the rejuvenating effects of a society whose citizenry exerted a major influence on their government, while not necessarily valuing mechanical devices such as the one-man one-vote system of election recommended by democratic agitators. In Rousseauan fashion they looked to a concept of consent that depended for its force on something wider than numerical majorities: Mill, in particular, worried about the injustices which a majority might visit on a less powerful segment of society. Their concerns focussed less on the mobilization of the masses, for whose intelligence and moral instinct they frequently expressed contempt, than on forms of government appropriate to various types of society. A fundamental question thus became, not 'Who should rule?' but rather, 'Within what framework should rulers be compelled to act?' Representation took a lower place on the agenda, that is to say, than the securing of independence and responsibility within the executive or the buttressing of the rule of law. Always an important hesitation in the espousal of democratic theory, this instinct acquired even greater importance, moreover, in the half-century after 1848 when many European states moved towards an expansion of their suffrage while the American dream dwindled into the nightmare of Tammany Hall, caucus politics and executive corruption. Resisting the European urge towards democracy had led political élites throughout the continent into some embarrassment and difficulty in the first half of the century; but in the very charged atmosphere of late-nineteenth-century Europe it provoked far more – not least because the burgeoning of socialist movements and political parties in most developed states added a significant pinch of ginger to the situation's ingredients.

Another characteristic of popular politics occasioned no less discomfort. Not only had the crowd reminded political rulers of its power throughout Europe between 1789 and 1848, but its members had also instilled among the intelligentsia of the west a new conception of mass behaviour. It seemed that the century had given rise to a new sense of the nation, a new image of its citizens as a *Volk*. States that had yet to win independence from superior powers or which as yet struggled to achieve a homogeneous nationhood fused their liberalism with their nationalism. In Italy, in Germany, in parts of Scandinavia, in the British dominions of Canada and Australia, liberalism would come to play some role as a vehicle of national identity and self-determination. But the sheer volatility of this emotion – a residue from the period of *Sturm und*

---

[4] Quoted in Preston King, *Fear of Power: an analysis of anti-statism in three French writers* (1967), 23.

Drang – prevented it from becoming a consistent liberal formula during the second half of the century when different moods supervened. More thematic in that period turned out to be the rise of militarist Prussia and its presiding genius, Otto von Bismarck; the emergence of empire alongside the promotion of democracy; the rapid expansion of western Europe and America into less developed parts of the globe during the imperialist fever of the 1880s and 1890s; the creation of an intricate system of international alliances that lasted long enough to witness the collapse of all liberal hopes in the summer of 1914. In formal terms the response of President Woodrow Wilson to the diplomacy that helped precipitate the disaster of the First World War seems in retrospect the only possible 'liberal' response. But among the statesmen and intellectuals of Europe this response by no means appeared automatically among liberals for whom the word 'imperialist' had come to seem a compliment rather than a complaint. The generation after 1870 produced liberals who not only tolerated imperialism but who believed in and advanced its claims as part of the revised priorities suggested by what they took to be the requirements of a new and distinctive epoch.

Internal instability and external aggrandisement doubtless helped shape that sense of newness. A third context, still masked in 1850, only made its presence felt acutely during the last quarter of the century but its effects would nevertheless prove serious in the recasting of liberal doctrine. The point concerns the international economy and significant shifts in its balance after 1870. Until that time the ramifications of industrialism had profoundly affected the economy of only one country inside the western states system – that of Great Britain. But over the next 30 years, and at a bewildering rate of acceleration, economic opportunities and anxieties helped remould the strategies of America and Germany and revised the ambitions of France and Russia. North American wheat sat heavily on the quays of European ports; South American meat crossed the Atlantic in refrigerated ships; German steel and Scandinavian timber invaded the western fringes from an opposite direction. And of course these shifts brought with them an obvious challenge to the conventional (and often rigid) financial structures of western states. Liberal theory had in no small measure validated the operation of those structures – their trading procedures, their fiscal mechanisms, the relationship between capital and labour – and inevitably it came under searching scrutiny. In its prescriptions for internal harmony, for example, some urgent recommendations seemed necessary to cope with 'the city' as a concept and its faceless inhabitants – the spawn of an industrialized economy – with implications for liberal programmes of taxation and welfare. Externally, the question became one of compete or protect, sell more or buy less. Here, indeed, Liberals came closest to unanimity. From Chicago to Copenhagen, from Glasgow to Genoa, whatever their disagreements over social deprivation, imperialism or war, most liberals in most places took a dim view of trading tariffs. In part their opposition reflected a relationship between liberalism and the acquisitiveness of a manufacturing middle class caught up in a *crescendo* of international industrialism. Yet habit had long since elevated itself into virtue and taught liberals that their commitment to free trade rested rather on right reason and morality.

What may already have emerged by implication from these preliminary remarks is some sense of the degree to which British liberal theory took its nature from a highly specific assemblage of moods and elements – one which differed in a variety of ways from others in which liberalism gained ground. Sheer historicity played some part in the process. The maturity of a parliamentary system taken by theorists to have its origins in a Saxon forest placed a formidable psychological barrier in the way of

radical recommendations. The ancient university system which allowed for a traditional freedom of comment in its dealings with the state contained an invented
tradition of moderate empiricism that adherents traced back to Locke. Not that the
tradition had remained static: shifts in priorities and social image through the great
age of science associated with Charles Darwin and the following generation
undoubtedly helped the late-Victorian British intellectual feel more self-conscious in
his status as a member of a distinct class;[5] but the relationship between the universities and the government nevertheless retained a sense of distance that had broken
down in France and, even more obviously, in the German Empire. If the University
of Oxford developed closer links with Britain's new bureaucracy under the leadership
of a man like Benjamin Jowett, it never contrived to resemble the University of Berlin
in that respect. On the other hand, most senior politicians passed through the 'staff
colleges' of Oxford and Cambridge and suffered some exposure to their atmosphere if
not always to their teaching. Where the political structure dovetailed into Britain's
subtle arrangement of urban and rural societies, the story of contrast continued.
Rather than present to their dependents a caste of notables seen publicly only in court
circles, the British aristocracy had evolved a strange commuting existence between
national and local levels, softening class hatred and offering a platform from which
Liberal dogma, cooled and moulded in the gentle rhetoric of the Whigs, could find a
voice.[6]

From within this framework British liberals approached democracy (in both
senses) with weaker presentiments of danger than felt natural in countries ravaged by
revolution or civil war. The English 'civil war' had, in so far as it had ever taken that
form at all, received a liberal baptism and become part of the proof that the British
had transcended tyranny during a period when continental Europe drifted towards
absolutism. In neither the 1790s nor the 1840s did Britain experience social revolution, though fear had run high at a few moments. The limited opening of a safety
valve in 1832 and 1867 had granted a new catchment of selected males the right to
vote; and although the franchise remained severely undemocratic before 1884 and
partially so thereafter, enough had been done to defuse the discussion and allow
political attention to wander elsewhere. Indeed, to the extent that the liberal intelligentsia saw itself as a liberalizing agency, their great victories came not over franchise
at all but rather through the gradual subversion of eighteenth-century ecclesiastical
power and the substitution through the course of the nineteenth century of something
approaching religious pluralism. Liberals could congratulate themselves more
plausibly on relieving the condition of Irish Catholics, English Dissenters and
immigrant Jews than on anything they had done to advance the political claims of an
urban working class. Nor should it be said that their *point d'appui* in itself lacked
realism or relevance. In holding back from both the over-heated erastianism that had
dislocated British politics in the 1830s and 40s and from the rampant anti-clericalism
that embittered the politics of much of Europe, British liberals introduced a critique
of Anglican conformity that avoided the perils of enthusiasm.

Nationalism – our second theme – certainly existed as a doctrine in nineteenth
century Britain but again it assumed a particular style, tone and vocabulary. The
union of England and Wales with Scotland (1707) and Ireland (1800) left little nation

[5] Thomas W. Heyck develops the idea of a new self-consciousness among British intellectuals after 1870:
see his *The Transformation of Intellectual Life in Victorian Britain* (1982).
[6] For the distinctiveness of aristocratic life-styles in Britain during the nineteenth century, see David
Cannadine, *Lords and Landlords: the aristocracy and the towns 1774–1967* (Leicester, 1980).

hood to create, at least in a formal sense, whereas many other states sought liberation or national self-consciousness through the second half of the nineteenth century. By no means all the initiative towards nationalism came from liberals in those countries: no one accused Bismarck of liberalism; even Abraham Lincoln, liberator of the Negro, had been a Republican. But Liberals everywhere found some emotional charge in the nationalist movements of the 1860s and drew strength from the examples offered by the northern States of America, by Italy, Poland, Denmark. Even the forlorn hope, imperial Russia, emancipated her serfs. In Britain, too, these developments caused some stir; yet no British version of nationalism could readily reflect them or deflect the public from its concern with parliamentary reform or cholera or cattle plague. Instead, the nascent nationalism of British politics flowed into a channel which Conservative politics made available in the 1870s and beyond. It became a doctrine about Empire.

The lust for colonial acquisition formed a continuo for British politics during the last two decades of the century and it heightened liberals' sense of difficulty in three ways. It helped stimulate and amplify a form of popular chauvinism that many liberals found distasteful; and by so doing it embarrassed the significant group (for this was no fringe section) who held that the British empire, properly conceived and responsibly administered, had a genuine role to play in extending liberty to less fortunate parts of the globe. Theorists whose writings pressed for the liberalizing of British institutions often mixed their liberalism with an emotional defence of high-minded imperialism on related grounds. By the outbreak of war against the Boers of South Africa that was to last from 1899 to 1902 that position had, admittedly, lost some of its innocence and given rise to a vigorous party-Liberal opposition which would itself make a major contribution to the fashioning of Liberal politics in the shadow of a Teutonic militarism that seemed more and more to have sustained itself in the nationalism of Hegel and Treitschke. A second difficulty for liberals arose because Britain's imperialism in the late nineteenth century cut across one form of Liberal strategy for Ireland. The story of that tension must be left until later in this account; but it should be made clear at the outset that Ireland developed simultaneously into a test case of informed imperialism and a key instance of its offensive results. And, finally, the mania for annexing territory in Africa and Asia brought with it of necessity a high-profile defence policy. That, in turn, meant money. Any student of Liberal history in Britain after 1880 cannot fail to notice how frequently Liberal governments and their apologists stumbled over the economic difficulties produced by their efforts to arm and provision military services equal to the task of policing the new colossus.

Individualist liberal theory contributed to the dilemma by insisting on the narrowness of options facing politicians. Perhaps the teaching of Mill and Fawcett and Sidgwick would have created problems in this area even if the economy had remained robust. The economic theme still demands some stress, however, because British industry and agriculture never fully emerged from the crisis of the 1870s with the vigour found among their rivals. Depression became a general condition in western Europe, certainly, and to that extent Britain merely shared in a common suffering; but the phasing and duration of the British experience could hardly mimic the rhythms of younger and more dynamic forms of industrialization. Since the problems posed by the British economy assumed an historical and structural form, politicians found the depression tightening about them with no obvious way to relieve the pressure, apart from turning the clock back or liquidating competitors. Patterns of landownership could not be recast overnight and liberals showed little enthusiasm before the turn of the century for recasting them at all. The rigidity of industrial and manufacturing processes also derived from three or four generations of successful practice when the world had been kinder. These considerations pressed hard on liberals and it may help our understanding of them to notice the paradox – perhaps one ought to call it an explanatory clue – that most of the period during which British Liberalism experienced its pivotal phase of development coincided with a period during which the great age of British economic success struggled and died. Whether that coincidence argues in favour of the senility of liberal theory and practice or rather suggests their potential for adapting to changed circumstances poses a question which must be left for a more contentious moment at the end of this book.

Peculiarities

These themes, then, gave rise to some echoes among British liberals as among European. Suppose one narrow the problem and ask, not about 'liberals' in the sense of people who might associate themselves with a certain cast of mind, but about the Liberals who consciously and deliberately supported or helped organize one of the many 'Liberal' political parties in existence throughout Europe by the end of the nineteenth century? A brief examination seems worthwhile because, if differences of national mood seem obvious between species of liberalism broadly defined, then the contrast stands out even more sharply when one considers the institutions through which liberal doctrine sought dispersion. Organizations seeking the support of specific social constituencies inevitably directed their attention towards concrete issues and grievances that promised to move an increasingly demotic electorate to applause or anger. Intoning abstract principles or lecturing about the nature of political economy might win converts in a university: it would hardly win votes. Even when one can recognize a 'Liberal' party as propagating some form of liberal doctrine, therefore, the currency of that message impresses more by its base metal than by any sense of its general convertability.

Consider first the diversity of the political structures that one hopes to compare. To speak of an identikit state that undergoes democratic agitation in 1848 and proceeds towards something like universal male suffrage by the end of the First World War voices just enough truth to sound plausible from a distance. But the differences are important and often go unremarked in the more 'whiggish' histories of the period. The only western European states with a claim to some form of democracy after 1848 were France and Switzerland. Yet France's political behaviour operated in a far from democratic fashion under the second empire and thereafter gave rise to a structure of politics in which party played a surprisingly minor role. Switzerland, on the other hand, despite granting the suffrage to males over 20, continued to organize its political life cantonally and produced nothing resembling Liberal party politics until the turn of the century. Other states widened their franchise, certainly. One could phase the order of their significant movements in this direction as follows: Germany (1871); Belgium (1895); Norway (1900); Austria (1905); Sweden (1907); Italy (1915).[7]

---

[7] For a useful comparative analysis of such data, see Thomas T. Mackie and Richard Rose (eds.), *The International Almanac of Electoral History* (1974, 1982). Against the raw figures one must set, of course, the operation of informal controls of which the lack of a secret ballot often proved most effective. In France, for example, Gambetta's remark that 'universal suffrage is the most interesting thing in the social

But such lists take no account of the environments within which franchise provisions operated. Often forgotten, to take the most simple among the complications, is the age threshold for voting in such countries. This often produced an older electorate than the one familiar in Britain. Twenty-five would have been a 'normal' age threshold for enfranchisement in a number of west European states in the late nineteenth century; and, rather than follow a pattern of constant reduction, these exclusions actually increased in some cases to offset the democratic thrust of franchise extensions. This was the case in the Netherlands in 1896 and Sweden in 1907, though neither matched Denmark's 1849 constitution which gave the vote to selected males over 30. The Danes did not reduce their age threshold to 21 until 1964!

Needless to say, the constraints within which constitutional niceties demand to be set run far beyond details of franchise. To make sense of 'Liberal' parties, where states other than Britain had one, the flavour of their political practice becomes far more important than constitutions and formal descriptions of their cameral structures. Perhaps the most economical way to review that practice might be to concentrate on one area at a time and begin at the beginning.

The world's oldest Liberal party arguably sprang not from Europe at all but rather from America. Jefferson and his followers embodied one form of liberal politics that struggled to find a successor. The creation of the second party system inverted some of the logic of the first and made Jackson's Democratic party in certain ways the custodian of Jeffersonian values. But the Jacksonians, for all the admiration that some British radicals of the 1830s felt for them, came too close to the soil to find any real fit with the British Liberals. Repatriated by force, they would probably have voted for Peel's radical Conservative party rather than the urban civic pride and industrial pushiness of Manchester Liberalism. Jackson's campaign against the Bank and his resistance to the Nullification movement did not mark out his party as a liberal identity, seen in British terms. With the Republicans exercising the greater grasp of the slavery issue, moreover, the Democrats entered a period of difficulty from which they were not fully to emerge for half a century. They discovered less heroic heirs in Garfield's party that found itself needing to struggle for every vote it won. 'The wonder is,' a recent historian of the Democratic party comments, 'that the Republicans lost a single presidential election between 1860 and 1912; only by a fluke could a Democrat win in much of the North. A financial panic, an election campaign slur against the Irish voters, or a split in the Republican ranks was needed to keep the Democrats from sliding into oblivion.'[8]

Parallels with the British experience exist, needless to say. The concern of American Democrats with the politics of race in Reconstruction society might go into the balance against the anxieties of British Liberals over the Irish and the containment of Celtic nationalism, for that problem undoubtedly had a racial dimension after 1870. Yet the balance remains very much uneven and any attempt to discern a common Anglo-American politics appears implausible. 'At the heart of much Anglo-American politics,' we are told, 'lay an argument over what image of the nation men should carry in their minds.'[9] Judgements of this kind fail through their sheer

life of France' might be placed against the view that no secret ballot was available in practice until the turn of the century. See Robert J. Goldstein, *Political Repression in Nineteenth-Century Europe* (1983), 15. For Gambetta, see Theodore Zeldin, *France 1848–1945: politics and anger* (Oxford, 1979), 254.

[8] Robert A. Rutland, *The Democrats: from Jefferson to Carter* (Baton Rouge, 1979), 108.

[9] Robert Kelly, *The Transatlantic Persuasion: the liberal–democratic mind in the age of Gladstone* (New York, 1969), 25.

inclusiveness: they say little about what made American or British 'liberal-democrats' evolve into the oddities that both variants became. When, indeed, an American radical like Henry George toured Britain to convert radicals there to his views about the centrality of rent among economic and social problems of the moment, his reception among the more articulate political classes and the intelligentsia suggests a divergence of language and tone between the two countries quite as striking as the 'influence' to which historians sometimes point. Both species of Liberal, again, suffered from Darwin. But then the American experience of social Darwinism proved distinctive: it did not follow the same channel that we shall need to explore in Britain. Both parties found themselves obliged to come to terms with doctrines that have been called 'progressive'. Yet both the nature of the challenge and the pattern of its reception reveal significant contrast. Assuredly the doctrines of progressivism played a considerable role in British Liberalism after 1900 and the term found some currency in other sectors of party politics. But those who used it did not self-consciously model themselves on American progressives in the way that, for example, British radicals of the 1930s looked to Roosevelt's New Deal. As Kenneth Morgan concedes in his study of transatlantic progressivism, the 'influence' ran more strongly in the East–West direction than vice versa. 'The impact of the United States on British reformers', that is to say, 'was intermittent and partial at best.'[10]

Across a narrower sea, the Liberal parties of Europe remained still more distant from British problems and perspectives. France, the home of European Liberalism, produced no distinct Liberal party but rather a smear of liberal persuasions across the entire centre of the party spectrum. The polarity of monarchy versus republic still exercised great power, one more effective than that of Left versus Right. With the demise of Napoleon III's second empire in 1870 and the foundation of the Third Republic that would last effectively until the Germans came back in 1940, politics moved in tighter channels than in the age of the Jacobins. The constitution was short; the new chamber of deputies was small (533 compared with 1,118 in 1789). Ministers came and went with their customary haste but, oddly, the structure itself displayed a good deal of stability. All the volatility seemed concentrated at a high-political level: indeed most of the changes of ministry took place between elections rather than as a result of them. Occasionally a politician of great ability and intellect might surface. Gambetta had a genuine interest in democratic theory. Ferry quoted at people Mill's essay on the subjection of women. But the average deputy lived in a less ethereal world dominated by localism to an extent more redolent of England in the eighteenth century than the nineteenth. Indeed Theodore Zeldin's characterization of the deputy's existence could almost have been written by Sir Lewis Namier:

> The emphasis on principle in their rhetoric was counterbalanced behind the scenes by constant attention to the individual complaints, demands and threats of each constituent. . . . As a result, they (the constituents) looked on him as being obliged to them for their votes and for his living. They pestered him shamelessly for favours. . . . For much of their time, deputies were concerned not with large issues of policy but with the satisfaction of petty particularist interests.[11]

[10]Kenneth O. Morgan, 'The Future at Work: Anglo-American Progressivism 1890–1917', in H. C. Allen and Roger Thompson (eds.), *Contrast and Connection: bicentennial essays in Anglo-American history* (1976), 251.
[11]Zeldin, *France 1848–1945: politics and anger*, 212–13.

Not that liberals withered away in this environment. They increased their purchase on the French centre, for example, when the radicals of the 1890s found some reinforcement, though also some criticism, from the *Gauche democratique* and *Gauche radicale*, echoing in a sense the uneasy discussion in Britain between main-line Liberals and their social-democratic wing. But the social dimension of these politics differed markedly from the British case and interacted with sharply-differentiated ideologies in the French political system to produce no real parallel. French business-men, like British, had a liberal tinge; but they also had a Catholic one, shifting them worlds away from the chapels of the Pennine slopes. They enjoyed corruption – a global pastime – but mixed it with an overt anti-Semitism which received less official encouragement across the Channel. 'Dreyfus' told a different story from 'Marconi'. And if the government proved more stable than first impressions suggested, first impressions none the less mattered. They confirmed the view at Westminster that the French had gone downhill. In the days of Guizot and Chevallier, British Liberals had looked to the French for their exemplars. No one did that in 1900. Rather than think of a great trade treaty like the Anglo-French agree-ment of 1860 on which Gladstone liked to dwell, those British who thought about the French at all called to mind a more dubious France by turn of century: one defeated by Bismarck, compromised by woolly-brained socialists, dirtied by Zola.

The desolation occasioned among Europe's Liberals by Bismarck's aggression (and especially after his first major *sortie* in the Prussian invasion of Denmark in 1864) found some compensation in the better prospects further south. Kossuth's Liberal nationalists in Hungary had attracted British interest and sympathy in the 1850s in the hope that Austria's grip on the weaker state might relax. That did not happen. The constitution-making of 1867 promised a new dual state in Austria-Hungary; but the pretended equality soon showed its hollowness as Vienna made plain which partner would prove predominant.[12] For Liberals the situation gave rise to a number of cross-grains, not only over the question of nationalism but also in response to religion, *laissez-faire* and the democratizing of urban centres. The Austrian liberals solved the last of these by refusing to extend the franchise in the towns. Their failure to solve the others has been colourfully caught by Carl Schorske:

> During the last quarter of the nineteenth century the programme which the liberals had devised against the upper classes occasioned the explosion of the lower. . . . A German nationalism articulated against aristocratic cosmopolitans was answered by Slavic patriots clamouring for autonomy. When the liberals soft-pedalled their Germanism in the interest of the multi-national state, they were branded as traitors to nationalism by an anti-liberal German *petite bourgeoisie*. Laissez faire, devised to free the economy from the fetters of the past, called forth the Marxist revolutionaries of the future. Catholicism, routed from the school and the courthouse as the handmaiden of aristocratic oppression, returned as the ideology of peasant and artisan, for whom liberalism meant capitalism and capitalism meant Jew. . . . Strong enough to dissolve the old political order, liberal-ism could not master the social order which that dissolution released and which generated new centrifugal thrust under liberalism's tolerant but inflexible aegis.[13]

Liberalism in Vienna became more of a café phenomenon than an organized political force, killed by a particularity of circumstance that gives little illumination to other configurations.

[12]A. J. P. Taylor, *The Habsburg Monarchy 1809–1918* (1948), 136–40.
[13]Carl E. Schorske, *Fin-de-Siècle Vienna* (1961, 1980), 117–18.

On the other hand, a new star had meanwhile emerged across the Alps in nationalist Italy whose persecutors – Austria, France and the Vatican – seemed unlikely to prevent the emergence of a strong Liberal state. The names of Cavour and Mazzini, even of the disreputable Garibaldi, peppered Liberal conversation in the early sixties at a time when an important emotional identification between British Liberals (other than Irish ones) and the Italian liberators gained ground. Yet over the next half-century that Liberalism became a sour sham as Italy's political structure ceased in practice to contain anything resembling a structure at all and degenerated rather into a noisy market for the touting of muscle, money and place. Some Italian Liberals tried to advance the ideals of the founding fathers, needless to say, none more successfully than Giovanni Giolitti whose influence made itself felt at many points during the period we are considering. Even his political survival demanded, however, that tariffs be sold to the agricultural lobby, that the remarkable industrial revolution of the north (unmatched in Europe after the 1890s) brought little benefit to the near-starving in Calabria, that anti-papal instinct stifle in face of the need to conciliate a centre Catholic party. Some extension of Italy's narrow franchise betokened a mild Liberal success. But parallels with British experience are otherwise hard to find once Italy's political parties are observed collapsing into a morass of personal and group affiliations in which only the anarchists learned organization. Even the intellectuals in the universities – in politics often the last to know – gave up the Liberals for dead. Italy's pre-eminent humanist thinker of the period, Benedetto Croce, later became a fervent Liberal; but in the pre-war years he continued a tradition of disengagement, understandably preferring poetry and historical thought to contemplating the plight of Giolitti.[14]

To discover a stronger resemblance to British Liberalism among European states, one must rather move north towards the Low Countries and Scandinavia. Belgium and Holland both showed occasional signs of the perspectives and issues that exercised British Liberals in the second half of the nineteenth century, especially through a joint concern (felt more keenly in Belgium than Holland) with supplying an unobstrusive resistance to universal suffrage and with the politics of educational reform. Yet although largely diversionary extensions of the British suffrage took place in 1867 and 1884, and although Dissenting religion played a highly significant role in focussing Liberal approaches to educational policy, neither concern became so shrill in Britain as across the North Sea. Anti-Catholicism doubtless found some reflection in British Liberal journalism; it never reached the temperature and comprehensiveness of the Belgian and Dutch varieties. Within British parliamentary politics the Liberal party may have received a bloody nose from the effects of its education bills of 1870; but it did not die. When Belgian Liberals crashed in 1884 following *their* attempt to push Catholics out of the state school system, the party lost its hold on power for the next 30 years.[15] Similarly, celtic nationalism may have tested the patience and resilience of Liberal governments in Britain, but it remained a skin-irritation compared with the malignancies of Fleming and Walloon that were to express themselves so bitterly in the twentieth century. Dutch Liberals retained more influence in the government of their country than did the Belgians in theirs. Yet that influence usually found its channel as in the French model: through an individual

---

[14]See Edmund Jacobitti, *Revolutionary Humanism and Historicism in Modern Italy* (New Haven, 1981). For Croce's politics, cf. Walter L. Adamson, 'Benedetto Croce and the Death of Ideology', *Journal of Modern History* 55 (1983), 208–36.
[15]See E. H. Kossmann, *The Low Countries 1780–1940* (Oxford, 1978), 229–309.

Liberal statesman's participation in a regime rather than through an organized political party's coming to represent a coherent doctrine. And the peculiarly Dutch version of anti-papalism, stimulated in Holland as in England by the re-establishment of a Catholic hierarchy in the 1850s, ultimately dominated the issues that most disturbed Liberals to a degree unmatched in Britain outside the 'Temple of Peace' at Hawarden. As in Luxemburg, where Liberals predominated almost throughout our period, Belgian and Dutch Liberals responded to a politics of highly distinctive colour – one far more vibrant than the subtle greys and pastels of the British experience.

Denmark, and to a lesser extent Sweden, edged a little nearer to that experience, at least in their issues and catch-cries. For despite Denmark's constitutional development having come rather late, its Liberal party – the *Venstre* of 1870 – pressed for the enhancement of a genuine parliamentary style of politics together with a programme of free trade and *laissez-faire*. A Radical Liberal party seceded from it in 1905, calling to mind the strains that British Liberal party managers knew all about through their dealings with their own radical wing in the decades since 1880. A threat also came to the Danish Liberals, as to the British, from the Right in a party whose programme centred on the strengthening of the powers of the second chamber and the promotion of a 'forward' defence policy. Sweden's Liberals had developed a cohesive politics by the 1890s and there, too, one senses a form of discussion by no means alien from those current in Britain. They faced a social-democratic challenge from their Left, but one that turned on the tariff question – a Liberal stamping ground. After 1900, indeed, the story, if not its outcome, has an audibly British sound: a battle over the status of the second chamber culminating in a deal with the Conservatives to support manhood suffrage in return for the adoption of proportional representation and the survival of a bi-cameral system.[16] In the face of these Danish and Swedish examples, one may object at once, of course, that the economic and social structures accompanying (if not determining) political questions in those countries show little resemblance to the British case. Industrialization was yet to achieve there the impact it had long exerted in Britain: one can hardly compare in any direct way agrarian societies throwing up a Liberal politics resting on the interests and ambitions of farmers and peasants with the most deeply-industrialized state of the western world whose politics presumably reflected the concerns of an entrenched middle class. On the other hand, a pre-industrial context may present parallels with a post-industrial one and it has been noticed by historians that Britain's industrial prowess had already turned into past tense by 1880 and given rise to a vocabulary better suited to a rural imagination than an urban one.[17] To that extent, the Scandinavian images may not seem completely *mal apropos*.

This brief survey of western countries has amounted to a nervous encirclement of Germany. The claims of the *Kaiserreich* to inclusion in any discussion of European Liberalism remain overwhelming. Germany developed numerous Liberal groupings. The economic environment in which they grew and fragmented bore obvious resemblances to Britain's in its industrial strength. Many of the differentiating peculiarities produced elsewhere by national or racial minorities did not operate

[16]Central elements in the Danish and Swedish political structures are briefly noted by Francis G. Castles in Roy C. Macridis (ed.), *Modern Political Systems: Europe* (Englewood Cliffs, 1963, 1983), 399–400.
[17]This point forms much of the argument in Martin J. Wiener, *English Culture and the Decline of the Industrial Spirit* (Cambridge, 1981), though Wiener makes no attempt to place Liberalism among the value-structures he describes.

there. The German intelligentsia, moreover, had manifested a habit of regarding British institutions and political practice as something of a model to emulate. The difficulty lies not in the reasonableness of parallels but in the high voltage carried by the concept of German peculiarity. All German historiography since 1945 approximates to a discrete account of the origins of the Third Reich; and in that story the Wilhelmine period obviously supplies important chapters. Liberal history has thus become enmeshed in an explanation for the 'failure' of the German middle class to follow a 'normal' pattern of development, and for its supposed collapse into impotence, thereby allowing the militaristic tendencies of certain sectors of German society to drag the nation along a *Sonderweg*, a distinctive road towards the catastrophe of 1933. That picture of German history has recently suffered a welcome acid-attack[18] but the discussion to which it has given rise stimulates too many theoretical perspectives to allow a thorough treatment here. A few introductory observations bearing more directly on the concerns of this book must suffice.

One might note as a fundamental point that the offensive against a notion of 'proper' development which Germany somehow 'failed' to follow has not brought with it any reconciliation in the histories of British and German Liberalism. Indeed Blackbourn and Eley stress the contrast between the two reforming traditions and see, for example, the behaviour of the British Liberal government after its electoral triumph of 1906 as 'best explained by a particular configuration of circumstances and events'.[19] Structural considerations go some way towards accounting for the discrepancy between these two histories. The unification of Germany and proclamation of the Empire in 1871 brought with it a constitutional framework in which any Liberal party would have struggled, even without the confrontation and accommodation with Bismarck which dominated parliamentary Liberalism in Germany until 1890. The disposition of power between Reichstag, Kaiser and Chancellor had no equivalent in Britain; nor did the singularity of a regional electoral system – that practised in Prussia; nor did the manhood suffrage that so disturbed the Liberal right-wing in Germany. The conservatism of the German bureaucracy and universities (helped by shrewd weeding) had some parallels but remained quite different in origin and flavour. Within the broader social environment, again, the Catholic regions helped underpin a Centre party that played a major role in German politics through to 1914 – a function that British Liberals had long since appropriated. Sometimes German historians write as though the situations could be transposed – quoting Disraeli on England, perhaps, as a valid description of German conditions, or seeing a German Left Liberal leader in the 1890s 'imagining himself playing Cobden to Caprivi's or Bulow's Peel.'[20] But the translation seems implausible, just as the unconscious allusion to the politics of economic protection seems very much to the point.

In Britain the resistance to a politics based on tariffs helped originate the Liberal party and provided a key element in its doctrines and sense of identity. In Germany the *Zollverein* antedated not merely the foundation of the National Liberal party but the establishment of the state itself. Bismarck had some of his battle won, therefore, in bending the Liberals towards a *rapprochement* with tariffs. He found yet more

[18]David Blackbourne and Geoff Eley, *The Peculiarities of German History: bourgeois society and politics in nineteenth-century Germany* (Oxford, 1984).
[19]*Peculiarities*, 104.
[20]Dieter Raff, for example, quotes Disraeli in two-nation mood in order to continue: 'Wie in England, so waren auch in Deutschland zwei Klassen entstanden . . .'. See his *Deutsche Geschichte vom alten Reich zur Zweiten Republic* (München, 1985), 105. For the Cobden example, see David Blackbourne, 'The Problem of Democratization', in Richard J. Evans (ed.), *Society and Politics in Wilhelmine Germany* (1978), 173.

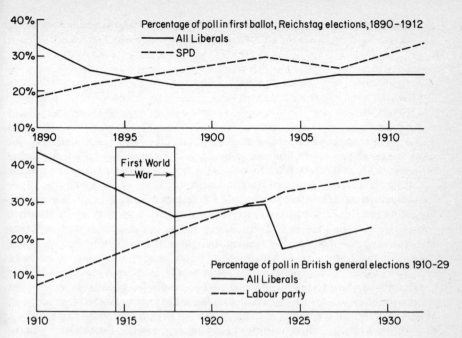

Figure 1.1: The Liberal–socialist relationship in Germany and Britain

powerful support, of course, in the early existence of a socialist movement in Germany and the appearance of a Social Democratic party that commanded a potential quite beyond the capacity of nascent labour organizations in Britain. Socialist candidates in the entire western world apparently received 438,231 votes in 1878.[21] True, less than half a million socialist voters hardly seem likely in retrospect to overturn the stability of the world; the point is rather that only just over 1,000 of those votes were cast outside Germany. German Liberals thus encountered the socialist problem earlier than did their British counterparts and did so within a more worrying franchise arrangement. The relationship between the Liberals and the SPD then followed a trajectory that differed from the British Liberals' confrontation with the Labour party. And because the First World War impinged on the latter argument, the difference turned out to lie not only in the dating of the curve but also in its shape. (See Fig. 1.1[22])

The language of German Liberals compares rather better, indeed, with the British Liberals of the 1920s than with those of the 1880s and 90s. Only during and after the First World War, with its world in ruins, did British Liberalism take on the sense of doctrinal crisis that so often marked German expression in the *Kaiserreich*. By then, it, too, faced a massive challenge from the Left in a context of universal male and some female suffrage. By then, too, it had lost its business and commercial ballast. An examination of the 128 National Liberal party representatives in the Reichstag in

[21]Cited in R. P. Morgan, *The German Social Democrats 1864–72* (Cambridge, 1965), x.
[22]The German component of this graph is based on a more complex representation in James J. Sheehan, *German Liberalism in the Nineteenth Century* (Chicago, 1978), 223.

1877 suggests that the German Liberals in any case never had one to match the British case. Sheehan finds the following disposition in their backgrounds:[23]

Land and rentier	26.4%
Businessmen	13.2%
Officials	49.6%
Lawyers	9.3%

The analysis should be compared with the portrait of the British Liberal party in the next chapter of this book. The role of business in German Liberal politics grew, certainly, in the 1880s but too late to present the face to the working class that Liberal businessmen sought to present during the heyday of British Liberalism.

As much in its value-structure as in its sociology, German Liberalism moved further away from Britain as the nineteenth century drew to its close. Its theorists went, some of them, the way of Treitschke and Sybel in a defence of the new Reich that tried to accommodate Liberalism within nationalism. Its historians, who had lavished so much attention on Britain earlier in the century, drew away to cultivate their own garden.[24] British observers also pulled away. Sedan spoke more loudly than the *Kulturkampf* that an English anti-clerical Liberal like John Morley admired.[25] By the time Morley and his Liberal colleagues found themselves pitched into office in 1906 with the greatest majority in living memory, German Liberalism had become a dead thing. British ministers went to Germany to study the Bismarckian welfare schemes; but they thought of them as state socialism rather than enlightened Liberalism. And they took them to have come about because the Germans had tried to fight Labour rather than transcend it – a useful rhetorical point when stressing the degree to which New Liberals at home supposedly listened to the demands of the working class.

> That is not so everywhere. It is not so, for instance, in Germany, and yet in Germany there is no Liberal Party worth speaking of. Labour there is very highly organized, and the Liberal Party there has been destroyed. In Germany there exists exactly the condition of affairs, in a Party sense, that Mr Keir Hardie and his friends are so anxious to introduce here. A great social democratic party on the one hand, are bluntly and squarely face to face with a capitalist and military confederation on the other.[26]

Other images of the nineteenth century take the mind far beyond the regimes of post-feudal Europe and demand recognition, though they do not alter the impression of British specificity. Imperial government, as it was understood by the Victorians, included an element of Liberalism-for-Export as part of a rationale for annexation that would suggest something more than a veneer for looting. In the colonies and dependencies British rule appealed to a Liberal justification that a radical like Mill found persuasive in the case of India. The dominions supplied an even clearer cameo as they struggled to turn the pieties of Liberal rhetoric into a workable policy. Canada and Australia bred politicians who might not have seemed out of place on the benches

[23]Sheehan, *German Liberalism*, 160.
[24]Charles E. McClelland underlines this swing away from Anglophilia in his *The German Historians and England: a study in nineteenth-century views* (Cambridge, 1971).
[25]See J. P. Parry, *Democracy and Religion: Gladstone and the Liberal party 1867–75* (Cambridge, 1986), 44.
[26]Winston Churchill at Glasgow, 11 October 1906, in Robert Rhodes James (ed.), *Churchill: his complete speeches 1897–1963* (8 vols., New York, 1974), I, 674.

at Westminster; and indeed some Liberal statesmen did have important experience of those younger constitutional structures. Canadians and Australians knew more about the operation of tariffs than their free trading *alma mater* in the second half of the century. They also both saw 'Liberal' administrations – in the case of Canada, a 'principled' one under Alexander Mackenzie. Yet even here the sense endures of a wide remove between the economic operations of British Liberals and those of a Canadian party striving to give a vast land area its tartan of railroads, just as the powerful and peculiar Australian Labour party found few parallels with the less advanced form of labour politics in Britain. In both dominions the strictures of geography and the patterns of occupation which that terrain enforced made a very different 'political nation' from the mother country's. Australian land usage and tenure, plus a strongly progressive bourgeoisie, dictated a brighter future for the Australian Labour party than its British equivalent. The significant advances of labour during the 1890s gave its organized wing considerable leverage in the new Commonwealth of Australia after 1901: not only could it constrain Deakin's Liberals but it also came to power in its own right by 1910. It also capitalized on a range of emotional commitments appropriate to the 'nationalist' phase of a young constitution – something hardly possible in a country that saw Liberalism as a tradition running several generations deep and Labour as an un-English deviation. Neither of these colonial styles of politics provided British Liberals with helpful examplars. The vitality of the Australian relationship between Liberalism and Labour suggested, unthinkably, that Britain rid herself of her past. The Canadian story, by contrast, suggested only the impossible. Could Britain somehow jettison her economic activities, she might share in the success of Canadian Liberals who, in the 15 years following the death of the Conservative leader, Macdonald, in 1896 had built a buoyant party more on wood pulp than on 'principles' as the Canadian economy enjoyed the boom that sent the total value of Canadian exports to twice their 1895 figure by 1910, and sent to England an indestructible opponent of Liberalism and free trade in Max Aitken, Lord Beaverbrook. Britain had no such resource to exploit. Her economy strangled in the grip of bygone success.

Wherever one directs a sideways glance at the Liberalism of other states, the incongruity seems too consistent easily to dispel. That lack of comfortable juxtaposition does not argue the pointlessness of comparative methods: indeed the decision to begin this inquiry into the nature of British Liberalism by looking elsewhere depends on an assumption about the importance of placing responses to wide-ranging phenomena such as industrialization and democratization within a broader framework than the one available between Inverness and Penzance. Rather, it implies a cautionary tale that suggests the danger of reducing the complexities of national experience to mere instances of subterranean processes running through the nineteenth century like volcanic faults – country becoming town, oligarchy creeping towards democracy, Liberalism snaking ever further Leftwards. Once history turns into the tracking of these tendencies, the point of it all lies simply in finding the correct point at which to stop the conveyor in order to explain any given case. We know, undeniably, that the countries of the western world developed industrially during the period under review here; we know that many of them extended their franchise and that several had approximated to manhood suffrage by 1918; we can see in every major state a party or section representing the Left and exposing the custodians of traditional centrist values to competition in votes or power. That these variables relate to one another in some way seems too obvious to brook argument. Yet to convert those relationships into judgements that crush out of awareness the hundreds of other variables that enriched each national experience relegates the history of Liberalism to a search for a handful of fictions few enough to grasp and coarse enough to grip. Our quarry here will at least prove more authentic, if also more elusive.

2

The British Liberal Party

On being Liberal

One could chase the word backwards through documentary sources at least as far as 1422 in the sense of 'Libral sciencis, that is to Say fre scyencis, as gramer, arte, fisike, astronomye, and otheris.' But in its political connotation 'liberal' has a clear anchorage in the decade following the end of the Napoleonic wars in 1815. It còmes into the language with a Byronic undertow, suggesting the romantic world of the *liberale* who championed oppressed peoples in general and the Greeks in particular and their efforts to liberate themselves from Turkish domination that had caught the imagination of British writers long before Admiral Codrington sent the Turkish fleet to the bottom of the sea at Navarino in 1827. At home it perhaps implied a flexible attitude over the granting of civil rights to Catholics or Dissenters without necessarily involving support for extending the franchise in the way demanded by Radicals and extra-parliamentary polemicists since the French Revolution. In the 1820s liberals belonged, that is to say, to the Whig party rather than vice versa. Only after the reform of 1832 did a 'Liberal' party come into existence in the form recognizable to late-Victorians. That it did so, moreover, owed little to the congealing of ideological sentiment and much to the political circumstances of the moment. In particular, the three elements occupying the ground to the left of Peel's new Conservative party – the Whigs, the Radicals and the Irish – discovered that they must remain forever impotent unless they could arrive at some *modus vivendi*. Each fragment depended on the others: a consideration that helped give Liberal politics in Britain over the next century its flavour of accommodation and inconsistency.

The first of these sections (and 'section' is a word we find increasingly used in contemporary criticism of the party's fragmentation) brought with it a history that Whigs believed had begun with the Glorious Revolution of 1688 when monarchy had, according to Whig legend, met its match among the far-sighted landowners of England who had limited its powers and pointed the way towards constitutional progress in Britain. All too apparently, the Whigs had forgotten how to be successful since then; but they kept their land, mixed it with assorted industrial developments and learned to thrive in the amphibious world dominated by the Industrial Revolution. They kept their families intact (indeed notoriously so) through careful selection of marriage partners. They clung to the sort of superiority that only land and blood can buy. Tories carried a farming patina, one that suggested soilworkers rather than landowners, and thus remained ever so slightly *coarse*. Manufacturers, nonconformists and Jews, while no less coarse, plainly required the leadership of a patrician class trained in the mysteries of government and the Whig–Liberal party spoke their language. Yet after mid-century the incidence of Whig vocabulary diminished as the Whigs themselves diminished into a band of isolated potentates anxious, many of them, about the future of property and unmanned by the Liberal party's lurches towards further democracy. By 1886 only five of the great Whig families still belonged to the Gladstonian Liberal party: the rest had slid across to Tory or Liberal Unionist benches or withdrawn to their town houses, leaving the party (at least in their own imagination) to an American-style caucus and offering their prestige instead to a railway company, an engineering firm, a merchant bank or a quality newspaper. Though the names of Earl Granville or the Earl of Rosebery, Sir William Harcourt or the Marquess of Crewe, would continue to recall a connexion sometimes generations deep, those men knew that the party they represented no longer relied on them and spent much of its time soliciting the good will of a very different kind of man.

At a parliamentary level many of those men would attract description in *Dod's Parliamentary Companion* as 'Radical' or 'Advanced Liberal', but the designation had itself taken on new resonances by the 1870s. The change reflected no simple slide from less extreme to more; rather it suggested alterations of social background and national priorities. Philosophic Radicals of the stamp familiar to a Macaulay or George Grote in the 1830s had given way to a northern manufacturing Radicalism supercharged by eccentric lawyers – part of a long tradition of volatility running into the past from Sir Charles Dilke or Sir William Harcourt through Henry Brougham and J. A. Roebuck to the parliamentary reformers and Corresponding Societies of the late eighteenth century. The priorities of Radicals had since switched from civil rights to political: from Catholic peasants, rural exploitation and supposed threats of revolution to the franchise, the Empire, the collapse of the countryside into depression, the new towns with their trade unions and socialists, the emergence of a new Ireland. Radicals distinguished themselves from main-line Liberals by their rhetorical purposiveness in face of these problems. Before 1880 few of them offered solutions that threatened the stability of Liberal politics as a whole, though many of their colleagues voiced the allegation. Simply by filling a significant proportion of Liberal seats, on the other hand, Radicals contributed to the tone of the Liberal message and the mental landscape of senior politicians whose thoughts about policy had to cope with the possibility of Radical resistance. Their precise number in parliament on any single occasion confounds assessment, not only because the frame of reference of the term 'Radical' alters but also because perception by others in any case dominates the selection of possible qualifiers. Purely as a rough indication of their size at the beginning of our period, Harcourt's figure of around 70 in the mid 1870s seems defensible, though modern analyses of voting behaviour find more than that in the division lists.[1] As a group, the Radicals never conquered the commanding heights of cabinet and senior party positions, though notable individuals such as John Bright and Joseph Chamberlain gained major influence. Of far greater significance were three forms of contribution: their talents in fomenting pressure-group activity; the

[1] See J. P. Rossi, 'The Transformation of the British Liberal Party', *Transactions of the American Philosophical Society* 68/8 (1978), 17.

journalistic flair that gave them a cutting edge in serious periodicals; and the spark of Dissenting religion that frequently fired their enthusiasm. They established limits to dissembling. They commented with mounting ferocity on social policy, especially from the 1880s. They played an ambiguous but prominent role in determining the party's response to the most pervasive and intractable question facing the Liberal party in the late nineteenth century: what to do with the Irish.

By the beginning of our period, even the oldest Members of the House of Commons would have struggled to remember the days before 1828 when the House contained no 'nationalist' Irish MPs. The comparatively comfortable period when Ireland translated itself as 'the Catholic question' seemed far away when Isaac Butt's Home Rule party established itself as a major force for the first time in the general election of 1874. To repeal the Act of Union with Ireland came as no new suggestion: the Liberator himself, Daniel O'Connell, had taken his party along that road in the 1840s. Nor did the need to work with representatives of Irish nationalism strike British Liberals as novel because two major deals, done with transparent opportunism, had already occurred in 1835 and 1859. But new elements intruded in the level of violence and ideological commitment that British governments of all colours encountered in Ireland from the end of the 1870s, and in the calibre of parliamentary leadership embodied in Charles Stewart Parnell through the following decade. Although the issue of Home Rule for Ireland turned quiescent in the first decade of the twentieth century, the damage caused by the explosion of 1885–6 and the spectacle provoked by its recrudescence after 1910 made Ireland a formidable problem for Liberals, one never far removed from their parliamentary tactics and rhetorical pronouncements.

These three pieces supplied part of the visible, tangible Liberal party. There were other parts. From 1877 the National Liberal Federation, through its meetings and monitoring of the constituencies, pulled together some of the regional Liberal groupings and helped lend a focus to electioneering and propaganda. The consolidation of a national and local newspaper industry through the second half of the nineteenth century likewise helped the process and reified those occasions crucial to local activism – the whist drive; the fund-raising bazaar; the garden fête; the agricultural show; the school prize-giving; the blessing of the boats; the laying of a stone; the planting of a tree; Mr Gladstone's coming visit; the annual general meeting, its chairman's excruciating hesitations and cutting collar now transcended in the neutrality of newsprint. But we know more about the notables behind these events than about their public – the people who read the newspapers (if they ever did), who saw the posters, heard the speeches – whose only incursion into public space took the form of putting a cross against the name of the Liberal candidate every few years, and only then if they possessed enough property to qualify them the vote and a local party busy enough to ensure that they received it. By 1880 over a million men in the United Kingdom were casting their vote for the Liberal party in general elections. Following the widening of the electoral franchise in 1884, their number never fell below 1,300,000 (in 1886) and peaked at 2,880,581 in the election of January 1910 in which 6,667,404 men registered a vote of some kind. But who were these men? Did they represent a class or a distinct economic interest? How far would the answer to such a question alter during the period, or depend on which area of the country one studied?

Questions of this kind pose resilient difficulties because historians have no way to approach them except by building models of voting behaviour. This period stands apart from earlier ones in that voting took place in secret after 1872: we therefore have very little evidence from which to demonstrate relationships between voting patterns and individual electors. Even before 1872 the incidence of published 'pollbooks' (lists of voters and how they voted, sometimes containing information about the occupations of electors) had greatly diminished but they still give some indication of the character of the Liberal electorate.[2] At the very least they demonstrate that curious consistency with which grocers voted Liberal and butchers Tory. But for the succeeding period the material simply does not exist and a plausible analysis of electoral sociology has to rest on a synthesis of indirect observations at a local or regional level. Much remains to be discovered through keyhole surgery of this kind and in the present state of knowledge few scholars would go to the stake for any conception of electoral behaviour in the half century after 1870, though some stimulating studies have appeared.[3] Perhaps it will prove most helpful in this short account to begin with the Liberal party at Westminster, about which a far clearer picture can be drawn, and then to proceed to the more intractable problems raised by popular politics and electoral geography.

In parliament

Power plainly comes first among priorities for a political party, so it will help readers new to the period between the passing of the second reform act in 1867 and the decision to enter the First World War in 1914 to note that the Liberal party held power on five occasions during those years: between 1868 and 1874; between 1880 and 1885; for a few months in 1886; between 1892 and 1895; and for the whole of the period between December 1905 and Asquith's invitation to other parties to join the Liberals in a wartime coalition in May 1915. In speaking about 'the climax of Liberal politics', therefore, there is no suggestion of a stranglehold on office. One is merely drawing attention to a period of pivotal political change that encompasses the remarkable governments of Gladstone and Asquith. For although historians disagree with some passion about the *meaning* of this phase of Liberal experience, they usually take all or some section of it as central to explaining the fate of Liberalism in the twentieth century. The period offers a repository of evidence which any theory of Liberal collapse or resilience will need to confront and explain. Much of the argument inevitably turns around the general elections in which power was won, but to compare Liberal performance across a broad sweep of time becomes difficult in face of the extension and remodelling of the franchise in 1884–5, which introduces obvious distortions into the data, and because of the splitting of the party into two factions in 1886 over the issue of whether Ireland should be granted a form of Home Rule. The dissident faction of 1886 formed a separate party, the Liberal Unionist party, which retained a distinct identity almost until the First World War, though in practice it had long since acted as a progressive wing of the Conservative party.

Disregarding distortions for a moment in order simply to sketch the shape of party performance in the general elections between 1885 and 1910, we arrive at a picture along the lines of Fig. 2.1. Of course this crude graph comments only on seats won, rather than the many more subtle indicators of electoral behaviour to which one might have recourse. Yet it announces clearly enough the consistency of Irish repre-

---

[2] For pollbooks and their use, see John Vincent (ed.), *Pollbooks: how Victorians voted* (Cambridge, 1968).
[3] This material will be considered in chapter eight. For a general perspective, see Peter Clarke, 'Electoral Sociology of Modern Britain', *History*, 57 (1972), 31–55.

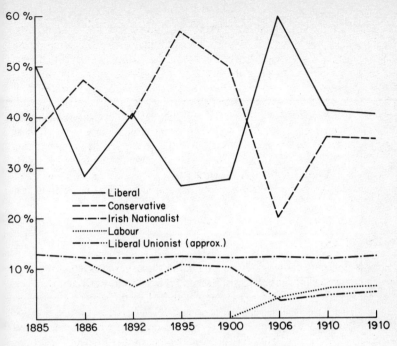

Figure 2.1: Percentage of seats held by all parties 1885–1910 (UK)

sentation through the period, the fading away of Unionism and the modesty of Labour's incursions into parliamentary power before 1914 – all important elements in understanding the Liberal story. In its simple oscillation of Liberal and Conservative predominance, however, the graph conceals a good deal. By generalizing the results it camouflages the situation in England (a worrying one for Liberal headquarters before 1906) by enclosing it in the healthier one suggested by Scotland and Wales. If we represent the English experience then Conservative strength becomes more marked (see Fig. 2.2). The addition of an 'average' figure for the period *before* 1885 goes some way towards silhouetting the problems faced after the party fissure over Home Rule. Indeed, there is a case for extending the procedure to the period as a whole. The result is perhaps fictionalized by its abstraction, but if we break the line at 1885 and 1906 the result, shown in Fig. 2.3, nevertheless seems startling. The degree of difficulty facing the party between 1886 and 1906 stands out far more starkly here and bears some witness to the effects of the schism. It also insists that the success of 1906 and later marked in one sense at least a reconquest of electoral influence won in the pre-reform period rather than a forging ahead to new heights. And of course extending the period after 1906 to the different electoral conditions obtaining after the First World War would give the Liberals a radically more pessimistic prognosis.

The sense of crisis in Liberal performance in the 1890s increases in intensity if one compares the data from English contests with that from the 'Celtic Fringe' of Scotland, Wales and Ireland. True, the Liberal position in Ireland had deteriorated rapidly after 1880 as Parnell's Nationalists swept the board and left the Liberals, even

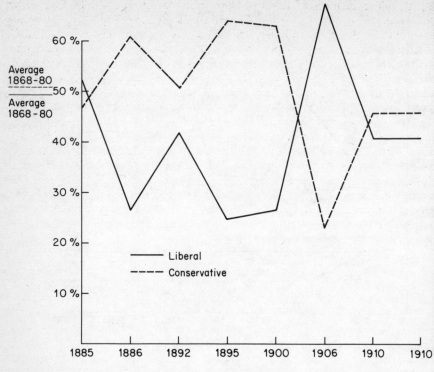

Figure 2.2: Percentage of seats held by Liberal and Conservative parties 1885–1910 (England)

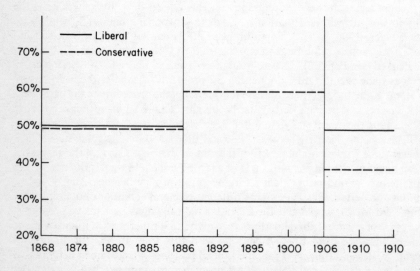

Figure 2.3: Average percentage of seats held in England by period

in the golden moment of January 1906, with only three seats. In their worst performance – that of 1892 – the Irish Nationalists still took 79 per cent of the seats in Ireland. On the other hand, the Nationalists never repeated their mistake of 1885 in allying with the Conservative party. From the beginning of Gladstone's attempts to force a Home Rule Bill through the British parliament, the Nationalists relied on the Liberals to realize their ambitions and the Liberals knew *pari passu* that they could retain Irish support so long as their commitment to Home Rule enjoyed some measure of prominence among their public priorities. In Wales, on the other hand, the most effective competition to the Liberal party came, by 1910, from the new Labour party; but neither the Conservative nor Labour challenges looked likely to dislodge the Liberals from the position of supremacy won after 1868. Even in the dark years after 1890, the Conservatives never won more than 8 seats out of 34 and that small segment withered away after the turn of century. In Scotland the curve matches that of the United Kingdom as a whole in its dip through the nineties but suggests the power of the Unionists, rather than the Conservative party, in deepening it. The picture of Liberal recovery after 1900 also appears more convincing in Scotland than in England (see Fig. 2.4).

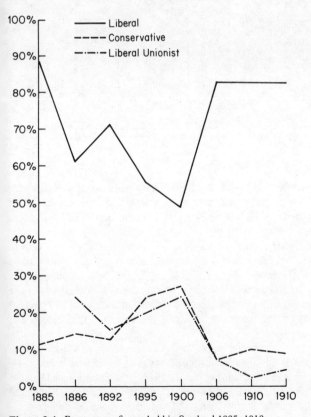

Figure 2.4: Percentage of seats held in Scotland 1885–1910

The rigidities of the British first-past-the-post electoral system encourage this concentration on seats won rather than votes polled. But any sensitive understanding of the Liberals' situation naturally requires that one know something of their share of the poll and the number of candidates they offered. This latter consideration may strike modern readers familiar with a situation in which serious political parties contest all constituencies as too arcane to cause concern; but in fact it exercised a particular importance during the 1890s when the Liberals performed so badly at the polls. Their failure to fight constituencies rather than to win them colours to no small extent the picture that one might form of their potential strength; so that, if we widen the terms of the argument by including these extra variables, a rather more complicated image begins to form. We might represent it diagrammatically as in Fig. 2.5.

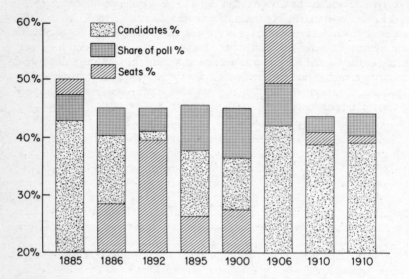

Figure 2.5: Liberal share of candidates, poll and seats 1885–1910 (UK)

The shortfall in candidates in 1895 and 1900 obviously goes some way towards accounting for the poor Liberal returns of these years, granted that the Liberal share of the poll remained consistent. Two other features deserve mention. One might notice, first, the immediate damage to the party as an electoral machine caused by the events of 1885–6. Second, the phenomenal success in seats won at the election of 1906 camouflages the marginality of the increase in the Liberal poll since 1885 and a substantial addition to their reservoir of candidates. Third, the poor share of candidates by 1910 suggests not so much a failure of resources as the effects of the Labour party's appearance as a major organization fielding candidates of its own (5.9 per cent and 4.7 per cent of the respective totals in the elections of January and December 1910).

Liberal candidates who returned to the House of Commons at any of the 11 general elections between 1868 and 1914 discovered themselves part of an established male world – no woman appeared in the chamber before 1919 – which radiated certain characteristics about its social background and assumptions. Naturally that world attracted some individuals whose eccentricities defy inclusion in any hypothetical description of 'the average Liberal MP', if one could agree about what such a description meant. Even convenient men, after all, spill over the edges of categories and definitions. Some statements nevertheless seem too banal to resist. In the second half of the nineteenth century, the power of land as a critical determinant of political affiliation and priority diminished and the influence of industry and the professions increased; thus common sense at least suggests that the Liberal parliamentary grouping must have shown some reflection of this shift of emphasis. Yet despite so modest a level of commentary, problems arise at once. Into which category should Sir Christopher Furness go? From 1891 to his death in 1912 he represented the Hartlepools, except for a few years in the late nineties, as a Liberal MP. Since he owned a shipping and engineering business he presumably ought to go into the column marked 'business'. But he also lived the life of a man to the manor born, at Grantley Hall near Ripon, and owned over 30,000 acres. Sir Charles McLaren (Lib: Stafford, 1880–6; Leicestershire, Bosworth, 1892–1910) presents similar difficulty. He held land in North Wales but was also a barrister and therefore ought, perhaps, to be counted as part of the Liberal legal complement rather than as a landowner. Indeed, a fairly regular photo-fit from the Liberal backbenches poses a problem: the man who takes a degree from Oxford or Cambridge, proceeds to the Bar but never actually practises, lives on a smallish rentier income from an inherited estate, but then supplements it by taking company directorships or funding a business of his own. In sociological terms a career of this kind looks like a plate of spaghetti; and the more one deploys boxes and labels, the more one wants to disown them.

Yet the feeling persists that the Liberals did, seen as a group, display qualities and connexions different from those common among Conservatives. Wealth, understood in any crude sense, is no great help in effecting the distinction because the Liberal party contained few working men in its parliamentary cohort while its Whig magnates commanded the resources to buy out many Tories without embarrassment. The contrast comes out better in the balance of interests which the two parties developed through the period in question. Suppose we examine individuals of both parties who succeeded in contested constituencies in the general election of 1892 – a helpful case since it falls in the centre of our period, reflects a post-1886 party structure and offers an instance in which the representation of the major parties turned out approximately equal. One possible apportionment of the occupations of those men would take the shape shown in Fig. 2.6.[4]

Interest	Liberal	Conservative
Land	8.1	28.5
Business and Finance	44.2	25.9
Law	24.8	24.1
Other	22.9	21.5

Figure 2.6: Background of Liberal and Conservative MPs returned at the general election of 1892 (percentages: UK totals)

[4] The analysis here is my own and rests principally on the biographies of MPs printed in Michael Stenton (ed.), *Who's Who of British Members of Parliament* (4 vols., Hassocks, 1976.81). It differs in detail, for the reasons suggested, from figures used by H. V. Emy in his *Liberals, Radicals and Social Politics 1892–1914* (Cambridge, 1973), 103; but the overall picture is similar.

Look first at the third row of figures which suggests one very important constant in the sociology of late-nineteenth-century political parties. One might note, too, that the significance of the legal dimension would markedly increase if the analysis were addressed at the 'high politics' of the cabinet room and the men of junior-ministerial status. But the first two rows of figures, commenting on land and business, point to a no less firm discontinuity, with business interests easily predominant in the Liberal party and land still a major constituent in the background of Conservatives. Indeed the latter thought is amplified when we recall that these figures include among the Conservatives a group of around 46 'Unionists' who often began their careers as Liberals and who included industrialists like Joseph Chamberlain and his Birmingham contingent of quondam Radicals. The fourth category opens the way to a number of interesting speculations. On the Tory side, any impression of randomness among these 'others' soon disperses. Over half of this group (and 16.3 per cent of the total sample) had ties with the army: the man whose *curriculum vitae* ran Wellington, Sandhurst, commission, early retirement, Conservative seat had some role to play in the quieter backwaters of Tory politics. The Liberals reveal a wider catchment. Here the military connexion, as one would expect, has far less prominence with only 2.7 per cent of the total displaying an army background. If any social category appears with noticeable regularity, then it is one spanning education and journalism. Taken together these comprise about 9 per cent of the 1892 sample and they doubtless helped to give confidence to the proclamation heard ever since that the Liberals are the party of Thought, even if everything else they represent has turned to dust and ashes.

This snapshot of Liberal parliamentarians in 1892 suffers through over-exposure. It also loses much portraiture in its sheer instantaneity. One needs a sense of change over time and that in turn requires an examination of Liberal background at a number of points in the chronology. Few such points are currently available but research has illuminated at least two areas: the early period of Liberal development in the 1850s and 1860s and the very important period just before the First World War. Selecting categories similar to the ones I have used for 1892, we could construct a small table

Interest	1859 – 74	1892	1914
Land	49.2	8.1	6.0
Business	30.1	44.2	40.0
Law	16.7	24.8	22.0
Other	4.0	22.9	32

Figure 2.7: Background of Liberal MPs at selected periods (percentages: UK totals)

(see Fig. 2.7).[5] Plainly the drift away from land as a predominant characteristic continued after the 1890s and one finds it as much a Conservative phenomenon as a Liberal. Business interests either held constant or declined slightly (depending on how one reads individual cases). Either way, something like 40 per cent of parliamentary Liberals held interests in this area, raising questions about the ability of an employer-dominated party to find the necessary flexibility to respond to changes in industrial Britain after 1900.[6] A proliferation of interests emerged meanwhile to place nearly a third of Liberals MPs in the amorphous 'other' category by 1914.

Of these various groups, the business element perhaps best illustrates the style of change. The traditional Liberal industrialist in the West Riding of Yorkshire or the Lancashire mills, stiff with pound notes, chapel principles and free trade, still existed on the Liberal benches in 1914. Indeed the weight of such Liberal industrialists remained in precisely those primary sectors of the economy that felt most acutely the cutting edge of competition. Other commercial activities had polarized more obviously by 1910 than might have seemed apparent in 1890. The popular image of the Tory party as a collection of bankers and brewers who had soured Gladstone's grapes when he lost the 1874 election does not bear scrutiny. If bankers appeared less commonly on the Liberal benches than the Tory they nevertheless appeared often enough to make their presence there seem natural. If Tory brewers like Charrington fitted Gladstone's accusations, then other brewers like Whitbread and Bass did not. Looking down the list of business interests in the 1892 Commons the impression is one of broad equilibrium: both parties contain a considerable amount of commercial experience; there is little sense of monopoly and only a mild surprise that a Liberal businessman and future leader of the Liberal party, Sir Henry Campbell-Bannerman, should have a Tory MP as an elder brother. That these impressions relate to a transitory moment seems very evident when the 1914 Commons is brought into comparison. By that time gin and beer had clearly flowed in the direction of the Conservative party which had also mopped up the interconnected milieux of insurance, stockbroking and accountancy.

Just as time conceals important shifts of emphasis, so the geography that lies behind these lists of names has something to say about the realities of Liberal politics. Professional and business MPs could hardly scatter themselves across the fields of Essex and Somerset. Light industry allowed a certain freedom in its sitting, of course, and a few brand names acquired political overtones: Colman's Liberal mustard, Spicer's Liberal paper, Stephens' Conservative ink. But for a concentration of Liberal industrialists one must go to a centre like the West Riding in the nineties where the dominance of Liberal wool and worsted was overpowering. Turn to Scotland and the flavour lightens appreciably: here Liberal doctors emerging from the medical schools of Glasgow and Edinburgh found their niche. Academics often swept aside merchants in this educated and formidable electorate – unless a man had the imprimatur of Glasgow with its exotic Indian connexions and a line, perhaps, in ships or linen or jute. In Wales an unsophisticated man had more chance, even a working man if the constituency could find the money (a thousand pounds, maybe more) to see

[5] These figures come from a variety of sources. For the early period I have used entries in John Vincent's tabulation in his *The Formation of the Liberal Party* (1966), 3. The 1914 figures come from John Ramsden, *The Age of Balfour and Baldwin 1902–40* (1978), made use of by Geoffrey Searle in an important article on 'The Edwardian Liberal Party and Business', *English Historical Review*, XCVII (1983), 57; but the figure for the percentage of lawyers (subsumed by Ramsden under 'Professions') I have taken from Emy, *op. cit.*
[6] See Searle, 'Edwardian Liberal Party', esp. 34–56.

him through. But a merchant with a fat wallet must have seemed a better buy, especi
ally if he could claim roots in Cardiff or Swansea or, more likely, in Liverpool.

In the country

Liverpool says much that is unrepeatable. Its peculiar version of Liberalism, near
strangled by the Tammany Hall Toryism of Archibald Salvidge and the Irish radical
ism of T. P. O'Connor, stands as warning to anyone wishing to paint a national
picture by enlarging local tints.[7] Abandon Liverpool for Manchester and the towns o
its hinterland, and the story shifts markedly to one of Liberal success and vitality afte
the turn of the century. Once cross the Pennines, however, and the descent into
Huddersfield and Halifax brings with it a descent into a different political climate
where the ILP and the unions carry more charge and Liberal employers, for all thei
continuing political power, have less time for the new-fangled.[8] Yet no sooner has the
historian expunged Liverpool, Manchester, Huddersfield and Halifax from hi
generalities than London, Birmingham and Glasgow begin to make their own plea
for uniqueness. Even bits of Liberal countryside kick and elbow one another in thei
claims to particularity within any of the categories that analysts seek to impose. One
must face the reality, then, that pictures of 'the country' and its opinions amount to
charcoal sketches: monochrome, free-hand accounts, worthwhile for their sense o
shape but fragile in their detail and firmness of line.

It follows that no agreed imagery comes readily to mind. In this area controversy
suffuses discussion from the outset and leaves little room for consensus beyond the
banal. The banal, on the other hand, has its uses when one comes to a new period with
little sense of its major reference-points; perhaps it sometimes takes even the
cognoscenti back to long-forgotten first principles. Asking which parts of Britain
proved most consistently Liberal seems at least a question that a map ought to be able
to answer, even if we cannot easily measure the intensity of Liberal adhesion. The
map of electoral performance between 1885 and 1910 is too complicated to help one
see any pattern, but we can corrode the surface by concentrating attention on areas
that, for example, returned Liberal MPs at all eight general elections through the
period. The result of this violence appears in map 2.1.[9]

Anyone unsure of the importance of the 'Celtic Fringe' within Liberal politics in
the late nineteenth and early twentieth centuries will find immediate reassurance
from an X-ray plate of this kind. Scotland, Wales and a sizeable chunk of the West
Country plainly provided a reliable base of support. The map of Liberal consistency
turns out not to be a map of central England but rather of the periphery. Suppose we
take a different axis: one measuring not the extent of Liberal territory but its type.
Notice how the acid has affected *urban* Liberalism. London is omitted from the
account, true, but then introducing it would only compound the impression because
London reflected a sharp swing towards Toryism after 1885. Plot the cities and the
industrial centres on such a map and the fit comes out badly. The Quaker Pease-dom

[7] The politics of Liverpool have been well analysed by Philip Waller: see P. J. Waller, *Democracy and Sec
tarianism: a political and social history of Liverpool 1868–1939* (Liverpool, 1981).
[8] Contrast the images presented, for example, in Peter Clarke, *Lancashire and the New Liberalism*
(Cambridge, 1971) with those in an analysis of Yorkshire politics, Keith Laybourn and Jack Reynolds,
Liberalism and the Rise of Labour 1890–1918 (1984). This contrast will be recalled in chapter eight.
[9] The map is based on Michael Kinnear's cartography in his *The British Voter* (1968), 83.

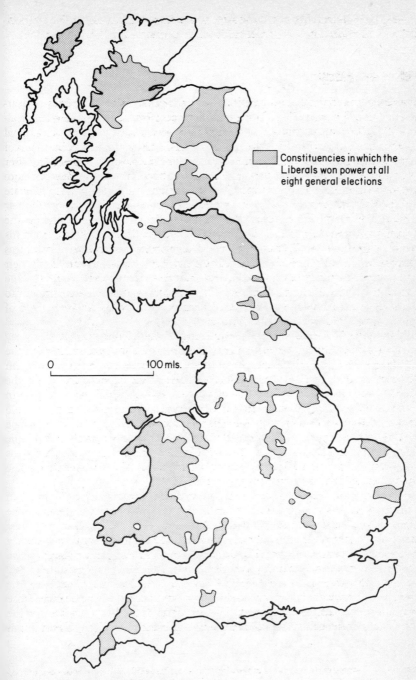

Constituencies in which the Liberals won power at all eight general elections

Map 2.1: The Liberal heartland 1885–1910

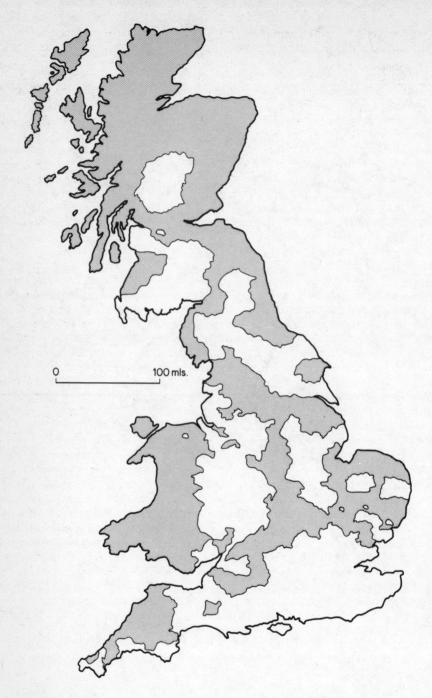

Map 2.2: Liberal territory (shaded) 1892 (London omitted)

of the north-east makes its Liberal impact, certainly. There exists, too, that finger of Liberal tenacity pointing inland from the Humber estuary, winding westward with the Aire and Calder towards parts of the West Riding and then over the Pennines into east Lancashire. But the story is partial and misleading. No small part of this territory consists of suburban or semi-rural enclaves within an area of heavy industry. And beyond those areas much of the industrial focus of the North lies outside Liberal monopoly because the ILP and Labour party have already made substantial inroads there before 1914. This is what has eaten away the towns of south Yorkshire and driven the Liberals back from the sea across the mining valleys of south Wales. Alternative forms of corrosion have also made their mark, of course: the Unionism of Chamberlain and his allies in Birmingham, the robustness of urban Toryism in central Sheffield or Hull. But taken together the impression becomes strong that, if we freeze Liberalism into a single block of experience across nearly 40 years of time, it seems to have achieved its greatest consistency of performance at general elections in areas outside the growing conurbations.

Yet history never did freeze satisfactorily; and in the impression offered by the stopping of the clock many features become obliterated. Some sense of the passage of time and what it did to the behaviour of Liberal voters plainly demands attention. One way of responding might be to examine the configuration of Liberal territory in 1892, the year on which our analysis of Liberal MPs rested, together with a later one taken from the years after the Labour party and the spectacular Liberal win of 1906 had become realities. The second election of 1910 seems a suitable comparison. By then the distortions, if such they were, of 1906 had died away and the major parties returned closer to the parity in representation they had known in 1892. In absolute terms, indeed, the return of Liberal MPs proved almost identical – 272 in 1892 and 271 in 1910. The latter election also proved to be the final one before the coming of the First World War and the fundamental reshaping of electoral conditions in 1918. Considering these events as slices through the chronology may, therefore, suggest something about Liberal developments and these two perspectives appear side-by-side as maps 2.2 and 2.3.[10]

Some obvious changes catch the eye at once. The spine of Liberal support running down the centre of England in 1892 has by 1910 fractured at its base in the west Midlands. Home Counties Toryism has joined hands with the Welsh Marches, cutting off residual Liberal constituencies and leaving them isolated in a Conservative environment. Further north and east, Labour accretions have come uniquely from Conservatives and Unionists: everywhere else the Labour presence appears in former Liberal areas. This is mostly as one would expect because, under the terms of the secret electoral alliance concluded between Liberals and the Labour Representation Committee in 1903, Labour still operated largely under Liberal licence. That the Liberal party felt it necessary to concede the licence nevertheless says a good deal about the power of Labour politics in some areas and the poverty of the Liberal machine in repelling it.

Against this mood of Liberal difficulty, one may read the map in a way that leads the mind in a different direction. The Liberal dominance in the industrial north in 1910 appears stronger than in the map of heartland areas we examined in map 1. An implication therefore deserves note. Although the Liberals may have wavered from

[10]These again represent selected information from Kinnear, *British Voter*, 23, 35.

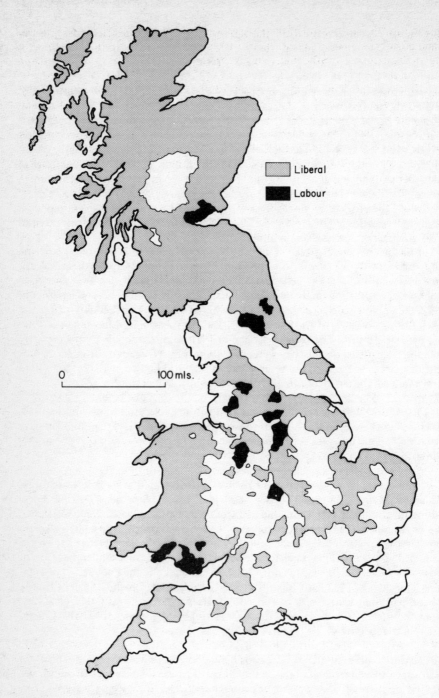

Map 2.3: Liberal territory December 1910 (London omitted)

time to time in their control of these areas over the quarter-century since 1885, the graph of success in many constituencies flicked *upwards* in the elections of the early twentieth century. Now the point is a contentious one and ought, perhaps, to wait until the final chapter for a fuller development. But it seems appropriate here to underline that the Whig view of the Edwardian period in which the Liberal party fares worse and worse against the problems and rivals that beset it does not fit a wide range of evidence. Map 2.3 collects only a few fragments of such evidence but it says enough to cast doubt on an understanding of Liberal history that turns on irreversible decline before 1910. Certainly the Labour party has made its presence felt as a new force; but the map shows clearly enough the scale of the challenge. It has not wrested industrial Britain away from the Liberal party. To say that it was about to do so and would have done so, had not the crisis in Europe pre-empted its advance by changing the character of British politics, does not amount to a stupid argument but neither does it offer a grounded one. What seems certain is that the Liberals continued to retain a broad base of electoral support after their remarkable achievement in 1906.

The maps make their point. Yet they cannot say explicitly what kind of social base the Liberal territories comprised. Nor, in these years of the secret ballot, can any other form of direct evidence: one must use a certain intuition and imagination in trying to illuminate the localities by turning electoral geography into social history. Placing the problem in a longer time-scale helps at least to establish some perspective. We know that Liberal voters in the towns after 1868 contained a new element from the 'respectable' working class in the householders and better-heeled lodgers enfranchised by the 1867 Reform Act. The towns brought into the representative framework for the first time in 1868 – among them Burnley, Darlington, Dewsbury, Middlesbrough, Stalybridge, Stockton and the Hartlepools – suggested the possibility of deepening northern Liberalism by exploiting this new catchment. The catchment, conversely, was not one for which Whig–Liberalism in its 1860s format seemed especially well-geared. Professor Vincent's image of a local Liberal environment whose workers looked like Adam Bede and Felix Holt[11] is well-taken and implies a world that did not die for some time. By the beginning of the 1880s, on the other hand, the afterlife of Adam Bede and Felix Holt had come to its end: they lay under stones in the churchyard, quaint mementos of a receding individualist culture. The towns had already begun their slide from societies differentiated by ecclesiastical denomination and occupational interest-group towards more impersonal and large-scale social units in which 'class' and 'status' found a thousand refractions in local behaviour and sharper reflections in the glint of money.

The Liberal party coped badly with this elision, not so much out of ideological aversion as through a lack of urgency. It lagged behind the Conservative party in the 1870s – organizing itself only after the Tories had hammered Liberal candidates in the large towns at the 1874 election. Its imagery of urban man as a rural transplant shielded the party from a realization that more would be needed if the towns were to remain Liberal. Besides, it made apparent sense to concentrate on the countryside when everyone knew that the next piece of franchise reform would have to involve extending the provisions of 1867 (or something like them) to the counties and give the vote to Hodge the Labourer. So for a time the parties stood on their heads: the Conservative party loosened its grip on the counties as they turned their attention towards thrusting themselves into the towns;[12] and the Liberals spent much of their energies

---

[11]Vincent, *Formation of the Liberal Party*, 57–8.

[12]For Conservative behaviour after 1867 see H. J. Hanham's enormously helpful survey, *Elections and*

looking to gain a foothold in the rural areas which their Whigs – an endangered species by the mid eighties – no longer controlled. But that strategy was a Radical one that reached its apogee in Joseph Chamberlain's Unauthorized Programme of 1885 and which lost impetus when he and his allies defected from the party over Home Rule in 1886. In concrete terms this probably did not matter much. We shall see that Gladstone did not understand the countryside. But Chamberlain and Lloyd George did not understand it any better. The idea that rural politics turned on land-hunger and rational economic decision-making dogged Liberal thinking for the next half century. Agricultural shows, meat-market morality and farmers' pub lunches projected into the twentieth century a form of consensual politics that Tories knew by instinct. Ruling that world by dividing it horizontally between Tory farmers and Liberal labourers looked a stronger option on paper than probably ever existed in fact. When Gladstone threw the paper in the bin in 1886 in order to make his Liberals talk about something more acceptable, the initiative in any case all but ceased and Liberalism began to address itself to the towns 15 years later than hindsight implies might have been prudent.

This did not mean ruin. It meant disadvantage. The Liberals knew about their difficulty and made considerable efforts, on a fragile budget that Herbert Gladstone worked hard to strengthen, towards improving their urban party machinery and preventing the Independent Labour party from gaining too firm a grip in working-class districts. Surveys by modern analysts of Liberal sentiment among those and other sections of society validate a few tentative observations. In many areas of heavy industry – coal, textiles, shipbuilding – the Liberal party maintained a credible presence before 1914. The decision of the Miners' Federation of Great Britain to transfer its political support to the Labour party in 1909 may have written much writing on the wall, but it seems clear that in most mining areas a Liberal candidate had a good chance of winning a seat in Edwardian Britain and in some of them a near-certainty of doing so.[13] Lancashire cotton and West Riding wool presented different faces of Liberalism – one new, one old – but both were remarkably consistent in their Liberalism before 1914, with spectacular irruptions such as the narrow but arresting win by Victor Grayson at Colne Valley following the departure of Sir James Kitson to the House of Lords in 1907. Free Trade played some part in this affinity, of course, especially in the Lancashire cotton trade, but so did more unspoken continuities. As Peter Clarke acutely observes in his portrait of Lancashire Liberalism after 1900, cotton men often believed in free trade because they were Liberals rather than in Liberalism because they were free-traders.[14] In other sectors the Liberal experience had become more chequered. Steel towns presented a complicated picture as, for example, in south Yorkshire where the tariff argument probably helped Conservatives and Unionists do better, on the one hand, and provided opportunities for Labour advance on the other as in the much-publicized win at Attercliffe in 1909. Taken together, then, the evidence from parliamentary elections does not suggest any form of annihilation among the Liberal working class so much as interesting regional complications in its pattern and conditions of support. The argument soon becomes a controversial one, however, and we shall, therefore,

Party Management: politics in the time of Disraeli and Gladstone (1959, Hassocks, 1978) and E. J Feuchtwanger, *Disraeli, Democracy and the Tory Party: Conservative leadership and organization after th second reform act* (Oxford, 1968).
[13]Roy Gregory's study of the miners in this period underlines the degree to which their Liberalism often held firm after 1909: R. Gregory, *The Miners in British Politics 1906–14* (Oxford, 1968).
[14]Clarke, *Lancashire*, 274–310.

defer further consideration of it until later sections of this book.

What about other parts of the social structure? The lower middle class deserves inquiry because the period after 1870 sees a significant phase in its emergence. For the moment the research remains too thin to permit broad-ranging comment[15] but a few points have entered discussions of Liberal potential. It appears from voting patterns in the south-east, for example, that a swing towards Conservatism occurred among the upwardly-mobile, though it would help to know more about the self-image of black-coated workers and small shop-keepers in the 1890s when the shift becomes evident. By itself, the electoral evidence never shrugs off a certain ambivalence: the greatest concentrations of lower-middle-class support certainly have a Tory tinge as the period progresses; but that result may be biased by the failure of many such individuals to gain the vote at all. Normally we think of this problem as a working-class phenomenon. The revised franchise of 1884 still contained a property qualification. It follows that individuals at the lower end of the social spectrum failed to cross that threshold and consequently could not vote. Indeed, the proportion of adult males affected by this disability may have remained as high as 40 per cent throughout the period.[16] But the qualifications contained *two* requirements – property and residence. The question arises: which sections of the population would have been most disadvantaged by the need to reside in the qualifying household for a full year before the electoral registers were revised? In so far as an itinerant class may have emerged, it seems likely that such individuals may have improved their social mobility at the expense of losing their vote.[17]

Another group of middle-class Liberals retained as firm an immobility as did the mills and factories they owned. The Liberalism of this group (and to some extent its workforce) depended on the geography and character of its components. That a business such as the Baldwin family iron concern in Worcestershire should have put an MP on to the Conservative benches in the 1890s (Alfred, Stanley's father) suggests that some old associations between the Liberal party and the business ethic no longer held true. On the other hand, the Baldwins worked in a section of the economy that had a clear tariff mentality by the end of the century. More to the point, perhaps, they were Anglicans. But the old connexion between, for example, mill owners, Dissenting religion and the Liberal party held strong in the northern Liberal heartland of the West Riding. On occasion that Liberalism fused with a curious mixture of environmental conscience and subtle social control in the Liberal settlements of Lever's Port Sunlight, or Cadbury's Bournville, or Rowntree's New Earswick. And the appearance of a Rowntree as MP for York for the *first* time in 1910 confirms the dangers of visualizing the period as a slow etiolation in the power of employer-Liberalism. Rather does it imply the relevance of questions about the potential within Liberal politics for adaptation and new initiatives in a post-Gladstonian situation.

Having recourse to the nonconformist churches as an instrument of explanation comes naturally to anyone concerned with the late-Victorian and Edwardian Liberal party. The evidence left by politicians comments persuasively on the degree to which they worried about what Dissent thought of them: even Lloyd George remembered from time to time to behave like a Baptist. When crisis promised to appear from

[5]Geoffrey Crossick has collected some papers on this theme: see G. Crossick, *The Lower Middle Class in Britain 1870–1914* (1977).

[6]Clarke, 'Electoral Sociology', *passim*; cf. Neal Blewett, 'The Franchise in the United Kingdom 1885–1914', *Past and Present*, 32 (1965), 27–56.

[7]Duncan Tanner, 'The Parliamentary Electoral System, the "Fourth" Reform Act and the Rise of Labour in England and Wales', *Bulletin of the Institute of Historical Research*, 56 (1983), 205–19.

around the next bend, Liberals knew that Methodists and Congregationalists would have something to say – especially if the issues involved the disestablishment of churches (i.e. the severing of their connexion with the state) or war and defence (about which the 'Left' of nonconformity held such strong opinions) or above all about education which in the period from 1870 functioned in the political domain as an encoded translation of dogmas and godly resentments. The map of nonconformity by the 1890s conforms fairly well to that of Liberal domination, after taking account of the Tory streak among Wesleyans and Unitarians and the 'Labour' tendencies of Primitive Methodism, many of whose members in the poorer rural districts would in any case have been unable to vote. Dissenting numbers turned into a downward spiral between 1845 and 1855 in the cases of the Methodist, Congregational and Baptist churches, though the diminution is best seen against the proportion of nonconformists within the adult population as a whole. Methodist membership in England rose, for example, by over a quarter of a million between 1871 and 1906 but as a proportion of the adult population that rise represented a fall from 4.1 to 3.6 per cent. Against that attenuation, on the other hand, we can place the very marked loyalty of nonconformists to the Liberal party: they stood in relation to non-Liberal nonconformists in a ratio of perhaps ten to one.[18] Besides, words often speak louder than numbers and Dissent had plenty of those. They could, moreover, make their words count through their preaching, their journalism and through politicians' fears that they controlled sections of popular opinion. A Liberal party conceived without R. W. Dale, R. F. Horton, Silvester Horne and Robertson Nicoll would be an impoverished and misleading piece of history.

Liberal churches, Liberal newspapers, their clubs, their sectional pressure groups: these elements did not act merely as satellites or acolytes. They became part of the way in which a political party needed to assert itself in what Kitson Clark called an expanding society.

> Turning and turning in the widening gyre
> The falcon cannot hear the falconer

So Westminster needed to shout louder, find more strings. We see a great acceleration in Liberal newspaper activity after 1870 and something approaching hegemony in the intellectual journalism peculiar to the heyday of Liberal editors such as C. P. Scott of the *Manchester Guardian*, J. A. Spender of the *Westminster Gazette*, Robert Donald of the *Daily Chronicle*, A. G. Gardiner of the *Daily News*.[19] Through such outlets, and at a more elevated level through the monthly magazines read by the leisured classes, a Liberal intelligentsia tried to tell Liberals what they ought to believe. Whether they succeeded in their mission (and which Liberals they converted) present important questions which this book must confront at a number of points. What cannot be denied is that the British Liberal party amounted to more than a collection of politicians, a few officials and a remote electorate. Above and between came a constellation of governing ideas whose propagators intended them to act as significant contributions to Liberal politics. To that extent those ideas and their thinkers may be seen as not so much a different story as a separate chapter.

[18]A. D. Gilbert, *Religion and Society in Industrial England: church, chapel and social change 1740–1914* (1976), 23–48.
[19]For the Liberal popular press, see Alan Lee, *The Rise of the Popular Press 1855–1914* (1976). The journals are explored by Stephen Koss in his *The Rise and Fall of the Political Press in Britain* (2 vols., 1981, 1984).

3

Liberal Theory before 1886

Individualists and their problems

'Of course,' said Lady Ambrose, 'it is necessary that some of us should look after politics, because if we did not somebody else would. But still – (are you a Liberal, Lord Allen?) – but still, within a limit, I think the *less* we meddle the better.'

W. H. Mallock, *The New Republic* (2 vols., 1877), II, 212

Intellectual politics, no less than aristocratic, carried the mind of its Liberal enthusiasts towards defining the limits of meddling within a society conscious of its stability and success during the last years of Palmerstonian England. The 1860s marked a high point for a number of Liberal theorists, over whom John Stuart Mill (1806–73) and Matthew Arnold (1822–88) had perhaps gained pre-eminence; and they made their mission the shaping of a distinctive Liberal culture through which the fundamental wholesomeness of British society might gain strength, and close its unnecessary fissures, without any sacrifice of capital, conscience or the individual's sense of personal responsibility for himself and his family. Both Mill and Arnold suffered from exposed roots: one network running back to the Benthamite utilitarianism of James Mill (1773–1836) who forever stained those parts of his son's mind that he did not actually destroy; the other carrying into middle age the muscular Christianity of his father's great public school – Rugby – and addressing a public to which Dr Thomas Arnold (1795–1842) had never been obliged to minister. Since the end of the Crimean war, they and some of the younger intellectuals committed to support of the Liberal party, among whom James Bryce, Leslie Stephen, Goldwin Smith, Henry Sidgwick, Henry Fawcett and Albert Dicey had won or were about to win major reputations,[1] had used the expansion of a high-minded monthly and weekly journalism as a vantage-point far beyond the boundaries of their natural environment in Oxford, Cambridge and London, from which to direct their opinions at a broader, but nevertheless still very exclusive, political public. Their message had a peculiar character. It differed, on the one hand, from the passionate outpourings of

---

[1] These and other Liberal intellectuals can be followed through in Christopher Harvie, *The Lights of Liberalism: university Liberals and the challenge of democracy 1860–86* (1976), *passim*.

German and French thought since the 1840s and, on the other, from the sophisticated programme which a new generation of Liberals came to espouse after 1890. In the absence of a more evocative name, this message may be described as a doctrine of individualism.

In our own day the description has come to suffer a bad press. Dicey's over-schematic division of political ideas into those connoting 'individualism' on the one hand, and 'collectivism' on the other, certainly required emendation, for one finds instead that the nineteenth-century idea of individualism had a compound character that allowed its adherents a choice of political parties and a wide range of priorities and emphasis. To place Mill and Herbert Spencer in the same 'individualist' camp would, for example, conceal more than it would reveal about their political positions.[2] But it remains the case that, between the 1850s and the 1870s, British Liberal theory often held at its centre the image of a desociated individual – what D. H. Lawrence would later call a single, paradisal soul – beset by the demands and rapacities of an industrial environment from which he expected governments to protect him. What he had no right to expect, according to Mill and his school, was the state's lifting from his shoulders the burdens that properly belonged there and nowhere else. In recommending the maximization of the individual's 'liberty', the spokesmen of mid-Victorian Liberalism aimed at giving him, indeed, precisely nothing – the commodity which Aristotle had identified as 'absence of restraint'. They did not wish government to take positive action in order to free the individual from the trials of living in a capitalist society; nor did they intend the individual to gain from government what he could not gain for himself – unless, that is, some artificial barrier had been placed in the individual's way. Exploitation, monopoly, unfair advantage, corruption, bigotry: these queerings of the pitch should certainly attract the attention of governments in order to allow the individual the opportunity to engage in free and fair competition with his fellows. That done, however, the game goes on with the batsman 'free' to score as many (or as few) runs as skill, weather and fortune allow under the scrutiny of a rather distant umpire. Above all one must not, as a Liberal, lose sight of the truth that what 'one does for people is only useful to them if it merely supports what they do for themselves.'[3]

A doctrine of this kind felt more comfortable after the economic upturn of the 1850s than it might have done during the darker days of the previous decade. Mill's relaxed sense of the present in the years of *On Liberty* (1859), *Representative Government* (1861) and *Utilitarianism* (1863) hardly reflected the doom that dominated the horizon of Thomas Carlyle when he wrote his *Past and Present* in the early 1840s. Looking forward to the repeal of the corn laws, Carlyle had envisaged a threshold of new activity from a recharged notion of government: 'A precious and thrice-precious space of years; wherein the struggle as for life in reforming our foul ways; in alleviating, instructing, regulating our people; seeking, as for life, that something like spiritual food be imparted them, some real governance and guidance be provided them!'.[4] Carlyle's ultimate 'governance' turned out to lie, of course, in an overt *Führerprinzip* through which the 'Mock Superiors' of Peelite Britain would find

[2] See Steven Lukes, *Individualism* (Oxford, 1973), esp. chs. 5 and 12; Michael Freeden, *The New Liberalism: an ideology of social reform* (Oxford, 1977), 32; Stephan Collini, *Liberalism and Sociology: political argument in England 1880–1914* (Cambridge, 1979), 13–32.
[3] Mill to Comte, 17 May 1847, quoted in Bernard Semmel, *John Stuart Mill and the Pursuit of Virtue* (New Haven, 1984), 97.
[4] Thomas Carlyle, *Past and Present* (1843), 185, 264.

themselves displaced by 'Real Superiors' of his own devising; and that solution held little appeal for Liberals whatever the state of the economy. Another style of activism current in the 1840s, one more palatable and even inspiring to Mill in his early years, originated in France. The father of French social science, Auguste Comte, exerted considerable influence in Britain in the forties and fifties when his 'positive' philosophy, which depicted the entirety of human experience throughout history as a necessary progression through three stages in the life of the social organism, lent a sense of law and progress to a generation conscious of the diffuseness of a German philosophy still reeling from the spiralling dialectics of the previous generation's most compelling thinker, G. W. F. Hegel, who had died in 1831. On the other hand, Comtean positivism undermined the character of Liberal individualism quite as readily as the Prussian authoritarianism seen by many as the likely outcome of Hegel's system of thought. Rather than die beneath the jackboot of a super race, the Liberal individual asphyxiated, in the care of Comte, through his immersion in a new 'society' that swallowed him up inside a larger reality and gave him no status beyond the privilege of participating in the life of the whole. 'Humanity is alone real,' Comte had warned; 'the individual is an abstraction.'[5] For the son of James Mill who had, in his youth, driven himself literally to nervous collapse in his battle to reconcile the robotic understanding of his father with a conception of individual psychology and morality, the loss of that individual had become unthinkable, for all the attractions of Comte's tidy sense of structure and process. Despite an important correspondence with Mill and a residual influence through Mill's disciple, Henry Sidgwick, Comte wrote no effective Liberal manifesto for Britain, though he found a more receptive audience among the more radical intelligentsia concerned to enhance the claims of Labour within the political nation.

For the functions of government the younger Mill saw, at least in the early phase of his thinking, a very restricted role. Even when, in 1872, he revised his early work on *The Principles of Political Economy* (1848), he did not move towards an expansion of executive authority except in the area of land ownership, for the nationalization of which he developed some sympathy in his last years. The necessary work of government he still confined to national defence and the provision of basic 'conveniences': coinage, paving, lighting, cleansing. 'No one . . . has ever objected to this.' Beyond this minimal framework the government 'surely must' also look after lunatics and infants. It ought to safeguard the rights of property, which Liberals believed necessary to moral behaviour and the development of a wholesome personality, and do so not merely through a structure of public order but also through a system of property laws – not least, again, because 'it has never been contended' otherwise. Once these minima exist within a society, the interference of government 'should never be admitted but when' – the hinge creaks audibly at this point – 'the case of expediency is strong'.[6] In the essays of the 1850s and 1860s the implications of this position for 'social liberty', the objective identified on the first page of *On Liberty*, received further thought and development but Mill's perspective on the scope of government intervention did not radically alter. Education, he thinks, must not become a state responsibility because it can only prove 'a mere contrivance for mould-

[5] Quoted in Robert Mackintosh, *From Comte to Kidd: the appeal to biology or evolution for human guidance* (1899), 26. Mackintosh had come under the influence of Edward Caird at Glasgow and wrote mostly on theology and ethics.
[6] *Principles of Political Economy* in *Collected Works of John Stuart Mill* (Toronto, 1963–), II and III (1965), iii, 801–4.

ing people to be exactly like one another.' (This three years before the Newcastle Commission on education confirmed the seriousness of underprovision for the education of the nation's children.) Intellectual development one must, on the other hand, somehow have. Indeed a properly-conceived system of representative government would introduce an intellectual test for the electors: one could, say, make them 'copy a sentence from an English book and perform a sum in the rule of three'. The extra vote for university graduates would, needless to say, remain. So would voting in public rather than by secret ballot so as not to introduce furtive citizenship into the body politic.

For his part, the Liberal individual of Mill's imagination must recognize the benefits which membership of a society confers on him by exercising his new-won individuality only 'in things which do not *primarily*' – more creaking – 'concern others'.[7] He must, in short, 'not make himself a nuisance to other people.' But Mill knew that nuisances often exist only in the eye of the beholder; and he took care to give his individuals large and searching eyes. They are encouraged to turn on those who incite riots or cause annoyance by waving placards. More than that, they are encouraged to help root out, through the public opinion on which Mill lays great stress, anybody who shows 'rashness, obstinacy, self-conceit – who cannot live within his moderate means – who cannot restrain himself from hurtful indulgences – who pursue[s] animal pleasures at the expense of those of feeling and intellect.' One might have thought these private matters suitable for discussion with one's lover, bank manager, doctor or bookseller. But for Mill it will not do to regard such deviancy as 'self-regarding' because it is inseparable from the unfavourable judgement of other individuals; and it remains the function of opinion in Mill's society to foster not only 'progress' but also 'virtue'. To this extent the notion of government by the people has a special connotation for Mill because the people (more precisely, those middle-class people who have acquired an education) are themselves called upon to supply, through their social policing, a mechanism for advancement that government itself cannot and should not provide. His 'liberty' can only emerge in a society which tolerates meagre forms of institutional interference together with maximal social monitoring of norms: anarchy plus the periscope.

Anarchy preoccupied Arnold more than Mill but he, Arnold, chose the same means to repel the evil. Rather than seek security in a concept of control, Arnold looked to the formation of a new culture which would render such restriction redundant. In his prescriptions for this society, described in his best-known work, *Culture and Anarchy* (1869), Arnold nevertheless went beyond Mill. That the world cried out for rescue from barbarians and philistines, Arnold had long since felt clear; and he shared Mill's opinion of what damage the common man might do to civilization if given his head. He also shared a faith in the power of education to raise discussion to new planes and shame ill-doers. But at the end of the day it is not enough. So deeply has the rot penetrated that the state must play its part in giving history the push it needs. In doing so, moreover, the state will not usurp the necessary functions of the Liberal individual but rather complement his fighting the good fight. Indeed, a page after recalling his father's approval of the Romans' logic in their practice of throwing rebels to their death from the Tarpeian Rock, he reports that:

---

[7] The quotations from Mill in this paragraph occur in *On Liberty* (1859), 45, 49, 50, 95; and *Considerations on Representative Government* (1861), 213.

in our eyes, the very framework and exterior order of the State is sacred; and culture is the great enemy of anarchy, because of the great hopes and designs for the State which culture teaches us to nourish. But as, believing in right reason, and having faith in the progress of humanity towards perfection, . . . we grow to have clearer sight of the ideas of right reason, and of the elements and helps of perfection, and come gradually to fill the framework of the State with them and to make the State more and more the expression, as we say, of our best self, . . . with what aversion shall we *then* not regard anarchy, with what firmness shall we not check it, when there is so much that is so precious which it will endanger.[8]

This hardly amounts to a manifesto but it perhaps implies more forcibly than had Mill what politicians ought to be doing to speed the birth of a Liberal state. For a time other thinkers went in a similar direction. Sidgwick decided, for example, at the beginning of the decade to lend his support to whoever would help form 'a Liberal Mediative party on the principles of J. S. Mill' and spent most of the 1860s as a Mill-and-Comte man. Mill himself gave the idea greater plausibility by becoming a Liberal Member of Parliament for a few years (1865–8). He joined Arnold among the marginalia of politicians' correspondence. ('I strongly recommend that you read the chapters of Mill, mentioned by me'; 'some good talks with Mat Arnold'.[9]) The second reform act of 1867 helped spur on discussion of democracy through its radical provisions to enfranchise a far wider section of the working class than had originally been envisaged. When William Gladstone took office as prime minister for the first time in 1868 it seemed – deceptively – the outcome of a series of Liberal advances in which the protean ideas of the intelligentsia had played their part.

Yet the mood did not last. By the end of the 1870s Mill and Arnold had become museum pieces and their 'individualism' the preserve of a diminishing band of anti-Liberal polemicists. Why, then, the change? No simple answer meets the case because it seems clear at once that developments both within and without Liberal theories played some role in re-orchestrating the message. Shifts in the political and economic structures underpinning their themes plainly acted as proximate causes. Reform in 1867 had, after all, shown an obverse face very different from the one that smiled on Liberal self-esteem. The acrid dispute in parliament, the press and various political pressure groups concerning the need to extend the male franchise in order to accommodate or evade the artisan classes of the towns had helped prompt within the intelligentsia a sense of urgency, and sometimes anxiety, over the safeguarding of civilization. Robert Lowe, the arch-sceptic of 1867, sat on the *Liberal* side of the House of Commons; those who shared Lowe's university background frequently shared his resentments. And if the education of one's new masters had become a duty, as Lowe contended, then little in Mill's programme seemed likely to accomplish it, while Arnold's reversion to the theme in *Culture and Anarchy* had more to say about the problem than about the solution. By the turn of the decade, galvanized by the radical programme of Gladstone's first government, there seemed a good deal of piety in the writing of the prophets but little guide to action for a generation increasingly conscious that only the state contained within itself the power to effect fundamental change in areas that would affect the lives of entire classes of people. The collapse of

[8] Matthew Arnold, *Culture and Anarchy* (1869), 203–4.
[9] Henry Bruce to Layard, 22 December 1866, and to his brother John, 27 November 1867, in *Letters of the Rt. Hon. Henry Austin Bruce GCB, Lord Aberdare of Duffryn* (private circulation, 2 vols., Oxford, 1902). I, 248, 252. For Sidgwick, see Sidgwick to Dakyns, 24 August 1861, in A. and E. M. Sidgwick, *Henry Sidgwick: a memoir* (1906), 69.

the government plainly bore some relationship to the collapse of the British economy in 1873 – a sharp downswing with which all governments would have to cope until well into the 1890s – and that, too, helped suggest the irrelevance of the Liberal truths which already felt faintly classical and better suited to the textbook than the boardroom where managers felt all too aware of the importance of American and German competition, or than the trade-union leadership questioning with mounting zest the optimism of an old guard who had taught that collaboration made more sense than revolt. For the landowner the depression betokened a crisis of rents. In the towns it would bring, after 1879, a degree of public misery not witnessed since the 1840s. The slide towards this situation turned out to be a Conservative responsibility for its early years coincided with Disraeli's government of 1874–80; but the policies of that government played no small part in raising Liberal consciousness about the changing functions of the political executive in an industrialized society. Through its social legislation of 1874–6 the Conservative party displaced the Liberals from ground they had traditionally claimed as their own. Through its callousness in face of the deepening social rifts apparent by the end of the decade, it pointed a direction which thinkers nurtured on Mill felt squeamish in following.

Some of them refused to bend what they believed to comprise fundamental statements about the Liberal individual in order to meet a local difficulty. The Duke of Argyll made himself into a theorist of rents and wrote articles designed to show that the relation of landlord and tenant could not, in 'the oldest and happiest of human industries', tolerate governmental interference. The former Regius Professor of Modern History at Oxford, Goldwin Smith, shared the priorities of the Liberty and Property Defence League and brought to the centre of his writing an insistence that property 'is not an institution but a fixed element of human nature. A state of things in which a man would not think that what he had made for himself was his own, is unknown to experience and beyond the range of our conceptions.'[10] No one trod this individualist path with greater realish than Herbert Spencer (1820–1903). As more and more Liberal thinkers abandoned individualism *tout court*, Spencer instead abandoned the Liberal party. As calls increasingly came for an element of compassion in policy, Spencer raised his voice in criticizing compassion as an abdication of policy. As Gladstone's second government of 1880–5 swung towards a mild attempt at the 'land question', over which Argyll resigned his cabinet seat and gave some credence thereby to the radicalism claimed by some Liberal MPs, Spencer issued his most extreme challenge to date in a series of articles republished under the title *The Man Versus the State* (1884). It left no one in doubt that Spencer, at least, remained unmoved by the teeming poor on whom everyone suddenly seemed to want to comment and lavish sympathy.

> 'They have no work', you say. Say rather that they either refuse work or quickly turn themselves out of it. They are simply good-for-nothings, who in one way or other live on the good-for-somethings – vagrants and sots, criminals and those on the way to crime, youths who are burdens on hard-worked parents, men who appropriate the wages of the wives, fellows who share the gains of prostitutes; and then, less visible and less numerous, there is a corresponding class of women. . . . Is it not manifest that there must exist in our midst an immense amount of misery which is a normal result of misconduct, and ought not to be dissociated from it? . . . To separate pain from ill-doing is to fight

[10]Duke of Argyll, 'The Agricultural Holdings Act', *Contemporary Review*, XXVII (March 1876), 521
Goldwin Smith, *False Hopes* (1886), 13.

against the constitution of things, and will be followed by more pain. Saving men from the natural penalties of dissolute living, eventually necessitates the infliction of artificial penalties in solitary cells, on tread wheels, and by the lash.[11]

The severity of this passage does not merely decorate the surface of Spencer's thought as a rhetorical device: it follows from his deepest premises concerning 'the constitution of things' and the political implications that must follow once one understands the nature of that reality. Where Spencer went, of course, virtually no Liberal could follow. The most faithful individualists of 20 years before found this position absurd and humiliating. Indeed by 1885, Henry Sidgwick, who had abandoned both Mill and Comte through the seventies, had come to see individualism 'of the extreme kind' as a doctrine that had 'clearly had its day'.[12] Its most passionate adherents apart from Spencer himself – men like Wordsworth Donisthorpe, Pleydell Bouverie and Auberon Herbert – contributed nothing to mainstream Liberal thinking and left behind a pool of ideas from which twentieth-century Conservatism would one day drink. But the position adopted by Spencer and his group deserves a place in any account of Liberal theory – less for its conclusions than for its assumptions which Liberals often did take on board in the later decades of the century and which they used for purposes which Spencer himself despised.

Science and its critics

That well-meaning Liberals often betrayed a community of mind with Spencer's leading assumptions about the universe suggests something of the subtle displacement in attitude that had occurred during the 1870s and 1880s. The timing was important for Liberal developments, as we shall see. But in order to understand their prehistory we must revert to some subterranean movements among the early-Victorian intelligentsia.

Perhaps the most significant of those developments arose from a new confidence about the value and potential of science. Spencer had figured among those who had helped generate a new mood when he turned to the working out of a synthetic philosophy through which he intended to rescue science from its status as a pile of unsorted empirical observations, as Frederick Pollock described it,[13] and reduce all social phenomena to manifestations of inevitable processes governed by laws. Unlike the generation that followed him, Spencer began with a social and political theory and moved towards a study of science in the second half of his life. The reason for this curious progress seems clear enough. Spencer had already reached maturity and made his living as a railway engineer and a journalist before the independent scientific inquiries of Charles Darwin (1809–82) and Alfred Russel Wallace (1823–1913) attracted notoriety among the intelligentsia with the publication of Darwin's *Origin of Species* in 1859. Spencer later claimed in his autobiography that he had already identified before 1859 the direction in which he intended to go; but the impetus of Darwinist thinking undoubtedly helped him along his chosen path. The conclusion that animals and plants compete for existence and succeed in perpetuating themselves only to the extent that their specific requirements as a species suit the

[11]Herbert Spencer, *The Man versus the State* (1884), 18–19.
[12]Sidgwick's Journal, 30 January 1885, in *Memoir*, 399.
[13]Sir Frederick Pollock, *For My Grandson: remembrances of an ancient Victorian* (1933), 98.

environment in which they exist lent extra righteousness to Spencer's resolution in sending the halt and the blind to the wall. Much anti-Liberal and anti-socialist thought drew inspiration from the same source through the nineteenth century, especially after 1890 when new developments in biological theory reinforced an assumption already current that European society had entered a phase of radical degeneration; indeed, it contributed to a pseudo-science of 'eugenics' and its application to enhance the 'health' of societies. Yet Darwinism cut two ways. If it added fuel to prevalent notions of social competition, despite Darwin's own insistence that his work should not be used as an *entrée* into some arcane theory of social engineering, then it at least took as its starting-point the proposition that the individual members of a species cannot be understood in abstraction from the conditions in which the supra-individual species flourishes or dies. By suggesting that human individuals must be conceived, not as atomic units in a crowd, but as related instances of a social organism, the implications of Darwinism pleased more than the priests of competition. Rich man and poor man now arguably inhabited the same body politic, for all their difference of function. One man contributed more than the other, possibly; but both remained essential to the body's survival and efficiency.

Liberals obviously preferred this form of Darwinist message to one that recommended brutal treatment for society's inadequates, but none of Darwin's postulates became party prescriptions in the short term. Even the emphasis on social interdependence had a conservative face, after all. It might encourage the view that the fortunate classes should not, on prudential grounds, ignore the plight of the less fortunate; it might also evoke, however, a Burkeian caution against interfering with the thriving of a living creature and its habitat: alter one element in the system and all the rest will suffer change also. So when Leslie Stephen adopted the language of organicism to describe political reform in the 1870s, his recommendations came closer to restraint than encouragement. 'It would perhaps be better to discard the metaphor of machinery for the closer one of the animated organism', he readily agreed with the reformers. But he also reminded them of the corollary: 'The mechanism with which we deal is not mere dead matter, but a living organ; we propose to modify a vital function, and not simply to substitute one set of wheels for another.'[14] To this extent, one can find Conservatives happy to use the same vocabulary to defend the status quo. Indeed, if the idea of organism held a specifically Liberal message, then it did not begin to emerge distinctively until the 1880s when 'scientific' assumptions ran together with other currents of speculation and began to overpower conventional views of the nature of sovereignty in the state.

Meanwhile a number of alternative dispositions had taken shape in the atmosphere created by Darwin, Wallace and their scientific followers. The most aggressive response grounded its differences from the evolutionist position in the doctrines of the Christian Churches – institutions that sometimes saw themselves as both outraged and threatened by the suggestion that natural history revealed rational processes other than (and perhaps inimical to) the unfolding of Divine purpose. A Liberal–Anglican reaction to the *Origin of Species* appeared almost at once in a collection of *Essays and Reviews* (1860) in which the sour Oxford don Mark Pattison (Casaubon in George Eliot's *Middlemarch*), Benjamin Jowett, Professor of Greek at Oxford, and Frederick Temple, the headmaster of Rugby, earned instant notoriety for their reasonableness in the face of Anti-Christ and advertised one version of

[14]Leslie Stephen, 'The Value of Political Machinery', *Fortnightly Review*, 24/18 (December 1875), 837.

Liberal intellectuality.[15] A more radical strand of Christian opinion sought relevance in the new climate through a form of Christian socialism associated primarily with F. D. Maurice and J. M. Ludlow and found in it a view of social compassion that exceeded the bounds of mid-Victorian individualism. A third possibility lay in the Comtean Positivism which, in its English incarnation, preserved a conception of 'scientific' inquiry together with a surrogate religion complete with its own ritual, a Catholicism without Christianity, as Huxley called it. But only Frederic Harrison among the Positivists exerted influence on the Liberal intelligentsia through his prolific articles in the periodicals that Liberals liked to think of as their own; and none of these various strains of opinion attracted Liberal theorists to the extent that philosophical Idealism succeeded in attracting the generation after Mill.

Sons of clergymen predominated among the future leaders of this Oxford school of thought which took its inspiration from a dynasty of late-eighteenth- and early-nineteenth-century German thinkers, most particularly from Kant and Hegel. But the liberal thinkers associated with the Balliol College of T. H. Green (1836–82) and Edward Caird (1835–1908) offered a view of the world that bore the marks of a Christian origin but lacked any cohesive Christian doctrine. Perhaps the spectre of a 'scientific' reduction of the universe to a collection of laws and principles helped promote the wish to run backwards to the difficult metaphysics of Kant and his followers; but again, as with Spencer, the older Idealists had begun their journey before the appearance of the *Origin of Species*. German thought had caught the imagination of scholars reared on Coleridge and Carlyle and whose prose would later abound in quotations from the poetry of Lord Tennyson and Arthur Hugh Clough. They reflected an increased awareness stimulated by the mediation of Schopenhauer (by John Oxenford) and the translation of David Strauss (by George Eliot). They announced, in recalling the thresholds of the 1780s and 90s, a determination to confront their present from the predicaments in which Kant had left philosophy at his death. For Kant had separated the conscious individual from the world in which he, the individual, believed himself to live by demonstrating on logical grounds the impossibility of his ever 'knowing' the reality of that world. Trapped inside his own head, man can do no more than carry out mental operations on the sensations which he believes to have been 'caused' in some sense by objects or events in the external world. Those sensations he knows: he can manipulate them, compare them. What he presumes to have sent those sensations – the things-in-themselves somewhere 'out there' – remain forever inaccessible except through elusive sensations structured and shaped by his own mind. This dichotomy between the world in its essential reality, on the one hand, and images of it formed in the mind of an observer, on the other, developed in the understanding of a generation of thinkers into an unbridgeable chasm between 'object' and 'subject'. And since the chasm seemed intellectually intolerable, one needed bridges. Kant himself had tried to unify the world through '*a priori*' categories which a transcendent God made available to his creatures. Fichte, Schelling and Hegel, in the next generation, built systems designed to show that the chasm should be seen as a mirage on the surface of a deeper, evolving unity. The British Idealists accepted none of these *in toto* but largely shared the frame of mind out of which they had emerged. They sought their own responses to questions which they accused British empiricists of never having asked.

These ideas are abstract, difficult and apparently non-political. What has any of

[15]See Mark Francis, 'The Origins of *Essays and Reviews*: an interpretation of Mark Pattison in the 1850s', *Historical Journal* XVII (1974), 797–811.

this to do with Liberal politics? The defence rests on three contentions: one, that British Idealist thinkers and their second-generation pupils amount in retrospect to something approaching an intellectual dynasty within the universities between 1870 and 1910 and demand consideration for the strength which this grip implies; two, that their politics were normally Liberal and often committedly so; and, three, that their politics followed from their philosophy just as surely as a visible stream surges from a subterranean spring. Within the varying emphases of Green's Idealists (for they were neither consistent nor systematic thinkers) there exists a continuity of concern with the nature and limits of knowledge and the character of man conceived as a dynamic consciousness, a creature in process of 'becoming' something better, more complete, more real, than he now seems. Only one perspective will allow light to enter this discussion from an Idealist point of view: the view from eternity in which inquiry begins with the *whole*, the totality of all that has existed, exists and will exist, and which then proceeds to consider the parts which the whole includes but also transcends. It became a joke in late-Victorian Oxford that Balliol had become a society for looking at things as a whole. But behind the irritating reliance on totality lay a serious point of view: a faith, for such it was, that the world could only be understood properly when conceived as what William James called a 'block universe' rather than as a plurality of bits; that the atomizing effects of scientific enquiry could only be resisted through an attitude of 'devout monism'.[16] And if that attitude supplied a weapon against science, it also offered a defence against those who saw societies as collections of individuals – human bits – rather than mosaics of relationships.

Granted the limitations which Idealists took to hedge round the possibility of learning about the world through a study of its disconnected phenomena, these men saw no reason to accept the scientists' claims to have invented a new age in the 1850s and 60s. Bishop Wilberforce's notorious reluctance to count monkeys among his ancestors found an echo in the disdain with which Idealists couched their judgements of 'evolution'. Sometimes they stood on Wilberforce's shoulders and screamed even louder than the Churchmen, as when the formidable Scot James Hutchison Stirling pitted Darwin against Hegel in a vocabulary which, as cynics said, enabled him to keep *The Secret of Hegel* largely to himself during the course of two substantial volumes in 1865:

> Monkey is the pass word! Sink your pedigree as man, and adopt for family tree a procession of the skeletons of monkeys – then superior enlightenment radiates from your very person, and your place is fixed – a place of honour in the acclamant brotherhood that names itself 'advanced'. So it is in England at present; this is the acknowledged pinnacle of English thought and English science now. Just point in these days to the picture of some huge baboon and superstition is disarmed, priests confess their imposture, and the Church sinks . . . .[17]

A no less formidable English Tory, William Hurrell Mallock, satirized the physicist William Tyndall from the same direction. 'No idle metaphysics have clouded my brain,' Tyndall's mouthpiece boasts in Mallock's novel, 'so I have been able to see these things clearly'.[18] But one could make the point less clumsily. Science could come under attack from so moderate a (Liberal) thinker as Goldwin Smith simply

---

[16]William James, *A Pluralistic Universe* (1909), 76.
[17]J. H. Sterling, *The Secret of Hegel* (2 vols., 1865), I, xxxi–xxxii.
[18]W. H. Mallock, *The New Republic* (2 vols., 1877), II, 60.

because, 'though true as far as it goes', science failed to offer an understanding of 'Being' unconstricted by space and time.[19] More directly, science could suffer from the undermining of David Hume's scepticism about relationships that still constituted the *ne plus ultra* of British empiricist thinking; and that objective played no small part in a critical commentary on Hume that appeared in 1874 – the first book of Thomas Hill Green.

In 1874 Green was nearly 40. Since 1860 he had held a Fellowship at Balliol College, Oxford, of which his former tutor, Benjamin Jowett, became Master. The Anglicanism of Green's childhood had gone but there always persisted a seamless spirituality, what he himself termed a 'modified unitarianism', which his marriage in 1871 to a sister of John Addington Symonds may have deepened. Two applications for major philosophical chairs had failed, though Green seems not to have felt as keenly as others the pressures of academic, or indeed of intellectual, life. Unlike Mill, he knew nothing of mental disturbance and nervous breakdown. The flame, such as it was, ejected no sparks. His prose was the same colour as his coat and trousers: black and grey. So the casual reader of anything from the three volumes of Green's *Collected Works* will see at once what the Cambridge Liberal, Goldsworthy Lowes Dickinson, meant when he described Green as a tired Oxford Whig. Yet, that said, Green's influence on his generation became compelling, partly through the charisma which premature death grants its victims – he died in 1882 after holding an Oxford chair for only a few years – but also through the practical and worldly politics of this most impractical and unworldly man. He did not, like Mill, enter parliament but he sat as a Liberal on Oxford City Council. He did not, like Mill, evade the state's responsibility to the young: indeed, it would do little damage to his position to place education at the top of Green's agenda. Though he greatly admired Mill as a human being – 'such a *good* man' – he pulled Liberal theory towards a doctrine of citizenship which required from the state more *dirigisme* than Mill had thought compatible with liberty. When Sidgwick began, in the mid 1880s, 'to find something wooden and fatuous in the sublime smile of freedom', he turned his face, whether he knew it or not, towards the Oxford of Green.[20]

Not that Balliol had become a collectivist cell. Green's *Lectures on the Principles of Political Obligation*, delivered in 1879–80 but not published until after his death, contain the fullest adumbration of his conception of the individual's relation to the state; and nothing in the text's endless qualifications and sub-clauses would have disturbed a Liberal anxious for the future of Freedom and Property. Had Arnold still been alive he could have read the section on the moral worth of individual ownership with pleasure: the distribution of property remained (and ought to remain) unequal; inheritance must not disappear: free trade continued its career as a commercial-cum-moral priority. Possibly land might one day come into national rather than individual possession, but then Mill had run to that. Green allowed a disgruntled citizen to consider whether a law infringed his 'rights'; and he saw certain circumstances in which the individual would have a point. But the qualifications are severe: the

---

[19]Goldwin Smith, 'The Ascent of Man', in *Letters and Essays* (1881), 99.

[20]Journal, 21 February 1886, *Memoir*, 439. For details of Green's career, see the memoir by R. L. Nettleship in Nettleship (ed.), *Works of Thomas Hill Green* (3 vols., 1886), and Melvin Richter, *The Politics of Conscience: T. H. Green and his age* (1964). The Cambridge critic on this occasion was Goldsworthy Lowes Dickinson, whose friend and biographer, E. M. Forster, would later identify true Liberalism with the progressives of the Edwardian period when 'the heavy, stocky body of their party was about to grow wings and leave the ground.' See E. M. Forster, *Goldsworthy Lowes Dickinson* (1934, 1962),

individual can campaign to have the law changed but only if his alternative conception of justice is 'founded on a relation to the social well-being' (defined by whom?)
and provided that he can persuade the consciences of his fellow citizens (how many?)
that his claim is legitimate. The suspicion endures that placards and riots still
condemn their creators to the Tarpeian Rock. On the other hand, the very language of
'rights' and 'duties' makes Green sound different from Mill and reminds the reader
recurrently of the teleological nature of the state that the text presupposes.

   This sense of purpose does not arise from some assumed point of origin for the state
in the forests of northern Germany or the swamps of prehistory. Green sees no 'social
contract' and has no time for the idea that collections of individuals met one day in
order to set up a society. Instead the moral purpose of society grows from within,
through the cunning of history. Man engages in a dialectic with his community, a
process in which the bad finds itself 'overruled' by the good until government
eventually matures into an agency for making moralized existence possible and ruling
over its citizens, not through the exercise of power, but by acting as the persuasive
instrument of their own better natures:

> The doctrine that the rights of government are founded on the consent of the governed is
> a confused way of stating the truth, that the institutions by which man is moralised . . .
> express a conception of the common good; that through them that conception takes form
> and reality; and it is in turn through its presence in the individual that they have a con-
> straining power over him, a power which is not that of mere fear, still less a physical
> compulsion, but which leads him to do what he is not inclined to do because there is a law
> that he should.[21]

Arguments of this kind helped erect a school of thought with a specific political
flavour, one that reached greatest intensity through the 1890s. The parts of the
message that depended on the technical characteristics of post-Kantian philosophy
plainly held less general appeal than those that blended easily with less abstract
concerns. Those who paled before the demands of the dialectic and the Absolute
could at least see the outlines of a caring society in the teaching and college sermons of
the 'society for looking at things as a whole'; and by the 1880s such a society could
only confirm the criticism of social particularism that had already reached crescendo.

Implications and challenges

By expressing the connexion between government and governed as one form of a
series of social relationships, writers in the last two decades of the century invested
the traditional understanding of sovereignty within a society – the ultimate location
of power – with a new meaning. Certainly sovereignty remained with the state so
long as it continued to fulfil its moral function and purpose. Yet despite the laboured
constraints of Idealist theorists, an idea had gained ground that ultimately power had
to reside in the community of moralized beings to which the activities of a political
executive must in the last resort remain accountable. The view contradicted a legal
tradition established half a century before, especially in the work of John Austin
(1790–1859), whose ideas gained wide currency during the ascendancy of the
Utilitarians. In Austin's view sovereignty within a state consisted of the ability of a

---

[21]*Lectures on the Principles of Political Obligation*, sec. 116, in *Works*, II, 429–30. For other quotations in
this paragraph, see *ibid.*, secs. 23, 31, 128, 144, 223–30.

determinate individual or institution to act executively without recourse to any superior body. But even as a three-volume edition of Austin's *The Province of Juris-prudence Determined* (1832) appeared in 1861, so its plausibility was undermined during the same year by the publication of Sir Henry Maine's *Ancient Law*. For Maine demonstrated that early societies possessed a conception of law, and therefore of sovereignty, before their political development gave them the institutions in which Austin believed sovereignty rested. Together with the reflections of other anthropologists such as Sir James Frazer and Sir Edward Tylor, these perceptions of social evolution left Austin looking rather too Euclidean for the modern world. 'One begins by thinking Austin self-evident', Neville Figgis wrote a generation later; 'one learns that qualifications have to be made, and finally one ends by treating his whole method as abstract and theoretic.'[22] By the end of the 1870s, indeed, a general reaction against the ideas of lawyers who had seen no further than the operation of *force majeure* in their thinking about political sovereignty had clearly set in. Consent, the feeling ran, had to amount to something more than passive acquiescence and, if it did, then it must also play a part in determining how power could be used. As one writer expressed the common instinct during the year in which Green delivered his lectures on political obligation, 'Society is an organism, and an organism is something more than the sum of its component parts.'[23] Hardly a month would pass over the next two decades without some journalist or academic introducing his opinions with a slogan of this kind.

But why terminate the argument after formulating a position about *internal* sovereignty in the state? The relevance accorded to thoughts bearing on the relationship between the individual and society presumably retained some weight when one considered questions of international and imperial cohesion. In the greatest age of imperial expansion ever seen in the history of the world, the relevance should surely increase. Sir John Seeley, Regius Professor of History at Cambridge (and Gladstone's appointee), certainly lamented a failure among imperial thinkers to approach the matter from a holist point of view; he wanted to go beyond the entities normally discussed by Liberals and draw their attention to 'that great whole, the πόλιs, or nationality, which . . . has really nursed the greater part of all moral sentiment.'[24] In the writings of Seeley and J. A. Froude, a debate whose terms had altered sharply since Disraeli came to power in 1874 came to the centre of consciousness. And in responding to those changed terms through the following decade, Liberal theorists developed positions that threatened the peace of Liberal politics quite as radically as had the supplanting of individualism by different values.

Of course the problem was hardly new. The British intelligentsia had taken exception to several forms of foreign policy, much of it 'Liberal', since the 1820s. The years of Palmerston's government between 1859 and 1865 had proved particularly rich in embarrassment, not least because the party's most unreconstructed Whig happened to hold power during a marked upsurge of nationalist and liberationist feeling in Europe and America. The Liberal 'Lights' ranged themselves, needless to

[22]Quoted in David Nicholl, *The Pluralist State* (1975), 49.

[23]H. D. Traill, 'The England of To-day', *Fortnightly Review*, 33/27 (January 1880), 135. Cf. Frederic Harrison, 'Austin and Maine on Sovereignty', *ibid.*, 30/24 (October 1878), 487–90.

[24]J. R. Seeley, 'Our Insular Ignorance', *Nineteenth Century*, XVIII (December 1885), 869. Cf. two classic texts in the literature of imperialism from the mid 1880s, Sir John Seeley, *The Expansion of England* (1883) and J. A. Froude, *Oceana: or England and her colonies* (1886). The relationship of such 'Whig' thinking to a broader Liberal understanding of the past is examined in John Burrow's *A Liberal Desecent: Victorian historians and the English past* (Cambridge, 1981).

say, on the side of the angels and frequently found themselves out of sympathy with the support which many Liberals lent to the darker forces, especially in the support of the American South over which even Gladstone burned his fingers. For Liberal governments to feel pressure from their Left seemed, on the other hand, a traditional and perhaps wholesome contribution from the intelligentsia during the 1850s and 60s. More worrying was the development of a splinter group on its Right sharing the anxieties of some politicians who worried about the effect of further increasing the franchise beyond its dimensions fixed in 1832. But the so-called Adullamites, led by the visionary Robert Lowe, did not develop an international or imperial position that might upset Liberal stability. Lowe in fact went on to construct an opposition to imperialism from the same premises he had used to validate his fight against democracy: both doctrines whipped up uncontrollable forces.[25] Mill faced in exactly the opposite direction but generated no greater threat. While he attacked the Liberal government of 1865 for its timidity over the franchise, and especially over its failure to countenance the enfranchisement of women, he did not develop a cutting critique of empire. He even assented to it – 'Despotism is a legitimate mode of government in dealing with barbarians' – so long as the 'improvement' of the natives remained its purpose.[26]

Whether in the mouth of Lowe or Mill, however, these views addressed themselves to an 'imperialism' very different from the variant described and recommended by Seeley and Froude. The earlier commentators did not need to react to a movement of overt territorial expansion or to the stories of expropriation, tyranny and atrocity that came in its wake. In retrospect the 1870s seem first to have provided the conditions for a more charged frame of mind about imperialism. Gladstone's first government of 1868–74 had lost its impetus by 1872; and since then Disraeli had tried to manufacture a new public appeal for the Conservative party through the idea of empire. To this extent his accession to power at the beginning of 1874 suggested the possibility of a major revision in the standing of imperialism as an executive theme. The government's purchase in 1875 of a substantial holding in the new Suez Canal (1869) implied a fresh focus of stategic and economic concern in north-east Africa. The bombast associated with giving the Queen the title of Empress of India in the following year continued the theme. For Liberals, however, a more significant development lay in Disraeli's sneering reception of reports in 1876 that the Turks had 'massacred Christian Bulgarians under their jurisdiction. Churches and universities in Britain became a focal point for a propaganda of resistance to the atrocities long before Gladstone decided to take a hand himself with his pamphlet on *The Bulgarian Horrors*, which sold in startling quantities and harnessed the Liberal party to the swelling agitation to expel the Turks from Bulgarian soil. The Liberal historian Edward Freeman made a prominent contribution towards galvanizing the national campaign and genuinely believed that the behaviour of the Turks had caused 'the mass of Englishmen' to lose sleep.

They shuddered, as well they might; and they not only shuddered but wondered. . . . [The] feeling which the news stirred up was a sublime national emotion such as had few parallels. Men came together as if to deliver their own souls, as if their hearts could not rest within them till their tongues had spoken. They came, as it were, to wash their own hands clean from the deeds of which they had just heard the tale. It seemed as if the common earth and the common human nature had received a defilement.

[25] Robert Lowe, 'Imperialism', *Fortnightly Review*, 30/24 (October, 1878), 459.
[26] Mill, *On Liberty*, 9.

Only positive action by the British government would help allay this sense of blood guilt; the immoral (and traditional) distinction between public and private morality could no longer stand in the face of overt bestiality.[27]

'Bulgaria' had an impact on Liberal theory, then, not by turning it into an anti-imperialist ideology, for many Liberals retained a belief in the missionary and civilizing benefits of British rule in 'backward' and 'primitive' countries, but rather by directing attention at an area of Liberal sensitivity that had not been thoroughly tested since the Prussian invasion of Denmark in 1864. Just as Sidgwick's individualism had deserted him in the 1870s, so had his relaxed imperialism shifted, by the time of the Congress of Berlin in 1878, to ruminations on the 'great danger' posed to Britain by 'her new responsibilities and her new temper'.[28] The Russo-Turkish war of 1877–8 and the Conservative government's failure either to appease or control the Afghans and the Zulus provided, with the memories of Bulgaria, the platform for Gladstone's campaign associated with his new constituency of Midlothian. So far as the Liberal intelligentsia was concerned, Gladstone judged, correctly, that intellectuals shared his revulsion at Tory excesses over the past few years. He interpreted that revulsion, erroneously, as a mandate for pursuing a policy of 'Little Englandism' when he returned for his second period of power in 1880. In fact the government's tergiversation over Egypt and, above all, over Ireland brought about a serious alienation of intellectual Liberalism from the party that had enjoyed its support, largely, since the end of the 1850s; and in this sense the international and imperial anxieties of Liberal theorists joined hands with their domestic worries to make Gladstone's last decade in political life a period of brooding tension.

The tension distracted attention from a further problem which grew in volume and weight through the 1880s. In speaking of 'socialism' in the 1860s, writers had tended to refer either to the populist cries that had accompanied the revolutions of 1848 or to a vaguer hope that an increase in the responsibilities of the state would usher in a better life for the working class. Leslie Stephen's brother, Fitzjames, trampled on such notions with an exuberant cynicism in his *Liberty, Equality, Fraternity* (1873). His view of socialism as a form of 'mistaken philanthropy' seemed convincing to minds even of a more Liberal cast, not because they shared Stephen's apprehensions about a coming depression of society to a common mediocrity, than because they feared the 'indolence' and 'pauperism' that would be bound to occur if the 'financial principles' of socialists found an audience. When a draft of Mill's *Chapters on Socialism* was published posthumously at the end of the decade, it served only to show how great remained the distance between those principles and the instincts of mainline Liberals.[29] Besides, socialist thought had already embarked on a path that would render that distance even greater. Those who drew their inspiration from Lassalle and Karl Marx remained for the moment a minority: Engels's English edition of *Das Kapital* did not appear until 1887. Indeed in many ways a thoroughgoing socialist message did not reach a wide public until the second half of the 1880s. But the language and imagery of German socialist thought – the so-called 'Socialism of the

[27]Edward Freeman, 'The English People in Relation to the Eastern Question', *Contemporary Review*, XXIX (February 1877), 490; Argyll, 'Morality in Politics', *ibid.*, 319. For a modern treatment of the crisis, see Richard Shannon, *Gladstone and the Bulgarian Agitation, 1876* (1963; Hassocks, 1975).

[28]Sidgwick to Dakyns, n.d. [1861] and to Roden Noel, 2 September 1878, in *Memoir*, 66, 339.

[29]See Henry Fawcett, 'Modern Socialism' in H. Fawcett and M. G. Fawcett, *Essays and Lectures on Social and Political Subjects* (1872), 25–9. For Mill, see 'Essays on Economics and Society', *Collected Works*, V (1967), esp. 707–8, 736; and Alexander Bain, *John Stuart Mill. A Criticism: with personal recollections* (1882), 90.

Chair' – made a noticeable impact in English periodicals after 1880 and gave a more urgent tone to Liberals' defence of land and private property. H. M. Hyndman's mangling of Marx's writings may have distressed purists as much as it incensed Marx, yet the popularity of Hyndman's books could only contribute to an awareness, however confused, of radical social criticism. His Democratic Federation of 1881, which became the Social Democratic Federation three years later, together with Henry George's lecture-tour of Britain with its evangelism against rents, helped locate in a new context the resignation of a landed Whig, the Duke of Argyll, from Gladstone's government in 1881 and the more *outré* provisions of the 'Unauthorized Programme' pressed by Joseph Chamberlain and others in 1885.

Here, as when discussing other facets of the relationship between theory and practice in the generation after 1868, the stimulus of events 'on the ground' in the awareness of commentators becomes manifest. From Gladstone's return in 1880 that stimulus increases markedly – in part because economic insecurity had already exposed the nerves of the intelligentsia, but also because a new current within parliamentary Liberalism presented custodians of party strategy with new perplexities. Of course, giving a radical lead to the sluggish forces of mid-century Whiggery had itself frequently proved trying and unrewarding to the men of Mill's day. At least the common rooms and editorial offices had then enjoyed, however, the pleasure of radical superiority: better to flog dead horses than go under the hooves of wild ones. Disraeli's turning the world upside down in 1867 had changed the relationship in an alarming way. For in its scrambling to keep up with the Conservative party, the decision-making centres inside the Liberal party had jerked both the Whigs and the intelligentsia sharply leftwards, leaving its prophets with an odd and dislocated sense of the world. Rather than see themselves as inspirators of a timid parliamentary body, Liberal theorists of the 1870s and 1880s found themselves speaking the language of constraint and moderation in their conversations with politicians. Over the empire, over socialism, with increasing shrillness over Gladstone, they proceeded through the *crise de conscience* stimulated by Gladstone's first government towards the *crise de nerfs* precipitated by his second. Over Ireland, their nerve broke. An understanding of that evolution depends only partially on an investigation of the theorists' worries about the Liberal party. The enlarging object of their anxieties had, after all, its own, very different history.

4

The Gladstonian Liberal Party 1868–1886

Legacies and prospects

Relinquishing in 1882 the editorship of the *Fortnightly Review* for the less elevated world of the House of Commons, John Morley told his admiring Liberal public that an editor exercised the influence of 25 MPs.[1] He had no evidence for that assertion and none has come to light since. Yet the assumption that the ideas and values of intellectuals played a formative role in political action fed from deep roots in Liberal attitudes. Whatever the power of an editor, the power of *thought*, understood as the outpourings of the universities, the churches and the press, struck Liberals as beyond question. The notion that politicians took their thinking from the quadrangles and courts of Oxford and Cambridge perhaps seems naïve to later generations soured by disappointment in their leaders; but when John Stuart Mill or Henry Fawcett or John Morley moved from theorizing to governing they believed themselves to be extending their former experience rather than terminating it. In the course of this chapter we shall discover remarkably little evidence for that view, either. The intellectuals became bad, in the sense of ineffective, politicians because they could not adjust to an environment that required new forms of behaviour and new styles of language. Earl Granville may have lacked the intellectual apparatus of Mill, but he had not become a senior politician without coming to understand the importance of these things. 'Mill has failed as a politician for the moment', he reported to Gladstone in 1869, 'not so much from advanced views, as from errors of judgement and tact.'[2] Mill's failure turned out to be neither temporary nor unique.

Intellectuals, administrators and constituency activists – people who spent their lives applying principles and doctrines to situations quite different from the ones which politicians normally needed to confront – frequently misread the options available to those directing policy. Possibly the central principles of Liberalism

[1] See John Mason, 'Monthly and Quarterly Reviews 1865–1914', in George Boyce, James Curran and Pauline Wingate (eds.), *Newspaper History: from the 17th century to the present day* (1978), 292–3.
[2] Granville to Gladstone, 14 January 1869, in Agatha Ramm (ed.), *The Political Correspondence of Mr. Gladstone and Lord Granville 1868–76* (2 vols., Royal Historical Society, Camden Series, LXXXI–LXXXII, 1952), I, 10.

seemed clear by the 1860s; perhaps by then, as James Bryce recalled, 'everyone roughly knew what a "Liberal" meant.'[3] Knowing that 'Liberals' tended to favour free trade, to mistrust imperialism and to urge the withdrawal of the state from areas where it had no business to meddle, nevertheless did little to guide Liberal cabinets of the day in manipulating immediate and complex problems, many of which had emerged from historical developments for which they had no responsibility, and some of which derived from the very nature of their party as a sprawl of sentiment and enthusiasm. A man of Gladstone's intellectual sophistication delighted in argument for its own sake. He prepared most of his policy positions by reading books about the subject in question. But he recognized, at least until his political judgement began to fade in the later years, that this framework formed no more than a stage from which to begin thinking politically. The first phase came quickly and easily: 'the state of my speculative mind,' as he told Henry Manning, 'is not the portion of me that I have most difficulty in exhibiting.'[4] The difficult part lay in finding some way of securing some of his objectives within a closely-textured society which he could not control and amid daily complications that no one could predict. Disraeli's cliché about the art of the possible had a distinct Liberal face, too, in the awareness that ideal laws could not be imposed by the Liberal party. One had to find instead what a group of diverse individuals (and their diversity showed every sign of increasing after 1867) could be persuaded to tolerate. 'This is the essence of *politics*,' the Whig Sir William Harcourt advised one of his Radicals, Sir Charles Dilke, in 1870; 'all the rest is *speculation*.'[5]

Comparatively few issues before 1865 left Liberals feeling a sense of divorce between their speculations and their politics. 'Democracy' had proved a pressing problem since the end of the 1850s in the guise of franchise reform and certainly over that issue the party had been made to feel its width. John Bright and the Radicals on the one side and a violently anti-democratic faction known, thanks to Bright, as the 'Adullamites' on the other, had kept the party leadership disturbed and the party leader, Lord Palmerston, confirmed in his antipathy to the political claims of those he called 'scum'. With Gladstone drifting leftwards by 1864 (the year in which he spoke about bringing the people within the pale of the constitution) and public opinion strengthening under the pressure of the Reform League and Reform Union's agitation in the country, the potential for a major disruption of Liberal politics had, for a time, looked formidable. Palmerston's death solved a great deal, therefore, in 1865. And although the Liberals' own attempts to carry a reform bill in 1866 had met with failure and their removal from office, Disraeli's determination to stay in power by doing something radical over reform did the Liberals a greater service than they realized.

At the time, Liberals spoke the language of treachery and disaster. Indeed there were those on the Whig side who never forgave Derby and his party for letting down the side of property by coquetting with the masses for party advantage. We hear Lord Kimberley still growling about it two years later when Derby's death reached the newspapers. 'How the man who could talk as he used to do of having undertaken to stem the tide of democracy, could have made himself responsible as First Minister for the Household suffrage bill, it will puzzle future historians to explain on any hypo-

[3] Quoted in Christopher Harvie, *The Lights of Liberalism: university Liberals and the challenge of democracy 1860–86* (1976), 67.
[4] Gladstone to Manning, 16 November 1869, in M. R. D. Foot and Colin Matthew (eds.), *The Gladstone Diaries* (Oxford, 1968–), VII, 171.
[5] Harcourt to Dilke, n.d. [1870], in A. G. Gardiner, *The Life of Sir William Harcourt* (1923), I, 216.

thesis which does not impugn either his honesty or his courage or his intelligence.'[6] But the private journal in which Kimberley groused tells one something about the fate of Liberal reactionaries: they could not grouse publicly once the second reform act became patent fact. The situation demanded acquiescence, adaptation, perhaps even celebration. All the timidity that Gladstone had shown in 1866 must never be repeated in these new and changed conditions. As Bright put it in a speech to an audience of working men in 1868, the Liberals were now, whether they liked it or not, 'standing on the threshold of a new career.' He went on with the open cheerfulness that so often led his colleagues to hide their faces in their hands: 'Being there, we need no longer have recourse to the arguments which we have often heard from platforms in times past, such indeed as I sometimes have been ready to use. . . . We now have to appeal to you'.[7]

The next 20 years showed that most Liberals did not believe that their central priority lay in appealing to working men. Nor was that the lesson of 1867. It suggested, rather, that the Liberal party had *survived* the threat of 'democracy' for the moment without splitting Liberal politics into warring camps of Whigs and Radicals. Other issues had posed moments of danger in that respect over the past decade, but they also had lacked the power to pull the Liberal party apart. The American Civil War had given the right-wing a difficult period because its instinctual admiration for the South, publicly proclaimed by Gladstone in a hopelessly-misjudged speech of 1862, left it looking the very reverse of 'Liberal' in the eyes of Radicals and provincial enthusiasts still damp-eyed over the victories of Italian Liberalism. For once, Bright took his imagery from the leading lights of Europe rather than Britain and revealed the poverty of Palmerston, Russell and Gladstone by contrast:

> How comes it that on the Continent there is not a liberal newspaper, nor a liberal politician that has said or has thought of saying, a word in favour of this portentous and monstrous shape [the Confederacy] which now asks to be received into the family of nations? Take the great Italian minister, Count Cavour . . . he had no difficulty in deciding. Ask Garibaldi. Is there in Europe a more disinterested and generous friend of freedom than Garibaldi? Ask that illustrious Hungarian, to whose marvellous eloquence you once listened in this hall. Will he tell you that slavery has nothing to do with it, and that the slaveholders of the South will liberate the negroes sooner than the North through the instrumentality of the war? . . . Ask any man in Europe who opens his lips for freedom . . . he will have no difficulty in telling you on which side your sympathies should lie.[8]

Yet Bright joined a Liberal ministry a few years later without any sense of entering the devil's kitchen; and the consequences of the Civil War remained stronger at the level of inspiration or disgust than in the undermining of party stability.

Indeed nothing in the noises made by Radicalism suggested the possibility of deep rifts in a party that still lacked any restrictive identity, which still rested so heavily on land as its base and whose backbenches had sufficient ballast in industrialists and

---

[6] Kimberley's journal, 24 October 1869, in Ethel Drus (ed.), *A Journal of Events during the Gladstone Ministry 1868–74 by John, First Earl of Kimberley* (Royal Historical Society, Camden Miscellany, XXI, 1958), 8.
[7] At Edinburgh, 5 November 1868, in John Bright, *Selected Speeches on Public Questions* (Everyman ed., 1907), 109.
[8] At Birmingham, 18 December 1862, *Selected Speeches*, 80–1.

cautious lawyers – '*waiters* upon Providence'[9] – to stifle inconvenient zeal. Even the Radicals had begun to lose their edge, or so it sometimes seemed by the second half of the 1860s. Richard Cobden was dead; Bright's anger all too frequently looked back to the great days of the 1840s and 1850s. The latter's speeches carry a noticeable amount of past tense: if the subject is foreign policy then the reference point becomes the Crimean war of 1854–6; if he turns to free trade then his audience has its attention directed back to the sugar duties and the attack on the Corn Laws. Always embarrassing to his leaders, he had none the less lost the ability to sound dangerous. Gladstone worried a good deal about Bright and the forces that he embodied; but he slapped them down when the occasion demanded and helped Bright to the margin of political activity where he became more a curiosity than the architect of Liberal policy.

Prospects of major friction had their origins elsewhere – not in the generation of Bright but in that of his Birmingham associates Jesse Collings and Joseph Chamberlain; not in the field of franchise and foreign policy but in social class, education, trade unionism, and the need to organize Liberal politics into a machine strong enough to deliver parliamentary power and dominate the opposition. For the moment these issues jostled for the attention of politicians more keenly aware of the need to say something about Ireland, whose affairs seemed to have reached new levels of crisis; but Birmingham and its threat to the entire shape of Liberal politics would soon have its day.

All threats remained muted, meanwhile, by the common need to find a way of dislodging the government that Disraeli had taken over from Derby in 1868. In any case, even Birmingham Radicals did not yet want to go beyond the vaguely individualistic recommendations familiar to Liberal theory. Bright, and most other Radicals, wanted a secret ballot, whereas Mill did not. But in his conception of politics as an arena in which God's spirit moved, Bright's assumptions reflected Gladstone's. When the latter, during the course of his famous 'Midlothian' campaigns of 1879–80, referred to 'that primary element of society, the sacred constitution of the family', he said nothing to offend the aspirations of Radicalism. When he confessed his belief that 'the operation of economic laws is what in the main dictated the distribution of landed property in this country', he refused to follow Mill's departure from individualism and he took with him many inside the Liberal party. When Bright expressed his scepticism about the value of trade unions, he merely echoed the opinions of the bulk of Liberal employers. When he pointed to social equality in a speech in 1868 – 'It is a long way from Belgrave Square to Bethnal Green' – he mentioned the question as only the sixth item of an agenda that included the secret ballot, Ireland, the land laws, administrative economy and education.[10] To speak of an individualist consensus in 1868 does little violence, therefore, to the opinions of most party Liberals.

Questions not yet asked none the less remained. How long could the doctrines of *laissez-faire* cope with the demands of subduing Irish nationalism? How long could the haphazardness of the Liberals' commitment to 'free trade' remain veiled? (All very well to argue 'the less we say the better'[11] but circumstances might arise in which

[9] John Mellor to A. J. Mundella, 23 January 1861, Mundella MSS, 6P/1/1.
[10]Second Midlothian speech, Dalkeith, 26 November 1879, and Third at West Calder, 27 November, in W. E. Gladstone, *Political Speeches in Scotland* (2 vols., Edinburgh, 1879–80), I, 84, 105; Bright at Rochdale, 2 January 1877, and at Edinburgh, 5 November 1868, *Selected Speeches*, 122, 248.
[11]Louis Mallet to Mundella, 13 November 1869, Mundella MSS, 6P/2/2.

action would become unavoidable.) How long would the teeth of religion – the schools – refrain from biting? Liberal leaders might have been disturbed, had they known of it, by Collings's letter to the future Sheffield MP A.J. Mundella in which, two years before W. E. Forster moved towards his major Education Act, the principle that '*no school that teaches any theology, creed or belief peculiar to any sect ought or can receive money from the Public Purse*'[12] received an alarming degree of stress. In their relief at finding themselves able to regroup, following their undeniable 'dishing' by Disraeli in 1867, Liberals could be forgiven for seeing little thrust in such things. Over the next 15 years they would feel their point. They would respond to the prodding in a variety of ways – some traditional, some new. They would leave a number among their party suspecting that Liberalism had lost its way and severed some vital arteries. For an individualist Whig like the Duke of Argyll, that process amounted to 'a manifest giving way to heresies and "deviations" of all kinds from the sound Liberal creed.'[13] For others it marked an attempt by convinced Liberals to redirect their party towards a position from which it could deal realistically with changed circumstances. Either way, the presuppositions of individualist Liberalism plainly faced a period of trial.

Practice: the first Gladstone government 1868–74

> Now gentlemen, I hope I am at least earnest and sincere in my intentions as to being what passes for a Liberal politician. . . .
> Gladstone, speaking at Blackheath, 23 October 1871

Briefly to portray the working of one of the most energetic and prolific administrations of the nineteenth century presents obvious problems. At one level of practice the history of the Liberal government formed by William Gladstone in December 1868 emerges best from the 23 volumes of *Hansard*, many of them running to 2,000 columns of closely-printed text, covering the period of office to his resignation in 1874, and from the piles of parliamentary papers to which he and his ministers gave rise. But a digest of even this mass of material would hardly suffice: all the surviving private papers of ministers and MPs await scrutiny in their carefully-arranged letter-books or, more usually, their jutting bundles of correspondence and envelopes tied in faded pink ribbon. Drowning in such detail has its own satisfactions, but they hardly seem appropriate to the more immediate task here of seeking a perspective on these years as a whole and asking wider questions of the events in order to make judgements about their relationship to what the more meditative Liberals believed party politics ought to comprise. Rather than attempt a tedious trudge through a chronology of commissions, committees, Bills, amendments and Acts of Parliament, perhaps we ought, therefore, to think about categories of discussion favoured by Liberal theorists and consider Liberal practice as a whole in their light.

We have seen that a highly-confined view of the place of the state in directing the conduct of society played an important role in classical Liberalism. Most of the activities of Gladstone's first government comment on that role, but one might distinguish between three forms of commentary. The government attacked certain areas of

---

[12]Collings to Mundella, 30 August 1868, Mundella MSS, 6P/1/8.

[13]Argyll to Gladstone, 18 December 1885, in Eighth Duke of Argyll, *Autobiography and Memoirs* (ed. Dowager Duchess of Argyll, 2 vols., 1906), II, 400.

monopoly with a view to liberalizing some social practices which tradition or super-seded ideology had made the preserve of a favoured group or identity. Terminating the power of the Church of Ireland – an Anglican élite in a Catholic country – comes under this heading, as does abolishing the 'purchase' of army commissions and removing from the universities of Oxford, Cambridge and Durham religious 'Tests' formerly applied to those wishing to hold academic posts and to candidates for university degrees. A second style of reaction took the form of using the power of government as an agency for compulsion in order to remedy social abuse, redress grievance or curb nuisance. In some cases the attack on monopoly had this justification also; but in others, the government took a firmer line to insist on prevent-ing harm from being done. A strong moral thrust characterized this area of policy and between 1868 and 1874 it appeared most prominently in the regulation of sex, drink and (an interesting association) trade unions. A third category comprised the small but bitterly-debated domain of policy in which the government chose to use its power in order to do something desirable rather than inhibit something undesirable. Whether Forster's Education Bill should contain compulsory school attendance among its provisions exemplifies the strain; or whether Ireland could be calmed without redistributing Irish land over the kicks and screams of its present owners; or whether the government could surmount the prejudices of generations by establish-ing a genuine university for the Irish. That the government came close to the rocks over each of these matters says something about the sensitivities of Liberals. That none of them achieved the transition from theory to practice says rather more.

The Irish Church began Gladstone's ministry because it had provided the lever for removing its Conservative predecessor. The problem of maintaining what had always been an alien Church had deepened into a major grievance among the Irish peasantry and the violent outburst of Irish nationalism over the past few years lent the status of the Church of Ireland a heightened sense of anomaly. Yet a problem does not normally become an issue until politicians choose to make it one; and some degree of party strategy certainly underlay the decision to impel Liberal policy towards the objective of disestablishing the Irish Church. Crushed by Disraeli's tactical victory over reform in 1867, Gladstone and his colleagues urgently needed a flag around which to regroup and the injustice of an English Church in Ireland presented an ideal mixture of high-mindedness and distance from the issues over which Liberals had no hope of agreement among themselves. Once the Liberals learned to live with one another, after all, Disraeli had no hope of continuing in power: his government still rested on a parliamentary minority. At the ensuing election in November–December 1868, the Liberal party increased its majority from 62 (in 1865) to just over a hundred: but their *English* performance played no part in the success. For the first time in British politics, the 'Celtic Fringe' exercised a decisive influence. As Gladstone himself saw, however, the difficulties of Ireland required more than the removal of its established Church. The disestablishment of 1869 left the vast problem of land untouched; and that problem threatened to open more wounds than it closed. It cut not only at monopoly, which Liberals disliked, but also at property, which they venerated.

The English Church suffered no major depredation. Indeed, Gladstone spent many of his waking hours as prime minister worrying about its bishoprics and how they should be filled. In removing barriers against the appointment of non-Anglicans to university posts, the government acted not only out of a respect for nonconformity but also from personal knowledge of the difficulties faced by intellectuals like Leslie Stephen and Henry Sidgwick following their loss of faith. But the weight of the

Liberal attack went against other institutions no less esteemed by gentlemen as employers for their younger sons: the civil service, the army and the universities. The opening of the civil service to competitive examination in 1870 merely pressed forward recommendations dating back to the Northcote–Trevelyan report of 1853 but it suggested a new mood none the less since other 'Liberal' governments had done nothing about them. Edward Cardwell's army reforms moved in a similar direction by proposing as part of the provisions the abolition of the procedure by which well-connected individuals could buy commissions in the British army, regardless of their military training or experience. Two stimuli came into play: the Peelite background of an 'executive' politician with a taste for efficiency and the fears for British defence provoked by Germany's whirlwind defeat of France in the Franco-Prussian war of 1870–1. A glare of hatred came inevitably from Top Brass; the backbenches debated the matter with a heat never generated by more serious issues; the peers threw out the Bill in a fit of blimpish temper and forced the government to put through their scheme by Royal Warrant, thus gaining their purpose at the expense of distressing Liberals who worried more about the constitution than about the army.

Less ambivalence seemed appropriate to the moral questions of the day and Liberals approached them with considerable panache. Prostitution – 'a painful subject, on which I cannot here enter into detail'[14] – occupied the time of government as much as the mind of Gladstone, though less from a wish to help 'fallen women' than to protect their clients. For this government completed the programme begun by previous Liberal administrations to compel the registration and medical monitoring of prostitutes in the vicinity of certain garrisons and ports, despite lurid reports from some of their own MPs about the evils of compulsory (and painful) examination. Only in the mid 1880s did Josephine Butler's repeal agitation succeed in removing these 'Contagious Diseases Acts' from the statute book. Drink struck nonconformist Liberals as no less painful and far more public; so Henry Bruce's Licensing Act of 1872 won warm support from those seeking further to curb the drink interest. It did not lose Gladstone the next election as some contemporaries believed, but it unquestionably aroused strong sentiments among critics who often took the precise ground of personal freedom as the starting point for their attack. Seen from the perspectives of the early twentieth century, these Liberal attitudes appeared quaint in their lack of complexity. A later generation found much greater difficulty in associating its state – the one conceived as an embodiment and realization of the better society – with pollutions of this kind: an interesting and significant shift of stance.

The conception of trade unionism as a form of social disease turned out more of a blunder. 'Personal freedom' found a home among the Liberals in this case as they struggled to prevent the intimidation of working men by unionists. Public opinion proved malleable over the issue because the so-called 'Sheffield outrages' of October 1866 and the inquiry that followed them implied a need to control the unions. In parliament, meanwhile, plenty of industrialists on the Liberal benches saw no problem at all in moving against them. Edmund Potter (Lib: Carlisle, 1861–74) 'had been an employer of labour for many years and forty-five years of experience had taught him that Trades' Unions did no good to the men, and certainly no good to the masters.'[15] Like Cobden in his early days, Potter ran a calico-printing business in

[4]Gladstone at Blackheath, 23 October 1871, in A. T. Bassett, *Gladstone's Speeches: descriptive index and bibliography* (1916), 414–15.
[5]In the House of Commons, 7 July 1869, *Hansard*, 3s, CXCVII, 1370ff.

Lancashire; as with Bright, his reforming enthusiasms deserted him at the mill-gate. The natural trajectory for such attitudes ran in the direction of the Criminal Law Amendment Act of 1871 which took away what the government gave in its Trade Union Act of the same year by having the effect of making picketing impossible without prosecution. This threw the unions into the arms of Disraeli from whom they earned the restoration of picketing rights in 1875; and Granville revealed only his lack of nous in this area when he advised Gladstone that the misalliance would have little political effect.[16]

The timing of the government's backlash could hardly have been worse. Over the next few years the unions won a good deal of public sympathy. In the case of Robert Lowe's notorious attempt to tax matches in the 1871 budget, for example, a national sense of victimization of match-girls who would lose their jobs caused some stir. The engineering dispute of the same year likewise won attention far beyond Northumberland and Durham where the strike began. More fundamentally, however, the government did not see – how could it? – that the economy teetered on the brink of a far-reaching economic downturn that would bring the relations of capital and labour far closer to centre-stage than Liberal politicians habitually regarded them. Even in these last boom years, Gladstone assumed a non-interventionist stance over wages that Peel would have endorsed without hesitation. At the Lord Mayor's dinner in 1872 he turned to the problem only at the very end of his speech in referring to what *The Times* winningly described as 'the revision of the terms of engagement between employers and employed.' His remarks contained an emptiness that Disraeli must have admired:

> Mr. GLADSTONE glanced at these facts before he sat down, and expressed a confident hope that habits of good sense and of mutual confidence and dependence which had been produced by generations of freedom would stand us in good stead under the present as under the former trial.[17]

This was porridge. In so far as the Liberal government had evolved a policy about the working class, its organizations and its conditions of life, the message seemed clear that liberties would grow faster than wages.

When the government moved beyond the anodyne, on the other hand, it ran into serious trouble with its own supporters. Two touchstones of resentment – religion and landed property – caused particular difficulty, not least because ministers chose to touch both of them in the same session.

Education reached the House of Commons first, in February 1870. Responsibility for the Bill to expand elementary education into a national system rested with the Vice-President of the Council, William Edward Forster, who hoped to remedy the undeniable patchiness of school provision on the part of the churches by making it possible for elected local school boards to add new schools. 'Our object', he said in a phrase that has stuck, 'is to complete the present voluntary system, to fill up gaps'.[18] To this extent the Bill comprised a major state initiative, judged by contemporary standards of intervention; it also commented on the failure of other approaches. Strange, then, that the Education Act of 1870 became the centrepiece of Radical attack against its own government. The reason stemmed from the close relationship

[16]Granville to Gladstone, 15 October 1871, in Ramm, *Political Correspondence* II, 274. Cf *The Times*, 16 October.
[17]Gladstone, reported in *The Times*, 25 July 1872.
[18]Forster in the House of Commons, 17 February, 1870, *Hansard*, 3s, CXCIX, 443–4.

between Radical opinion and nonconformist politics. Gladstone gave little lead in the direction of pulling the schools from the grip of the Anglican Church. The subject hurt him. Besides, he had other obsessions at the time – the Irish land problem and an unending mental turbulence over whom to appoint to the vacant bishopric of St Asaph. Forster came to the Commons with a feeble compromise reflecting the coalition between Anglicanism and Dissent that his party represented over this question.

That the Radicals would tolerate no sectarian teaching in the new schools became apparent at once; but they felt it unworthy of their party that they had to force their own government to accept an amendment – the Cowper-Temple clause, named after its mover – in order to insert that provision into the Bill. But at least they won. They lost over clause 25 (as vivid a slogan to Gladstonian Radicals as clause 4 would later become to Labour's) which allowed local Boards of Guardians to pay the *Church* school fees of necessitous children. They also lost over the question of compulsion. Radical pressure, most especially from the Birmingham-based National Education League and Joseph Chamberlain, had massed behind compelling school attendance. The Act shrank from this and Forster never recovered his reputation among nonconformist Radicals. Gladstone came to believe by 1873 that the education issue 'will eventually either split the party, or fatally cripple it for a time in regard to Parliamentary action.'[19] He exaggerated the case, but certainly no other issue had so plainly established the divide between his party's Centre and Left. Outside parliament, moreover, the damage ran deeper in giving educational radicalism a 'country party' flavour that it never lost before the onset of a secular system.

If Birmingham drove wedges between the Centre and Left, so Ireland created new fissures in the relationship between the parliamentary party and its drier Whigs. Many of the Whig grandees drew an appreciable slice of their rentals from Irish estates. In turning to the problem of the tenantry and its claims to extended rights in Ireland, therefore, the cabinet had already felt the weight of what Granville had called a landlord view of the matter. Now Gladstone might well, left to himself and his books, have taken a radical perspective and led the party in the direction of major concessions to the tenantry. But his antennae told him that his Whigs regarded this approach as closed from the outset; and he responded with great political sensitivity. When Bright made public noises about giving more of the land back to the Irish, Gladstone squashed him. When Whigs from the aged Russell to colleagues such as Clarendon, Cardwell, Fortescue and Hartington expressed pain and grief, he oiled their feathers, reaffirmed his commitment to the rights of property and his opposition to 'wild agitation for laws which as I understand them would destroy the relation of landlord and tenant.'[20] Consequently, the Land Act of 1870 offered a mild improvement in the lot of the Irish tenant but did not give him the security of tenure and freedom from the threat of eviction that stood at the top of his agenda. It disappointed the Radicals and left their opponents in the party sour and suspicious.

No simple path led from the Whigs' anxieties over Irish land policy to their revolt over the Irish University Bill in 1873. Their fears had been compounded along the way by the introduction of the ballot, the distance Gladstone seemed willing to go in his (unsuccessful) attempts to keep Bright in the cabinet, by general qualms about the leftward tendency of the world. But it had certainly done their self-confidence no good and made them edgier than they might have been when Gladstone pressed Fortescue to start thinking about higher education in Ireland. Because education

Gladstone to Granville, 3 September 1873, in Ramm, *Political Correspondence*, II, 405.
Gladstone to Cardwell, 21 September 1869, in *Gladstone Diaries*, VII, 135.

posed the problem, religion balked its solution: only this time Catholic, rather than Dissenting, advocates made their presence felt. Fortescue's removal from the Chief Secretaryship in 1871 – Gladstone and he had never got on – removed one difficulty, though his replacement by Hartington, heir to the Devonshire fortune and Irish estates and a man whose political grasp and interest reflected a certain inconsistency, promised little better. In fact Hartington saw the nonsense of the University Bill as quickly as anyone else. It offended not only an ascendancy mentality but also raw common sense to propose setting up an Irish university in which major subjects in the humanities would be banned in order to avoid contradicting Catholic teaching on them. The idea was little less than crazy and when the Commons threw it out, the government took the chance to ask Disraeli to assume office so that they could run away to the country. Disraeli had more sense than to allow them that luxury, of course, and they staggered on for another few months. But the government never recovered from the Whig resistance that led to its defeat.[21]

Nor had offending the Whigs brought any compensation in pleasing the Radicals. Indeed by 1873 the government's timidity over a clutch of issues had left them acidulated. Historians often quote Joseph Chamberlain's article on the Liberal party and its leaders that appeared in the *Fortnightly Review* in 1873 with its complaints about the timidity of a leadership 'exclusively occupied of late with its own dissensions' and 'deaf to the growing desire for radical reform which occupies the minds of the great mass of the people, upon whom it ought chiefly to lean for support.'[22] But this was the calculated outburst of an aspiring professional politician seeking to cut a figure and looking for a seat. One can illustrate the mood, with its venomous criticisms of Liberal leadership and method, from other sources. Take, for example, the doctrine of free trade. Gladstone made it a part of his rhetorical message to insist on Liberalism's standing for that if nothing else; he frequently referred to the Cobden Treaty of 1860 as the model of economic diplomacy. But Louis Mallet – an official of the Board of Trade who had played a part in those negotiations; the man who had privately hoped that the Gladstone government would say as little as possible about free trade – found before the end of the first year of that government that he could no longer contain his fury at its *lack* of doctrine or concerted thought. 'Empiricism' is the word that comes to mind in the twentieth century. He reminds us that it did not escape his in the nineteenth:

> The last ten years have been *wasted*. No one knows better than I, how cold and apathetic every Govt has been on this subject since Cobden's Treaty. I have always told them, unless you considered that measure as a part of a great policy, it was an act of empiricism & deserves the fate with which it is threatened – but Gladstone never regarded it in this light. He never took the slightest interest in the policy, if indeed he ever understood or accepted it. . . .[23]

Of course, no political act is value-free and to represent Gladstonian Liberalism as an 'empirical' politics would seriously distort its sense of mission. The first Gladstone government had attempted to realize objectives which it would never have entered the mind of the first Disraeli government to attempt. And whatever the

[21] For the background to the Whig politics of these years, see J. P., 'Religion and the Collapse of Gladstone's First Government 1870–74', *Historical Journal*, 25 (1982), 71–101.
[22] Joseph Chamberlain, 'The Liberal Party and its Leaders', *Fortnightly Review*, 14/20 (1873), 287–302 and esp. 291.
[23] Mallet to Mundella, 21 November 1869, Mundella MSS, 6P/2/14.

constraints under which it struggled with its problems, the common identification with a Liberal language about rights and justice guaranteed of itself a certain ideological coherence. If the Radicals had come to define their Liberalism in markedly different terms from any comprehended by their Whig colleagues, they all at least asserted a communion of intention. But the identity remained fragile and largely non-prescriptive; it grew out of the sociology of the parliamentary party and perceptions of its public in the country more than the textbooks of its theorists. Where its actions converged with formal doctrine, they did so rather along the line of least resistance than along the road to Damascus.

Edinburgh via Bulgaria

It must have been late afternoon or early evening when the train finally reached Waverley station. Thousands of people lined Princes Street and choked the station's approaches. On the platform stood the young Lord Rosebery who had arranged to accompany Gladstone in an open carriage through the crowds to Dalmeny for a night's rest before the campaign proper began the following day. Gladstone had already made three short speeches on the way up from Hawarden – at Carlisle, Hawick and Galashiels – and left each audience in no doubt that today, Monday, 24 November 1879, marked a decisive moment in the history of British politics and the beginning of the Liberal party's surge towards power. A century later that claim seems only mildly extravagant. Within six months the Liberal party returned to government after a painful five years. The object of Gladstone's venom during these 'Midlothian' campaigns – the foreign policy of Lord Beaconsfield, as Benjamin Disraeli had become in 1876 – did indeed drown in the general election of 1880 and its author with it: borne down in a torrent of prayer and indignation. A new phase in the history of Liberal policy no less certainly developed over the next few years, even if many of its characteristics bore little relation to the emotional promises made in 1879 and 1880 in the villages and halls of Midlothian. Yet (and easily within the memory of every political observer) a Liberal administration led by Gladstone had collapsed in ignominy at the beginning of 1874 and provoked its leader into resigning from public life in order to devote himself to speculation and writing. The route to Edinburgh had proved circuitous to a degree unfathomable in 1875. The party that travelled it had, moreover, changed and aged no less noticeably than its messiah.

Two changes in the second half of the seventies impress at once by their potential significance for the future: first, a swing away from domestic issues towards international and imperial ones; and, second, the modification of the party's organization and parliamentary character. Together these developments altered the public face of Liberalism and presented a clear message to the party about its leadership.

Thinking back to the first Gladstone government from the years of Beaconsfield's global adventures confirmed one of its more easily-missed features: the extent of its quietude in foreign policy. Important issues had emerged, of course, most obviously in the Franco-Prussian war; but, seen as a whole, the problems posed by distant parts of the globe did not impinge in the degree to which they would when the so called 'new imperialism' made its presence felt. The ministers who controlled policy realized perfectly well the preponderance of domestic issues. We see Gladstone remarking on the extent to which his mind is concerned with domestic problems, or one of his colleagues observing how out of touch Gladstone seems to be when the discussion does become international, as it had to do over the German attack on

France.[24] Two other matters caused some indigestion. The Foreign Office spent a difficult period negotiating compensation to the United States for Britain's allowing the building in Liverpool during the Civil War of a Confederate ship, the *Alabama*. And Gladstone's own instincts against foreign adventure came into friction with colleagues over an expedition to bring the Ashantis to heel in 1873. Placed alongside the controversies fomented by domestic reform, however, these remained back-burner matters. The change of direction came only after 1875 and as a result of decisions made by Disraeli's Conservative government.

As though to amplify the theme begun in their opposition speeches as early as 1872, the Beaconsfield government sought explicitly to pull public attention away from home affairs in order to exploit the unifying possibilities of a positive foreign policy. Disraeli's elevation of the Queen to new heights as Empress of India made an early signal of how the Empire would predominate. The remarkable purchase of a major block of shares in the new Suez canal showed how it would be maintained. But the public concentration on external themes owed more to events that did not originate with the government. The first and most spectacular of these concerned the Turkish massacre of Christian subjects in Bulgaria in 1876. Disraeli believed, quite apart from his long-standing admiration for the Ottoman empire, that nothing the Turks did in Bulgaria would shake the British government; and he was correct in that judgement. He none the less severely underestimated the amount of noise that a determined opposition might make over it. He also failed to recognize the life-line that so uplifting a cause might come to represent for the Gladstonian Liberal party.

The adjective 'Gladstonian' has considerable importance in this context. For that version of Liberal politics – the one that had emerged in the regrouping over the Irish Church and found its main force in a concentration on moral issues through which a sense of political purpose might be articulated – certainly needed saving. One can argue that it might have proved better for the Liberal party in the long run had it drowned. For then the other elements that had already given the leadership some anxiety, and especially that of industrial Radicalism with its nascent programme attacking the problems of social injustice conceived as inequality rather than as monopoly or mischief, would have reached prominence far earlier than they did.[25] With Gladstone in retirement (and in something approaching a sulk), Birmingham came many a mile nearer to Westminster. But Bulgaria brought Gladstone back. He may not have returned as leader in any formal sense; but all senior Liberals recognized that none of them could realistically claim the stage while Gladstone waited in the wings. By his reaction to what he called 'the Bulgarian horrors', Gladstone rediscovered 'the Irish Church' in a European setting: an over-whelming moral case that would pull Liberals together and make them act as *Gladstonian* Liberals should.

Just as over the Irish Church, Gladstone's involvement in the Bulgarian agitation took the form not of an initiative but a response. His pamphlet on *The Bulgarian Horrors* appeared only after other propagandists among the intelligentsia had whipped up a substantial public indignation against the Turks for their barbarism. The extraordinary sales of that pamphlet in the first few months, and the speeches

---

[24]E.g. Gladstone to Lawley, 10 February 1870: 'In truth the period since we came into office has been one of universal & almost total silence in the H of C with regard to foreign affairs.' Printed in *Gladstone Diaries*, VII, 235.

[25]For this view and the background to Gladstone's behaviour in 1876, see Richard Shannon, *Gladstone and the Bulgarian Agitation, 1876* (1963; Hassocks, 1975).

Gladstone made, re-established the style of Liberalism as a champion of the oppressed and gave it a sense of acceleration after the stagnation since 1873. Behind the new thrust lay Gladstone's determination to make the party once again an agency for action:

> My opinion is & has long been that the vital principle of the Liberal party, like that of Greek art, is *action,* and that nothing but *action* will ever make it worthy of the name of a party.
>   You can muster them [i.e. Liberals] for votes of religious liberalism (so to call it) and for little else. And the party lukewarmness on the aristocratic side is about as injurious as, & less excusable than, the rampant disorderliness on the radical side.[26]

Here the Gladstonian preoccupation appears at its clearest as a device to transcend the inertia of Whiggery and the anarchy of Radicalism by a call to arms. The call ultimately mattered more than the weaponry. It gave the Liberal leader the relationship with his public that he wanted and left even a former Chartist like Thomas Cooper convinced by 1880 that he had made his mark again with the masses. 'The *people* want Gladstone.'[27]

Liberal momentum rested on far more than Bulgaria. Between 1876 and 1879 Beaconsfield's government found it necessary to address itself to difficulties in the Balkans over which Russia and Turkey went to war in 1877. In particular it needed to defend the peace treaty negotiated with other powers at Berlin in 1878, some facets of which – especially the annexation of Cyprus by Britain – had given Gladstone further ammunition. An ill-judged war against the Afghans in 1878 gave still more and brought back echoes of the expansionist strategies of the 1840s in the north-west of India. The disastrous campaign against the Zulus, finally, not only reinforced allegations of reckless imperialism but also attracted to the government the less elevated criticism that they could not even win a war when they had begun one. Each of these episodes deserves a detailed exposition but the reader must turn elsewhere for that.[28] Here we ought rather to note the monotonous build-up of crises in foreign affairs that would give Gladstone his major platform when he arrived to open the campaign against the government at his new constitutency of Midlothian.

By that time it had become apparent in most Liberal circles that the attempt by Hartington, Granville and Forster to provide a surrogate leadership had thankfully come to an end. Yet beneath the surface of Liberal politics a non-Gladstonian initiative had nevertheless emerged. The National Education League, which had given Forster so many headaches over his Education Bill, had played a significant role in promoting the foundation in 1877 of a new Liberal organization called the National Liberal Federation. To speak of it as an initiative pays it an unwonted compliment: it appeared as a belated reaction to the Conservative party's revamped organization in the wake of the Reform Act. Its Birmingham base reduced its national profile, moreover, for some time. What it signalled nonetheless assumed considerable significance over the next few years. The constituencies (and therefore in practice the activists who controlled them) had provided themselves with a machine with a long-term capacity to change the way the Liberal party worked and the assumptions on which its

[26]Gladstone to Granville, 19 May 1877, in Ramm, *Political Correspondence,* I, 40.
[27]Cooper to Mundella, 5 April 1880 Mundella MSS, 6P/13/10.
[28]A recent and accessible account of the impact of these developments is presented in Marvin Swartz, *The Politics of British Foreign Policy in the era of Disraeli and Gladstone* (1985).

leaders operated. Having welcomed its birth, Gladstone soon regretted its survival. The Birmingham idea of cementing local Liberal opinion through a caucus and an effective electoral apparatus had helped revive spirits at a bad time and to that extent had been beneficial. 'But it is like a tonic good at a certain stage of recovery from disease, and inapplicable to other stages.'[29] In February 1880, when Gladstone expressed that view, he regarded himself as having reached a quite different stage.

Gladstone began his Midlothian lectures (they hardly amounted to less) in the same term that T. H. Green began delivering his lectures on political obligation. There are some shared resonances: a language of community, rational decision-making, a defence of property. But Gladstone, when he talked about the state at all, kept it as far away from his audience as he had distanced himself from it when rousing the faithful in 1868. Not all the speeches consisted entirely of declamations against recent foreign policy – the Fourth was the first to take that form – and each offered something of a local or domestic tinge to lighten the exposition of events in distant lands. Yet the silence over economic strategy screams from the pages of these printed speeches. The moment when farmers had just suffered the notorious harvest of 1879 ought not to have seemed propitious for advising them to try growing strawberries instead. Telling them to pay lower rents rather than higher likewise struck the more hard-bitten among his audience as nursery wisdom. But worse was to come.

> It is, more broadly, in a serious and manful struggle that you are engaged, in which you will have to exert yourselves to the uttermost, in which you have a right to claim every-thing that the Legislature can do for you; and I hope it may perhaps possibly be my privilege and honour to assist in procuring for you some of those provisions of necessary liberation from restraint; but beyond that, it is your own energies, of thought, and action, to which you will have to trust.[30]

'Necessary liberation from restraint': nothing more. 'May perhaps possibly': not the firmest of commitments. With the rural and urban economy in severe slump, the auguries for such a policy could hardly inspire confidence over the prospects for Gladstone's next government. Indeed, even the magniloquent pledges to destroy imperialism might turn out harder to achieve than proclaim.

Practice: the second Gladstone government 1880–5

While Gladstone talked about Afghanistan and Zululand, Beaconsfield discussed Ireland. This had the advantage of allowing him to talk less about India and Africa. It also allowed the Conservative party to direct attention at a major threat to the rule of law and the rights of property; and it brought back memories of the mess into which Gladstone's party had sunk over Ireland in the early seventies. Besides, Irish nationalism had turned into a genuine issue since Michael Davitt's Land League became a focus of rural unrest during 1879. Beaconsfield's decision to make the need to resist calls for Home Rule central to the election did Gladstone's Liberal party more harm than anyone realized at the time. For it meant that, when the Liberals won the election and returned to power, they set off on just the foot they would have hoped to avoid. The ministry began with Ireland; it became, at least publicly, obsessed with Ireland; it destroyed itself over Ireland. And because the Liberal crisis over Home

[29] Gladstone to Granville, 18 February 1880, in Ramm, *Political Correspondence*, I, 113.
[30] Third Midlothian speech at West Calder, 27 November 1879, *Political Speeches*, I, 101.

Rule seems in retrospect to wait in the future for the Liberal party to strike it and founder, so the temptation mounts to read Gladstone's second government backwards from the nightmare of 1885–6 and see all events running on rails towards that common, fatal junction. It is a great mistake.

Ireland had lost its missionary function for the Liberals since 1873: during the past few years Gladstone had pacified nobody. A certain paradox, indeed, arises from the thought that the years since the foundation of Isaac Butt's Home Rule party in 1874 had proved the very period in which the interest of Liberals in Ireland had demonstrably waned. They probably saw their agenda dominated in 1880 by the cleansing of the imperial stable and by the need to do something for rural distress at home, not least by extending the vote to the agricultural worker to complete the task begun by Disraeli in 1867 and do the party some good in the counties. In fact three themes dominated their period of office: the attempt to cope with Egypt without losing the Radicals; the strategy for coping with democracy without losing what was left of the Whigs; and the hopes to quieten Ireland without alienating one kind of Liberal opinion through coercion and suspension of civil rights for the Irish or the other by dangerous revisions of the privileges attached to an absentee landowner class. All of these cut close to the knuckle and made the central activity of political practice – the cultivation of a satisfactory language in which enlightened pragmatism might find a home – more difficult to devise than a predominance of more remote issues might have allowed. The procedure of 1869 no longer held good. Even if the Liberals could sweep Ireland away in the first year or so, they would not have the luxury of selecting pieces of minimal 'reform' across a broad front. Westminster had become a more claustrophobic place in which to conduct the great game. Unlike the situation following the dislocation of 1867, the new Liberal government discovered itself heir to a complicated continuity that it could alter but not easily evade.

Perhaps the constraints of their inheritance help explain why the ministry seems, in its conversations with theory, to fall into two halves, hinging around some point in 1883. So many difficulties pushed the Liberal government into uncongenial policy positions by the end of 1882 that much of the framework in which they were to act over the next few years already existed by the time Gladstone went off to Cannes to recuperate from a state of nervous collapse at the beginning of that year. Indeed, Allen Warren's suggestive point that Irish policy took on its essential character very early (between 1880 and 1882)[31] strengthens by extension. In most areas of first-rank political concern, with the partial exception of the reform act promised in 1880 but not enacted till 1884, the first two years provided an echo of 1870–2 as a kernel of executive activity. By the end of 1882 one Radical – John Bright – had resigned (again) from the cabinet because he took the government to have contravened Liberal doctrine over imperialism. Before even that point one senior Whig – the Duke of Argyll – had resigned because he believed Gladstone's Irish policies implied a Liberal desertion of the landed interest and the principles embracing property and the sanctity of contract on which it rested. Before climbing on the train to go to France, Gladstone himself had muttered obsessively about the need to give the Irish some form of local government:[32] the position beyond which he almost certainly

[31]See Allen Warren, 'Gladstone, Land and Social Reconstruction in Ireland 1881–7', *Parliamentary History*, 2 (1983), 153–71.

[32]'He, however, said to me incredibly *We must have a Local Government Bill for Ireland.*' Harcourt to Spencer, 17 January 1883 (emphasis in original) in Peter Gordon (ed.), *The Red Earl: the papers of the fifth Earl Spencer 1835–1910* (2 vols., Northampton, 1981, 1986), I, 238.

never intended to go until new threats and contingencies assaulted his dwindling judgement in 1885.

Imperialism hurt the Liberals in those early years by illuminating the valley between what Gladstone had preached at Midlothian and what the Liberal party practised when in power. No cohesive group of imperialists yet existed within the parliamentary party, though one would emerge after 1886; but the presence of establishment figures like Granville and Kimberley ensured that an imperial perspective remained available during the formation of policy. That Gladstone's host at Midlothian had himself been a strong imperialist said something for future frictions, even if Rosebery did not enter the cabinet until the very end of the ministry. In the meantime, the government's recall of Sir Bartle Frere as a reprisal for his having fomented the war against the Zulus failed to atone, in the eyes of Radicals at least, for the government's quaking before their duty to kick the Turks with their bags and baggage out of Europe, and for its unwillingness to withdraw convincingly from Afghanistan. In the eyes of the British public, the government's timidity in meeting the uprising of white Transvaalers that culminated in the killing of the British governer at Majuba Hill in 1881 likewise did it little good. But the graveyard of Midlothian idealism was dug rather in Egypt. The purchase of the Suez shares had provided Gladstone with some of his righteousness for the castigation of Beaconsfieldism. Yet what price moral indignation if the Liberal government could reveal itself capable when once in power of bombarding Alexandria with gunboats, as though Palmerston had returned from the dead to inspire the premier? Admittedly the nationalist revolt of Arabi Pasha gave both the British and French governments, which exercised a dual control in Egypt, severe problems to confront. But the Liberals' solution left the British government taking single-handed responsibility and allowing itself to be drawn militarily into Egypt with consequences that reached their climacteric at the beginning of 1885 when news reached Britain of the death of General Gordon. Only Bright resigned. But questions persisted and rumbled far beyond Gladstone's private pain over these events.

Ireland represented a slice of empire: different from India or Egypt but in its special way a fragment of imperial argument. The fear and pain that Ireland aroused did not depend, at least initially, on an intimation that Gladstone intended giving it away. Whigs worried more about the government's practising forms of generosity on behalf of the Irish tenantry that would mean more expense for them on their Irish estates and cause major embarrassment if imported into England. At the outset Gladstone had tried to encourage the more landed among his colleagues with disavowals of interference. 'Not all the Governments on earth,' he had reassured one Whig in 1880, 'can do for a community certain things it ought to do for itself.'[33] Nor did his subsequent behaviour suggest that he had undergone some personality change over the issue of Irish land. Returning to the subject at all doubtless gave him considerable discomfort since it argued the failure of his own Act of 1870. In retracing his steps, moreover, he avoided abstraction and began with specifics. Those who did not, like the economist Bonamy Price, caught his sense of satire rather than his enthusiasm. As he told the packed House of Commons when he introduced his Irish Land Bill in 1881, 'Mr Bonamy Price, is the only man – and to his credit be it spoken – who has had the resolution to apply, in all their unmitigated authority, the principles of abstract political economy to the people and circumstances of Ireland exactly as if he had been

[33]Gladstone to Harcourt, 12 December 1880, quoted in Warren, 'Gladstone, Land and Social Reconstruction', 158.

proposing to legislate for the inhabitants of Saturn or Jupiter.'[34] But the concession of the famous '3Fs' (fair rents, fixity of tenure, free sale of improvements made by tenants), for all the drafting acumen that had gone into making them far less sweeping and accommodating than they at first appeared, not only drove Argyll to despair and resignation but also pushed other Whigs towards the position of those who, like George Joachim Goschen, had refused to join the government at all for fear of where it might go.

Goschen, and other Liberals whom Gladstone thought weak-kneed, grounded their apprehensions about this government in its promise further to extend the franchise. In fact, the degree of democratization attempted by the Liberals in 1884 proved very limited: they gave the agricultural worker an electoral status similar to his urban counterpart; they increased the total electorate in the United Kingdom from around 3 million adult males in 1880 to 5,700,000 at the election of 1885; they removed, in the Corrupt Practices Act of 1883, some of the grosser abuses of money and influence common in elections. Some observers announced the falling down of the sky and the end of England. Not a few convinced themselves that Britain had tumbled into a democratical republic from which one could expect nothing better than spoliation and anarchy. From the higher vantage point offered by a century of political change since the 1880s, it seems plain that these fears missed the point. The Liberal government had not embraced revolution but rather side-stepped all talk of one by dealing quietly (and privately, for the most part) with a widely-conceded priority to complete the settlement of 1867.[35] Where radicalism made an appearance at all, it took its power not from action but from rhetoric and the *frisson* caused by the decision of the Liberal government to include Ireland within the terms of the Reform Act. Doing so hardly precipitated a revolution in the Irish counties where a franchise reform in 1850 had long since initiated the decisive shift.[36] But the half a million increase in the Irish electorate provided by the government seemed another instance of Gladstone's buying off Parnell – another warning that British Radicals wanted to shake hands with Irish ones in a common cause.

Fears about the fusion of Radicalism into a cohesive bloc in fact made little sense.[37] The British and Irish Radicals held completely different objectives: one group seeking national liberation on an Italian model of liberal politics, the other looking for a twist in the content of official Liberalism to point it in the direction of social equality and a consciousness that Gladstonian policies had become outmoded. Their sociology contained no common denominator. In one faction representatives of the brilliant intellectual élite of Dublin confronted the difficulties of a rural tenantry. In the other, men who epitomized civic pride and aldermanic values leaned against cleverer men to press them to consider the depressed cities and the atmosphere in which they – the English industrial Radicals – had always drawn breath: a mixture of steam and cigar smoke. In so far as anyone had made a Radical *motif* out of Ireland, Lord Randolph Churchill had invented it for Tory Democracy. For the Radicals of the Liberal party, Ireland's function was more modest; it simply got in the way. With their local contacts still fresh, they recognized, as Gladstone increasingly could not,

[34]Gladstone in Commons, 7 April 1881, *Hansard*, 3s, CCLX, 895.
[35]The Cabinet and party politics of the Third Reform Act are explained in detail by Andrew Jones in his *The Politics of Reform: 1884* (Cambridge, 1972).
[36]For details, see K. Theodore Hoppen, *Elections, Politics and Society in Ireland 1832–85* (Oxford, 1984), 26–33.
[37]See the helpful remarks of Alan O'Day in *The English Face of Irish Nationalism: Parnellite involvement in British politics 1880–86* (Dublin, 1977), 79–92.

that Ireland bored the British public when it did not actually disgust it. Little more than a vague anti-landlordism emerged from their commentaries on Irish affairs during these years. That sentiment at least merged with a range of domestic imperatives about the damage done by Whigs who failed either to toil or spin.

The famous castigation of the Liberal right-wing came from Joseph Chamberlain in 1883. By then he had been in the House for seven years and made at least as great an impression as Churchill. Yet one should distinguish between Chamberlain's Westminister persona as a cross-party phenomenon – a coming man in high politics – and his effectiveness inside the Liberal party. What seems plain at once when considering the power of Radicalism is that before 1885 its parliamentary successes were few and minor. Of course one must go beyond so limited a view to take account of perceptions that by no means followed from hard-nosed results. Yet even seen in this way the future of Radicalism looked dark by 1885. Gladstone had over-estimated the power of Bright and the style of Radicalism he had embodied in the 1860s and 70s; one can document moments when Gladstone receded from policy positions in order to placate him. Chamberlain he persistently misunderstood and grossly underrated. Birmingham Liberalism struck him as an offensive, half-baked socialism and Chamberlain as an ambitious climber using it for his own ends. Whatever his thoughts about Home Rule for Ireland in 1885, Gladstone felt fully persuaded by the intrigues and provocations of the last two years that he did not want home rule for Birmingham.

To argue that the Liberal leadership moved towards conceding one form of Home Rule in order to avoid the other goes beyond the evidence. It remains the case that this new development in British Liberalism, which propelled the party in a direction quite different from that indicated by most of its theorists and backbenchers, developed in a highly complicated party environment in which Ireland comprised only one element.[38] Some intellectual conviction and preparation there unquestionably was: Gladstone spent much of his time in 1885 reading books about the Union with Ireland, just as he had become absorbed in the literature about the Irish Church in 1868. Yet the 'conversion' appeared alongside a series of decisions concerning Gladstone's wish to retire; his determination to ensure that Hartington succeeded him when he did; his certainty that the temporizing Liberalism of weak-kneed Goschen was no more desirable than the swollen head of Chamberlain; his rejection of the Radicalism contained in the language of the Birmingham men and especially at the provisions of the so-called 'Unauthorized Programme' in which Radicals had taken the novel step of 'going public' with their criticisms of official policy. Gladstone radiated a sense of mission: he always did. But the content of the mission had as much to do with preserving the structure of Liberal politics in England as with securing peace in Ireland or the palliation of Parnell.

When coping with the Adullamites in 1868, Gladstone had re-absorbed them into main-line Liberal politics by finding an issue different from franchise reform and one that had the potential to direct party energies into a single moral purpose. The success of that plan made a great impression on him; he looked back on it as a great triumph and a model of how Liberal politicians ought to proceed. In offering the Irish a heavily-qualified form of self-government, the Gladstonian Liberal party reflected a concern with its recent lack of direction and a determination to put the party back on the road. So the revelation by Herbert Gladstone in December 1885 that his father

[38]See A. B. Cooke and John Vincent, *The Governing Passion: cabinet government and party politics in Britain 1885–6* (Brighton, 1974), esp. 3–60.

had come to believe in Home Rule for Ireland owed nothing to naïveté or stupidity. Rather, it provided a calculated point of departure for those who wanted to keep the Liberal party Gladstonian. In the three months that followed, the extent of the damage (or salvage) became apparent. The Whig section of the parliamentary party felt the blow as if hit by a falling log when even the more pessimistic among them had thought another last straw their worst scenario. Only a handful of the great Whig houses continued their loyalty to the Liberal party. On the Radical side, the casualties included not only Chamberlain and Collings, but also the vision of the future they had cherished for the past two years.

The magazine articles that the Radicals collected into their *Radical Programme* in 1885 had already turned – as the Gladstonians had meant them to turn – into 'one of the outstanding dead-ends in British political history.' Of course, the Radicals themselves had taken pains in their propaganda to broadcast their status as the party's broad base instead of a narrow band of pilgrims. More than that, Radicals had tried to present themselves as a loose confederation of practical men urging specific remedies. 'It [Radicalism] is not the creed of mere theorists, but is practical alike in its objects and its methods.' But no one could effectively conceal the degree to which Radical assumptions differed from those of the sluggish centre-men. Perhaps the eccentricities of Frank Harris would only find their true appreciation when he published his autobiography; but even now his politics, at least, contained a dangerous streak. He wrote the section of *The Radical Programme* that dealt with the problem of the cities and the urban poor; and his remedies ran closer to the new theories of social organism than many Liberals would think appropriate:

> The State has too long made itself the champion of the rights of the individual: it must now assert the rights of the many – of all. It is apparent that in open competition the fittest obtain more than they deserve, and the less fit come too near perishing. If co-operation is not to supersede competition, the worst effects of this struggle for existence must be at once mitigated.[39]

Mitigation, not supersession: capitalism, not socialism. The discomfort remained. Gladstonian Liberalism would find even so limited an approach to the state a struggle against the current of that moral politics it had evolved so successfully in the 1860s. Those whom Chamberlain called 'the "respectables"' put their faith where Gladstone had told them to put it, in the undoing of error and the punishment of mischief. By 1885 that doctrine had petrified because the mischief required re-definition. It took Chamberlain and his colleagues a while to see that the Gladstonian failure to reshape its image of the state lay not at the margin of Liberal politics but at its core. Eventually the enlightenment came. 'I think the Gladstonian period is slowly coming to an end', Chamberlain wrote to his fellow victim, Dilke, in 1888. 'It will leave great confusion behind, but its central idea is doomed.'[40] Jettisoned by the party he had hoped to take by storm, Chamberlain had at least the satisfaction of watching it go down.

---

[39]T. H. S. Escott, 'The Future of the Radical Party' and Frank Harris, 'The Housing of the Poor in Towns', both printed in D. A. Hamer (ed.), *The Radical Programme* (Brighton, 1971), lv–lvi, 91.
[40]Chamberlain to Mundella, 12 October 1885, Mundella MSS, 6P/18/27; Chamberlain to Dilke, 31 December 1888, in J. L. Garvin and J. Amery, *The Life of Joseph Chamberlain* (6 vols., 1932–69), II, 407.

5

Towards an Organic State: Theory 1886–1906

In the space of less than 12 months Gladstone had largely lost the intelligentsia. Its members had seen themselves, like their fathers and grandfathers, as the vanguard of political opinion; but the prime minister had run faster than those who expected to guide him – a reversal of the roles of 1876 when Bulgaria had fired churchmen and academics before Gladstone ignited his own enthusiasm. Home Rule discomfited the universities and the editorial offices of serious Liberal journals quite as markedly as it nonplussed the cabinet and backbenchers. Together with a crescendo in socialist activity and an overt race among the imperialist states of western Europe to annex and garrison parts of Africa, it left political thinkers to discover new principles for themselves or, more naturally, to insist on the rediscovery of old ones. The challenge would, seen in a broader perspective, help to generate significant developments within the classical Liberal position and result in the proposal of what came to be called a 'new Liberalism'. Less ultimately, meanwhile, the comforts of individualism seemed an attractive form of right reason in the face of Gladstone's apparent obsession with pressing the Liberals leftwards towards a position within nodding distance of the socialists. Mill may have had his tepid moments, after all, but he had never suggested giving India back to the Indians or, until late in his life, interfering with the fundamental rights of property at home.

Backpeddling took place in a number of areas directly linked to the policy positions adopted by the party, but a more profound instance of it concerned the mood in which intellectual Liberal 'lights' re-examined the concept of an 'organic society'. No one could turn back the clock to the days before Darwin but an instinct persisted none the less that a helpful notion had recently gone wrong. It had reminded political society that sovereignty lay with the people and not with party leaders or executive institutions: all well and good. But for the latter-day individualist, those 'people' remained what they had always been – a collection of distinct, identifiable, independent human creatures, each with a unique personality and a peculiar compound of intelligence, ambition, virtue and vice. Collective terms used to describe those individuals had no validity, therefore, beyond connoting a sum of constituent parts. People had lives of their own, no doubt, but *the* people had no life of *its* own, separable from the units on which its meaning depended. Subtract all the individuals from 'society' and one would be left with no remainder, no ghostly forces or metaphysical wills or intangible *mentalités*. By 1886, indeed, so luminous a Liberal 'light' as Goldwin Smith had lost patience with those who could not see the force of this argument.

> What is the State? People seem to suppose that there is something outside and above the members of the community which answers to this name and which has duties and a wisdom of its own. But duties can attach only to persons, wisdom can reside only in brains. The State, when you leave abstractions and come to facts, is nothing but the Government, which can have no duties but those which the Constitution assigns to it, nor any wisdom but that which is infused into it by the mode of appointment or election.[1]

Not all reactions to 'organic' thought reflected a measured tone, and individualists untroubled by Liberalism allowed their language to develop a degree of hysteria that made Goldwin Smith seem a paragon of socratic method. Sterling's vocabulary about monkeys found many an echo in writers of the 1880s who no longer could stomach arguments that depended on analogies with organisms. 'Social organism!' one commentator exploded in 1893. 'As well talk of an ant-organism, of a beaver-organism, or of a wolf-organism. As well argue about a bird-organism held together by the common medium of the air. If we were all stuck together like the Siamese Twins, then the term "organism" might do; but until this event happens, such a word taken in anything like a literal sense, is a gross and unreasoning exaggeration.' One might go further. Persons who used this language of the birds and the bees might suffer not only from self-deception but also deliberately deceive others by pretending that vicious policies had some ground in the concepts of interdependence and the general will. It could be that 'the State is only a veil interposed to give decency to the robbery of Peter for the payment of Paul.' Perhaps, by the same token, 'a free break-fast table means a table where one man eats and another pays; free education is where one man begets a child and another man pays for his schooling; just as a freebooter means a man who is free to take money from one man's pocket and put it into another's.'[2] Doubtless opinion of this kind found its wavelength in the Tory tavern more than among intellectual Liberals and certainly some prophets of an individualist utopia – 'anarchy *plus* the police constable', as one writer put it[3] – would have understood Spencer's drifting in a Conservative direction.

But it is important to grasp that collectivism and organicism did not amount to the same thing. A Liberal, even a 'New' one, could recommend an expansion of state activity to secure certain social ends without lending the concept of the state a metaphysical dimension of the kind that disturbed Goldwin Smith. The distinction bears a relationship to one drawn by Peter Clarke between 'moral' and 'mechanical' reformers among social-democratic theorists.[4] Advocates of a 'mechanical' approach to the task of improving society demanded no fundamental redrawing of the individual's personality or role within the social whole: they sought merely to expand the opportunities which membership of an organized society theoretically made available. One could suggest a programme which might take individuals as Mill understood them, for example, and then subject their social arrangements to changes of which Mill would himself have disapproved, yet do so without needing to turn

---

[1] Goldwin Smith, *False Hopes* (1886), 21–2.
[2] M. D. O'Brien, *Natural Right to Freedom* (1893), 14; E. Fry, 'The State as a Patient', *Contemporary Review*, LXVI (December 1894), 854.
[3] Thomas Mackay, *The English Poor* (1889), x.
[4] Peter Clarke, *Liberals and Social Democrats* (Cambridge, 1978), 4–5.

those individuals into different people or to assume that they possessed some as-yet-unrevealed social potential. Graham Wallas represents this strand of social democracy rather neatly, as a recent comment on his work suggests:

> Starting from the proposition that the nature of capitalism had made it easier for some individuals, as individuals, to oppress other individuals, Wallas' collectivism was simply an organizational solution for the amelioration of those individual injustices and inequalities. It was a machinery to ensure the maximum social good for the greatest number of individuals in an urban-industrial society.[5]

For the moral reformer, on the other hand, true progress demanded not merely better machinery but better people; and creating them involved a re-evaluation of the individual's nature and its relationship with the kind of society that gave individuals their nurture. The persistence of moral and mechanical recommendations within Liberal doctrine has lent it an ambivalence from which Liberals have never successfully divested themselves. To what extent, in order to achieve a Liberal society, must one transform not only the framework that tolerates illiberality but also the essential nature of the individuals whose social existence the framework is supposed to enhance? If no clear answer emerged from *fin de siècle* Liberal theory, it could at least reasonably claim to have fielded thinkers who seriously faced the question for the first time.

Idealism

Giving individualism a social dimension involved rethinking the elements of individuality. The world had to be changed not so much by inventing ever more sophisticated devices by which the State could impose itself on social frameworks as by reconstructing the idea of what it meant to be an individual and implying thereby a new understanding of state and citizen. Thinkers who turned their mind to this problem sometimes concluded that the individual had no concrete existence at all; 'he is a mere abstraction – a logical ghost, a metaphysical spectre, which haunts the habitations of those who have derided metaphysics. The individual, apart from all relations to a community, is a negation. You can say nothing about him, or rather it, except that it is not any other "individual".'[6] Now the writer was not Comte or Marx but a Liberal Idealist, D. G. Ritchie, whose *Principles of State Intervention* (1891) played a significant part in taking Liberalism further along the road to reconciling liberty with the forces for good believed to inhere in the concept of *communitas*. Ritchie merits a moment's pause, moreover, not only because his ideas have a representative importance within Liberal thought in the 1890s but also because he symbolizes a significant presence in the typology of second-generation Idealist Liberals: the Balliol Scot.

The Snell exhibition tenable at Balliol College, Oxford, helped sustain a vigorous relationship between Scottish universities and Oxford in the last third of the nineteenth century. The story might run as follows. A young man would establish a glowing reputation at Glasgow, Edinburgh or St Andrews; he would proceed, after his first degree, to Oxford (often by way of a German university – perhaps Leipzig,

---

[5] Terence H. Qualter, *Graham Wallas and 'The Great Society'* (1980), 138.
[6] D. G. Ritchie, *Principles of State Interference* (1891), 11.

where the Idealism of Lotze attracted disciples, or Göttingen or Berlin); there he would read for another degree, probably in *literae humaniores*. Thereafter he would move to an Oxford Fellowship for a while. But the generation of Ritchie did not obtain the purchase on Oxford established by that of T. H. Green and R. L. Nettleship; so increasingly its members moved away to the English capital (like Bosanquet) or the provinces (like Muirhead) or, as in the case of Ritchie, they returned to Scotland. He himself spent three years at Balliol during Green's high period (1875–8) and tutored in philosophy there following Green's death in 1882. Yet his main contribution came from the years during which he held the chair of Logic and Metaphysics at St Andrews between 1894 and 1903.

Where Ritchie's thought extended Green's was in the direction of science and especially in the effort to bring inside a common frame the thought of *Hegel and Darwin*, the title of one of his books. In the preface to this study he announces a project which 'expresses my endeavour to reconcile a qualified acceptance of the general principles of that Idealist philosophy which is based on Kantian criticism . . . with a full recognition of the revolutionary change in our intellectual universe which is due to the historical method of studying ideas and institutions, and in particular, to the influence of the biological theory of natural selection.'[7] Idealism and history could be made to work well together, in Ritchie's hands, to undermine the reality of the individual and to boost the status of a Rousseauan general will that characterized the totality of individuals in a way which no single one of them would ever be able to grasp:

> This sovereignty of the people, this general will, is only an idea, it will be said. It is an idea; but not therefore unreal. It is real as the human spirit is real, because it is this very spirit striving for objective manifestation. It lives, and grows, and becomes conscious of itself. It realises itself in different forms, in the family, the clan, the city, the nation, perhaps some day in the federation of the world.[8]

Notice that this last sentence may be read not merely as a list of examples but also as an historical progression of stages in a process of 'becoming': it is not unusual to find Ritchie and his fellow Idealists implying a 'Whig' view of history. A timeless proposition about Ritchie's ideal state will often begin life as a fragile statement about what 'history' shows. 'The history of progress is the record of the gradual diminution of *waste*', he will begin. It is then made to follow that 'An ideal State would be one in which there was no waste at all of the lives, and intellects, and souls of individual men and women.'

The discussion initiated by Darwin and Wallace did not compromise this position, in Ritchie's view, but rather confirmed the importance of thinking historically and treating human affairs as a domain characterized by interdependence. Herbert Spencer had come this far, of course, but Ritchie took him to have gone off the rails in failing to see what a thoroughgoing organicism would imply. Doubtless Spencer's readers would be 'delighted to learn . . . that the Houses of Parliament . . . resemble the cerebral masses in a vertebrate animal', but they formed from such nonsense an erroneous sense of the power conferred on social thought by the analogy. For where Spencer had disappointed the hopes of organicist writers was not in his use of the metaphor but in his timidity in failing to make the resulting 'social' individual

[7] D. G. Ritchie, *Hegel and Darwin* (1893), v–vi.
[8] Ritchie, *State Interference*, 69–70.

organic *enough*. Peopling this mental world with individuals of the kind invented by the utilitarians sapped the strength of the argument at the outset. One must also locate in the individual the stamp of nurture which, no less than his or her genes, will determine the potential of the person to develop into − to become − something different and better. And once placed under this light, the argument swung away from the recommendation that nature should take its course and towards the view that nurture should be given one; it pointed to a communitarian society, holist and caring, accepting responsibility for the well-being of the individuals which it does not merely 'contain' but has, in a very real sense, created. Darwin therefore moves to embrace Hegel in recommending the establishment of a social-democratic state instead of a competitive state of nature, red in tooth and claw. 'The conception of organic growth, if properly grasped, clears away mischievous abstractions in politics and in history; but politics are not thereby turned into branches of imaginative biology.'[9]

If the individual now had a new status − not so much an impermeable brick out of which a 'society' might be built in the manner of a wall as a soluble crystal dependent for its consistency and usefulness on the medium that surrounds it − then certain conclusions followed for the place of compulsion in defining the relationship between state and citizen. Over the next 20 years those conclusions would appear in various forms both in Liberal theory and practice concerning a wide range of policy discussions: the framing of welfare minima, the taking up of more 'forward' positions on the part of the state in assuming responsibility for the old, the sick and the unemployed. More immediately they impinged on education. Ritchie's writing reflected the consolidation of state initiatives in the provision of elementary and secondary education (1870, 1876, 1892). The theories of Mill and Arnold had long since lost their credibility except among the hyper-individualists who shared M. D. O'Brien's hysterical hatred of the 'force-fanatics' (among whom he counted Ritchie) and who deemed it 'better that a continually diminishing number of children should go uneducated, than that the State should usurp the natural and morally-disciplining functions of parents'. 'Ignorance', after all, 'is a trifle by the side of State communism.' This *Natural Right to Freedom*, as O'Brien's book was called, struck Ritchie as a deeply confused benefit which presented a *reductio ad absurdum* of unlimited individualism by representing a national scandal as a form of virtue. 'The freedom of opinion of those who cannot read and write and will not let their children learn,' he wrote, 'does not seem to be a very precious thing.'[10] But philosophical Liberalism soon demonstrated that it could also undermine less flimsy positions behind the receding lines of individualist theory.

The story of this transition belongs to the history of post-Gladstonian Liberal party politics and we shall recognize some of the threads and themes on returning to a consideration of the party's difficult years under Rosebery, Harcourt and Campbell-Bannerman. Yet the 1890s occupy a no less significant place in the development of Liberal theory as it further digested the proposals contained in the writings of numerous authors who contributed to an energetic discussion of central elements in the consciousness of the intelligentsia. That the Boer War of 1899–1902 terminated that phase, in a sense, has helped the nineties retain in retrospect a certain insularity before the remoulding of national psychology by the events in Africa. The events, indeed, themselves helped form a critique of imperialist politics

[9] Ritchie, *State Interference*, 20–2, 31, 49, 100.
[10] O'Brien, *Natural Right to Freedom*, 47, 57; Ritchie, *State Interference*, 117.

that would prove of great importance within Edwardian Liberalism. At a more fundamental level, however, the preoccupations of Ritchie – Idealism and Darwinism – acted as underpinnings for a series of Liberal stances throughout the decade.

Idealist doctrines maintained a secure hold on British speculation for most of the 1890s. By 1892 Green had been dead for a decade; but his disciples lived on to take the message further and deepen its analyses. They also took them, as we have seen, beyond Oxford. Not that the citadel surrendered easily: the arrival from Glasgow of Green's pupil Edward Caird to succeed Benjamin Jowett as Master of Balliol in 1893 promised some continuity as did Francis Herbert Bradley's reclusive tenure of a Merton College Fellowship for fully half a century after 1870. Bernard Bosanquet (1848–1923), described by Green as the most able man of his generation, had resigned his Fellowship at University College in 1881 after coming into family money and moved to London where he spent most of his working life until he succeeded Ritchie at St Andrews in 1903. A near-contemporary of Bosanquet was no less important to Liberal doctrine but emerged from an entirely different background. For Henry Jones (1852–1922) overcame extreme poverty in rural Wales to establish himself, as Caird's pupil, in a distinguished career at Glasgow and St Andrews. J. H. Muirhead (1855–1940) and J. S. Mackenzie (1860–1935), on the other hand, began in Scotland: they both originated in or around Glasgow. The first followed the Oxford route before taking the chair of philosophy at Birmingham. Mackenzie chose Cambridge, unusually, and held a Fellowship at Trinity College from 1890 to 1896. Now the point of offending the eye with this jarring list of names is not to insist on the importance of any one of these observations. Rather, it helps create an impression of an academic dynasty that established a stronghold within the universities. This matters in the history of British thought. It matters even more in a history of Liberal thought because the politics of these people remained for the most part distinctly and self-consciously Liberal.

In encouraging a persistent congruence between Idealism and Liberalism (one hardly to be found in Germany) both biography and philosophy played some part. Sons of the vicarage and the manse appear with sufficient regularity among the leading Idealist figures to suggest the suspicion that they sought some surrogate religion: a faith that turned on no question of ritual or dogma but simply resurrected 'society' and 'state' as creators of 'the good life'. Reaching that destination required something beyond the pursuit of individual ambition under the guidance of an imagined but unseen hand that would direct the sum of each enterprise towards the common good. Instead, the good life depended on the making of good people – moralized individuals who would see both in the state as a whole and in their own immediate communities a portrait of their own better natures – and a conscious concern with the purposes for which societies had come into existence and in which their 'real' nature consisted. Perhaps for this reason, a conception of the family and neighbourhood receive considerable stress in Idealist writing; it also ministered, of course, to an intellectual need to present social reality, as all other forms, as a dialectic between part and whole. Yet it seems hard to resist the impression that this emphasis derived too from a residual imagery taken from the Anglican parish and a collective conscience with which these writers may have invested it. Their depiction of the future shared some of the symbolism of Christian hope. When pressed to define the good life that may become possible for future societies they chose a vocabulary that echoes the Athenasian creed no less than the Hegelian dialectic in the 'losing of a lower self to find a higher one – "a dying to live" ', in a 'larger community [which] is itself the supreme community; the guardian of a whole moral world'.[11] Their moral world reflected the rectory in a pool of opinion about class and poverty. The work of Bernard Bosanquet and the Charity Organization Society best illustrates the ambivalence, taken by its enemies on the Left to comprise slack-minded timidity, of Idealist views about the responsibility of society toward its unfortunates; and even when the distinction drawn between a 'deserving' and 'undeserving' poor disappeared from the Society's *modus operandi*, as Bosanquet claimed it had done by the 1890s, the tone of moral censure called forth by any perceived spinelessness, improvidence or (Caird's frequent flashpoint) flippancy, flourished into the new century with all the timelessness of the cathedral close.

By no means all Idealist Liberals exposed this stratum of their thought: one has to dig for it among the interstices of more formal philosophical remarks.[12] At a more accessible level, the part/whole argument received greater rehearsal and often in a more Hegelian vocabulary. Haldane probably came closest to a full Hegelian position among the British Idealists but it is hard to read McKechnie, for example, and his language of 'lower categories' evolving into higher ones and his sense of the state's comprising 'not only all its citizens (without annihilating or absorbing their individuality), but also the infinite series of relations of every kind that unite them to one another and to the central organization', with no echo of his master's voice.[13] By the 1890s , however, the 'German' generation had passed its peak of influence, despite the appointment of Wilhelm Dilthey, a central figure in the formation of twentieth-century attitudes, to the Berlin chair once occupied by Hegel himself. British political philosophy seems rather to have turned in on itself in these years, content to respond to the mood of aggressive Darwinism that had made 'organism' almost a piece of street language through its many popularizers and to resist the implication that a true social existence could ever develop in an environment dominated by competition and struggle. If Green's distinctions between man and dog had become wearisome, it remained an urgent task to separate the future of mankind from Darwin's prognoses for pigeons and iguanas.

One line of attack had appeared in Ritchie's application of the survival-of-the-fittest ethic to the domain of ideas. Why should one not speak of a competition for survival among competing ideas – one in which only the most powerful would pass muster? Granted that a species survived because it possessed characteristics that bestowed advantages in exploiting the natural resources provided by its environment, might not the philosophy of social interdependence overcome that of fragmentation and war because it better addressed itself to the challenges of modern industrial civilization? This line of argument did not entrench itself within Idealism but it did give rise to a strain of social-democratic criticism such as that voiced by Hobhouse, as we shall see. Within Idealism the battle-lines followed an older pattern through the nineties; they took their shape from the need to show that competition between individuals was not only unwise or anti-social but depended on the incoherent view of individuality that Idealists had been attacking for some years. Quite simply, the objective became one of demonstrating that one individual could not attack another without also attacking himself, just as neither 'society' nor 'the state' could molest their component

[11]W. McKechnie, *The State and the Individual* (1896), 176–7; B. Bosanquet, *The Philosophical Theory of the State* (1899), 302.
[12]See Andrew Vincent and Raymond Plant, *Philosophy, Politics and Citizenship: the life and thought of the British Idealists* (Oxford, 1984), 97.
[13]McKechnie, *State and the Individual*, 3, 20–1, 43.

individuals without damaging their essential – their Ideal – natures. Edward Caird often dwelt on this dialogue between citizen and collectivity, as in a private letter of 1893:

> It is the savage, and selfish man that seems to be merely an *espèce*, one of a lot, that is on the borders of being lost in a genus, and the more he fights for himself, the less there is to fight about. If we are to generalise from this, we should gather that the more life loses itself, in one sense, in the universal, the more it becomes individualised; and progress can never mean the extinction of individual life, but must be the removal of hindrances to it.[14]

Removing 'hindrances' suggests more of a return to Mill than a march into the future but the recurrence remains deceptive. For Caird's individuals had no flesh and bone: each had rather to be identified as a focus of relations and dependencies. Certainly one might observe a crowd of them milling in a busy city street, but the image distorted reality by abstracting the individual from a fuller context. Every man should, to retain perspective, appear with a wife or lover, each child with its parents, each parent with every relation, every relation with every friend – each network of blood and love, sympathy and support, with all those neighbouring networks that supply shape and social location. By himself the individual struck an Idealist as no more 'real' than did a quaver in a symphony. Indeed, Idealists had begun by the 1890s to move towards an explicit denunciation of Mill for his failure to perceive 'the social universal in its differences' and his consequent myopia over the need to allow the state to extend itself on behalf of its members. His 'peculiar prejudice that the criterion of its justifiability lies in the boundary line between self and others, rather than in what coercive authority is and is not able to do towards the promotion of good life' disturbed Bosanquet because of what he saw as a fundamental confusion in the formulation of self-regarding and other-regarding categories.[15] Nor had more recent thinkers overcome the difficulty. They had transcended Mill, admittedly, in their insistence that state action must prefigure genuine social advance, but the individuals whom they wanted to help had no more substance than had Mill's. In his preface to *The Impossibility of Social Democracy*, a work by the German writer Schäffle which appeared in Britain in 1892, Bosanquet 'thoroughly assented to the author's conviction that the basis of Socialism is as yet individualistic, the State being regarded not as a society organic to good life, but as a machine subservient to the individual's needs *qua* individual.' If only the 'State' and the 'individuals' could be represented as classifications along a single continuum, on the other hand, fears that 'the good life' would carry too high a price in the onset of autocracy would soon evaporate.

Because their proposed continuum between society and person came close to the centre of their social thought, Idealists rested their understanding of the state on a philosophical ground of a rather inaccessible kind. Bosanquet reflected on many of its characteristics in his treatment of *The Philosophical Theory of the State* (1899) which attempted to pull many contemporary threads into a single argument. To the modern ear his definition of the state seems convoluted and contrived, but then the very totality of Idealism predicts that partial enquiry will seem unsatisfactory. One could not develop a '*complete* reflective conception' of the subject until one had worked out

---

[14]Caird to Mary Talbot, 2 June 1893, in Sir Henry Jones and J. H. Muirhead, *The Life and Philosophy of Edward Caird* (Glasgow, 1921), 187.
[15]Bosanquet, *Philosophical Theory*, 62, 171.

'a *complete* idea of the realization of all human capacity.' Still, the salient characteristics of this necessary state seemed obvious enough. It

> includes the entire hierarchy of institutions by which life is determined, from the family to the trade, and from the trade to the Church and the University. It includes all of them, not as the mere collection of the growths of the country, but as the structure which gives life and meaning to the political whole. . . . The State, it might be said, is thus conceived as the operative criticism of all institutions – the modification and adjustment by which they are capable of playing a rational part in the object of human will. . . . It follows that the State, in this sense, is, above all things, not a number of persons, but a working conception of life.

What also followed was that social and political institutions, 'made by minds at their best', embodied through the state the will and intellect of the people themselves. When, therefore, the state seemed to employ compulsion in order to secure obedience to its laws, the people in fact obeyed their own directives for those comprised the basis of the state's acts. Green had taught that the state depended not on coercion but on Will. The exercise of that will could not be reduced, then, to a 'question of the "interference of the State with the individual" – an antithesis which is meaningless so far as it implies that society can be interfering with the individual and not interfering with itself; but it is a question of how far and in what way the use of force and the like by the State is . . . a hindrance to the end for which the State, the social power, itself exists.'[16]

So by this point the two meanings of 'idealism' have converged. The State exists not only as a conceptual construction rooted in the mind and will of its citizens, but it also implies a beautiful destiny, remote from the tawdriness of self-interest, corruption and scandal, the balance of power, the arms race, war between state and state. To say no more than this is already to imply a fundamental innocence about Idealist Liberalism which cannot long be avoided in discussion of the politics it produced. It did not lie in isolated moments of naïveté, such as Bosanquet's refusal to believe that the state might 'actually order a theft, murder or the like' – a prospect he thought 'barely conceivable'.[17] After all, at the time when Bosanquet wrote his book, Benito Mussolini's violence did not extend beyond the occasional knifing of a classmate, Adolf Hitler was a 10-year-old boy, the name of Marconi had not acquired the reputation it shortly would win and the Russian pogroms against the Jews had not caught the public mind in Britain so strongly as they would by 1904. It demands too much of Bosanquet's generation to insist that they should have predicted the bestialities of statism in the new century. Less excuse can be found, however, for the Idealists glossing over the evidence, palpable in their evening newspaper, of international jealousy and war. During the writing of *The Philosophical Theory of the State*, Britain and France had come to the verge of war in the Sudan. In the year of its publication the mounting threat of war in South Africa became actual. Yet the Idealists failed to see the potential for harm in uniting state with *Volk*. Enough evidence of aggression and imperialism had emerged by the 1890s greatly to weaken any theory of the state that did not place conflict and the defence of national interests at the centre of its concerns. In that area contemporaries naturally came under the influence of writers who had more to say about competition than harmony

[16]Quotations in this paragraph are taken from Bosanquet, *Philosophical Theory*, 140–1 (emphasis added), 142, 171.
[17]Bosanquet, *Philosophical Theory*, 300 and n.

and who dwelt less on the nature of the good life than on the implications of the struggle for survival.

Science

Since 1859 Liberal theorists had made sporadic efforts at killing Darwinism by kindness. The Church had baptized it through the reception of evolutionary theory into the argument of *Essays and Reviews* (1860) and Charles Gore's edition of *Lux Mundi* (1889).[18] The Idealists, among whom Gore is sometimes counted, had extended competition to new domains in order to reveal a higher struggle for dominance. The vocabulary of 'organism' had revived its currency among Liberals who despised the ethic of the struggle for survival but who hoped that one could speak of the interdependence of individuals without stressing their competitive condition. But in the 1890s this optimism came under challenge from two directions, both of which held lessons for Liberal theorists. A new generation of young intellectuals had, in the first place, spent their formative years in a Darwinist environment and could not remember the harmonious universe that older commentators took to have preceded it; and in their willingness to bring Liberalism closer to the realities of imperialism and class ambition they pointed in new directions. Second, the development of biological theory in the 1890s suggested that Darwinism itself had evolved into a higher stage of development. The transition towards a more austere understanding of the determinants of heredity – the arrival of 'ultra-' or 'hyper-' Darwinism – left Liberals with higher mountains to climb if they hoped to persist with their declared intention of 'improving' society and operating as midwives to 'progress'.

In particular, two Liberals of the decade suggested a good deal cooler frame of mind than the school of Green with its elegiacs and exhortation. Both men – L. T. Hobhouse and J. A. Hobson – owed something to the atmosphere of Idealist Oxford yet neither remained content in it. The concept of society as an organism pervades their work; their writings on the confusions of individualism contain passages that might (and did) draw praise from the Idealists; they shared Oxford's preoccupation with questions of appearance and reality. Rather than merely diagnose social complaints, however, they sought to compose prescriptions. Lamenting the unregeneracy of man seemed insufficient: how to cope with it presented a more pressing problem. At the centre of their analysis they placed a conception of the state of nature which sounded closer to Hobbes than to Mill or Green. Their commitment to *social* action ('social evils require social remedies')[19] followed from a view of what would happen if individuals were given their head in a universe characterized by unequal intelligence, enterprise and muscle and a maldistribution of resources in the world that the individuals hoped to control. Here, as before, the realization of 'the good life' plays a positive role in their political plans; but securing it will demand a radical restructuring of social opportunity and the economic activity of the state. The Idealist R. B. Haldane gladly contributed a preface to Hobhouse's *The Labour Movement* in 1893. But he correctly identified a shift of emphasis in the book's contents; for while the 'real life of the common whole' endured as an objective, he

[18]*Essays and Reviews* (ed. J. Parker, 1860) and Charles Gore (ed.), *Lux Mundi. A series of studies in the religion of the Incarnation* (1889).
[19]Hobson in his *Life of Ruskin*, quoted in Michael Freeden, *The New Liberalism: an ideology of social reform* (Oxford, 1977), 107.

noticed that the author 'belongs to a school which is rapidly growing, a school the leading tenet of which is that the problem of today is *distribution and not production* and that better distribution requires the active intervention of the State at every turn.'[20] He might have added that the very idea of a book devoted to a mere section of the social whole would strike some Balliol minds as counter-thematic.

At Corpus Christi College, Hobhouse had come in contact with the eccentric College President, Thomas Case, whose irrascible campaigning for science as the saviour of the world from metaphysics and superstition came close to rivalling among his priorities the promotion of Conservative politics and the resistance to women in the university. If Hobhouse took from Case nothing but a respect for scientific enquiry, the nineties (a decade that left many observers with an obsession for dissecting social processes) pulled Hobhouse away from harmony and towards – his own word – friction. 'There is no greater mistake,' he wrote in 1896, 'than to suppose human society to be at any time a perfect organism. So long as the primary object of each man is his own good, conduct, though doubtless kept within limits by the power and requirements of the social system, will never spontaneously and perfectly adjust itself to the needs of the whole, and so far there will always be friction.'[21] Locating and lubricating the friction became for him the subject of scientific study, albeit within the constraints of a Liberal outlook that accepted most of the propositions accepted by Mill but also emphasized as its guiding principle that 'intelligent organization' must eventually prove preferable to a 'haphazard interaction of unintelligent forces' in bringing about the desired ends. Once grant that 'the withdrawal of collective control leaves industry to the interaction of blind forces producing mixed good and evil, with no necessary tendency to progress, no pre-established "economic harmony" between self-interest and the common weal' and the way will be open (say) to recommending a minimum wage for workers to be enforced by the State.[22] Hobhouse did not take his thinking very far in the 1890s: his more important statements matured in the following decade. He had nevertheless begun a journey towards the Webbs, in whose London School of Economics he became the first Professor of Sociology. Residual Idealism certainly played some part in his thinking in the years before the Boer War, but Beatrice Webb's insistence that '*we must apply the scientific method to social questions*'[23] had already found an echo.

It evoked a similar sympathy, perhaps a stronger one, in the mind of John Hobson. As an economist concerned with a field of study which had, in the hands of Stanley Jevons, seemingly turned into a variant of applied mathematics, he had a disposition to think heretically. Certainly he took seriously the notion of an organic state. He used it, however, less to reassure Liberals that the sky would not fall down if their government took a collectivist view of its objectives than to legitimize the political measures that a capitalist economic system implied if it were to be adequately controlled. These measures bared two sets of teeth. One of them threatened a major redistribution of wealth in order to correct a non-alignment in the relationship between saving and spending – one that made effective consumption impossible until more wealth could go into the pockets of the broad mass of people who produced it. Because wealth lacked this wide distribution in Britain, saving outstripped

[20]See L. T. Hobhouse, *The Labour Movement* (1893), xi (emphasis added).
[21]L. T. Hobhouse, *The Theory of Knowledge: a contribution to some problems of logic and metaphysics* (1896), 588.
[22]Hobhouse, *Labour Movement*, 53–4. For the minimum wage, see *ibid.*, 12.
[23]Beatrice Webb to Charlotte Payne-Townshend, 28 June 1896, in Norman Mackenzie (ed.), *The Letters of Sidney and Beatrice Webb* (3 vols., Cambridge, 1978), II, 47.

spending and expressed itself in investment that often, in Hobson's judgement, went overseas in search of higher returns in colonial ventures. He therefore identified a link between an imbalanced domestic economy and political annexation abroad: a relationship which greatly impressed Lenin 15 years later though he naturally found Hobson's analysis naïve in holding out the hope of anything better from capitalism. The scramble for colonies that so disgusted some *fin-de-siècle* Liberals acquired in Hobson's argument an observable 'economic taproot'[24] which Liberals would surely need to cut out. And the only instrument powerful enough to accomplish that task would presumably be the state which could, through an appropriate programme of taxation, redistribute wealth in order to liberate the spending power that an undirected economy had allowed to atrophy.

Hobson aimed a second threat at current conceptions of representative democracy. It seemed to him disingenuous to adopt an organic view of the state while privately wishing that the implications would remain theoretical. 'The question is one of supreme practical importance,' he argued in 1902, one 'involving, among persons capable of rational politics, the complete re-adjustment of their conception of Democracy and of the means of attaining it.' Nor was the restriction placed on persons incapable of rational politics lightly meant. Following a section about physical organisms, redolent of Spencer at his crudest, Hobson moves towards a description of the élite who will act as the cerebral forces of the new body politic:

A developed organic Democracy will have evolved a specialized 'head', an expert official class, which shall draft laws upon information that comes to them from innumerable sources through class and local representatives, and shall administer the government subject to protests similarly conveyed. . . . On the other hand, we should have the knowledge and desires, the will of the people, transmitted either directly and informally by public meetings, and other methods, or formally through elected representatives who would confine themselves to the work of representing, for which they were chosen and were competent, and not to the work of making laws, for which they are utterly incompetent. It is plain that when a rational Democracy is formed, laws, like hats, will be made by persons specially trained to make them.[25]

Through his cult of the expert Hobson took longer strides than Hobhouse towards the Fabian ideal: his writing throws back more than an echo of H. G. Wells. His joining the Labour party after the First World War seems to that extent a consummation of earlier thinking, notwithstanding his unhappiness about the sectionalism of Labour's ideals. *Per contra*, Hobhouse never let his early interest in the Labour idea slide that far; he continued a party Liberal.

Both men usually stood back from the worst excesses of biological analogy that threatened to turn what Hobson called a 'convenience in language' into grounds for a belief in social degeneracy or racial destiny. The mood that sanctioned this shift of emphasis emerged suddenly: we can date it fairly precisely to the first half of the 1890s. Two men contributed to it with noticeable effect – a German biologist, August Weismann, and a British popularizer of evolutionary theory, Benjamin Kidd, whose *Social Evolution* (1894) gained a wide readership and became a considerable

[24] J. A. Hobson, *Imperialism: a study* (1902). Cf. V. I. Lenin, *Imperialism: the highest stage of capitalism* (1916) and, for a modern discussion, D. K. Fieldhouse, *Economics and Empire 1830–1914* (1973, 1984), 1–103, 459–77.

[25] J. A. Hobson, 'The Re-statement of Democracy', *Contemporary Review*, LXXXVI (February 1902), 262, . 271.

succès d'estime outside the ranks of the intelligentsia. But in order to understand the significance of the argument one needs to go back, not only to Darwin himself and Alfred Russel Wallace, but to the conventional wisdom current among biological thinkers before the breakthrough of the mid nineteenth century. In particular we need to consider the idea of heredity and its relationship to political theory: a theme of massive importance after 1850. And because that relationship may strike some readers as a little arcane, the next paragraph will require patience.

Consider – as did so many nineteenth-century social theorists – the giraffe. For biologists the length of its neck posed a glaring problem. Everyone could see the 'purpose' of it: to allow easy access to the giraffe's staple food, acacia leaves. But how did the animal *acquire* the neck in the first place? Three answers became available during the course of the nineteenth century. God, the first and earliest answer, simply made it that way: end of problem. A second and secular answer gained currency during the first half of the century, not least through the writings of Lamarck (1744–1829). Here the argument assumed that the giraffe had *grown* its neck over countless generations through a reflex action stimulated by hunger: repeated straining and stretching by parents bringing about the generation of new tissue in their progeny. This mechanism for passing to the young an aspect of parents' life experience came to be called 'use-inheritance' or 'the transmission of acquired characteristics'.[26]. Through it, the babies of a species can begin their existence with advantages somehow grafted onto them by their parents; and they, in their turn, will, quite literally, pass on the benefit of their experience to their own offspring. Now for the giraffe substitute a human being; for the neck substitute the attainments of a particular individual in education or morals or physical strength or cultural development. Does such a person have the capacity to encode that prowess in the starter-pack of his or her children? For prowess substitute catastrophe: lunacy, deformity, criminality. Will *those* characteristics inhere in the next generation? It perhaps begins to appear that this discussion of giraffes, far from rehearsing a trivial controversy as far removed from politics as alchemy or phlogiston, raised fundamental questions about the ability of human society to progress by passing on to future generations the fruits of its work and genius.

After 1859 the reaction of Darwinist theorists to this line of thought proved ambivalent. 'Natural selection' obviously provided for a third answer to the giraffe problem by providing a comprehensive account of heredity within which the problem might be subsumed. It offered the theoretical possibility of rejecting 'use-inheritance' because the operation of the doctrine about the survival of species most fitted to their environment would, over the immense time-scales assumed in the model, account for the 'evolution' of organs required for success in the competition for feeding and mating. Long-necked giraffes would secure food more consistently than short-necked ones: they would therefore survive and mate. In the next generation the same process would occur. Darwin himself did not throw over use-inheritance quite so readily; he continued to believe *both* in the operation of natural selection and in the validity of some form of transmission of acquired characteristics. Darwin's rival, Wallace, took a more austere view and saw the struggle for survival as the sole determinant of heredity. What is of great importance for an understanding of the input of 'science' into political theory in the 1890s is a shift from the Lamarckian view of the central issues to those held by Wallace and Weismann.

---

[26]For a helpful discussion of these ideas, see D. R. Oldfield, *Darwinian Impacts: an introduction to the Darwinian revolution* (Milton Keynes, 1980).

August Weismann (1834–1914) had taught comparative anatomy and zoology at the University of Freiburg since 1863. From a study of hydrozoa in the early 1880s he had concluded that no means existed whereby what he called 'germ plasm', which he took to carry imprints from parents, could be modified by an individual's life experience. He later qualified that view but by then his reputation had run before him and made him into an academic celebrity widely believed to have made a major modification of Darwin's theory. Relations between the two men certainly went downhill in the nineties because of the dispute over acquired characteristics. Weismann's Romanes Lecture of 1894 on 'The Effect of External Influences on Development', his controversy with Spencer (who defended the Lamarckian viewpoint) in the *Contemporary Review* during the same year and the publication of Kidd's polemical work on social evolution, which referred to Weismann's work, spread these views far beyond the laboratory or university seminar. Political writing in Britain became saturated with biological metaphor and reasoning based on the new doctrines about heredity. Mendel's research on mutation and the appearance of a school of 'eugenicists' under the leadership of Karl Pearson and Francis Galton deepened the mood in the first decade of the new century.

Exploring their arguments and disputations would take us too far from Liberal theory to grant it space here, beyond emphasizing two points. The first stresses the sheer necessity of reacting to these biological assumptions on the part of all serious or systematic political thinkers after 1890. Witness the name that invades a peculiarly appalling verse by Rupert Brooke in 1909:

Prof. Weissmann [sic]
Can *hardly* be a nice man,
If he thinks that to be a Blakian mystic
Is merely a recessive Mendelian characteristic.[27]

This doggerel also illustrates the second item wanting stress: the repugnance in which Liberals tended to hold the new Darwinism. The comfortable idea that Darwin's ideas would encourage Liberal opinions rather than impede them had lost most of its comfort by 1895. 'Social organisms' could still be talked about, needless to say; they continued to offer a base from which to construct a theory of mutual care and support as well as to suggest a model of ruthless competition. As late as 1897, indeed, the historian Holland Rose persisted in his belief that Darwinism had, through its insistence on orderly development, undermined the claims of both 'the Toryism of pre-reform days' and 'the abolitionist mania of the succeeding generation'; it had demonstrated 'the folly both of immobility and of sudden and reckless change in the political world.'[28] But for many Liberal thinkers the dangers of biological thought had long since come to outweigh its attractions. Kidd's amateur speculations had amounted to little more than an appeal to revive religion, but other writers had recommended the taking of steps by the state to ensure that the purity of the species be not defiled or a drift towards national sterility countenanced. That argument pointed in a direction that few Liberals would want to face – a direction that one might plausibly term national socialism. It implied a doctrine that would urge an expansion of the functions of the state for social purposes but then (a parting of the

[27]Brooke to Geoffrey Keynes, January 1909, in Sir Geoffrey Keynes (ed.), *The Letters of Rupert Brooke* (1968), 155.
[28]J. Holland Rose, *The Rise of Democracy* (1897), 166–7.

ways for Liberals) establish the validity of those purposes by the degree to which they furthered the vigour of the Teutonic race and the setting of wider still and wider bounds to the British empire. This new shape in scientific discussion thus provided a cutting edge to the debate about the value of imperialism that had divided and disturbed Liberals since the Irish crisis of 1886.

Imperialism

Contemporaries strongly sensed the newness of their country's imperialism and argued about it in the vocabulary which Idealism and Darwinism had helped make current. The most shrill statements appealed to racial destiny and the need to save inferior races from the consequences of their own barbarity; they contained a conception of British (or Western) history as a source for demonstrating the cleverness, energy and enterprise of Aryan man; and they urged the place of empire in the nature of things – something impossible for a great power to avoid. Liberals did not bulk large among the more extreme apologists of empire although, as the Liberal MP Sir J. L. Walton showed in 1899, they certainly had their moments:

> Why are we Imperialists? As well ask the owner of an estate why he is a landlord. . . . We are, and shall be Imperialists because we cannot help it. . . . The argument may be digested thus. The energy of our race gave us empire. Nature has supplemented the bequest by the qualities which distinguished our ancestry. Government is the organ which expresses the faculties and tendencies of an Imperial people. Its policy is the line of action which their wishes and opinions dictate. If this political line is in harmony with the genius of the race it will be Imperialist. If it ceases to be Imperialist then either the harmony is destroyed, or the character of the race has suffered change.

'The basis of Imperialism,' that is to say, 'is race'. Lawson's exposition, almost every sentence of which says something interesting about a Liberal imperialist mentality, drew an immediate rebuff from the radical Liberal scientist Russel Wallace who reminded Lawson that imperialism had its 'seamy side' and that 'in these days every triumph of expansionism is a rebuff to Democratic Liberalism. Expansionist Imperialism means more Despotism abroad and more Aristocratic recrudescence at home.'[29] Much of the dead John Bright lives on in this complaint with its memory of Bright's castigation of great-power politics as a system of outdoor relief for the upper classes.

That passion flooded discussions of imperialism in 1899 will surprise no one familiar with the chain of events that brought Britain and the Boers of South Africa to the point of war later that year. Other developments also played some role, of course: the controversy among Liberal parliamentarians surrounding Gladstone's obsession with Home Rule for Ireland after 1885, the race for influence in east Africa culminating in Rosebery's annexation of Uganda in 1894, the threats of incursions by other powers into states where Britain had interests. But South Africa came at a critical moment: it served not only to crystallize attitudes but also to change them. Before 1895 Liberals could rub along with imperial politics, except at moments of crisis such as the bombardment of Alexandria in 1882. With the Jameson raid of 1895, however, and the heightened effect of Chamberlain's alleged involvement, doubts developed

[29]J. L. Walton, 'The New Imperialism', *Contemporary Review*, LXXV (March 1899), 306–7; Wallace, 'The Seamy Side of Imperialism', *ibid*. (June 1899), 799.

about African policy – the more so after 1898 following the accession to the Liberal party leadership of a man who would later warn that he was imperialist enough only for any decent man. Salisbury's view that democracy was no way to run an empire collided with the radical allegation that empire was no priority for a democracy. Indeed the Hobsonian plaint would be that empire had only emerged in the first place because British democracy had been distorted and misused. In this section of its pre-occupations, the Liberal party and its supporters underwent significant change between the electoral disaster of 1895 and the golden moment of 1906.

Where and when Liberal sympathy for empire originated seems hard to identify with precision but the sentiment certainly predates the *éclat* of Gladstone's conversion to Home Rule and probably emerged from responses not so much to the Irish problem as the Egyptian. Even Gladstone's government, for all the indictment of imperialism in the Premier's recent Midlothian speeches, found itself drawn into the vacuum created by French inactivity and the internal volatility of Egypt's relationship with the Sudan. Its most distinguished consul-general, Lord Cromer, and its historian, Alfred (later Lord) Milner, belonged to the Conservative side of politics. But it is noticeable as late as 1900 that the Liberal Idealist Muirhead took Milner's *England in Egypt* as a model description of great imperialism, illustrating 'from every department of administration what Imperialism can be at its best, and what it must be if it would be anything at all.'[30] But of course Gladstone had apparently brought all to nought by his failure to rescue General Gordon from the murderous Mahdi at the end of 1884; and the intellectuals added their voice to the popular cry for atonement. Coventry Patmore interrupted the flow of his verse to lecture the prime minister on his sins of omission. For 'it is to a Gordon, with inimitable courage and honour, . . . that [the people] will look with abiding reverence, and an elevating instinct that such men habitually move about in worlds by them unrealised.'[31] This mood helped the intelligentsia stand firm behind the Union with Ireland in 1886 and encouraged many of them to switch their electoral support from the Gladstonian Liberal party to the new Liberal Unionist party of Lord Hartington and Joseph Chamberlain.

Yet often that defence of the Union floated free from any general theory of imperialism. It reacted to a specific sympathy for Anglo-Irish property, a sense of the deep historicity of British relations with Ireland, and perhaps also to the general willingness to entertain assumptions about the inferiority of the Celt that found a larger exposition and audience after 1870. Indeed the more global defences of imperialism frequently betray a similar cast of mind, suggesting a position rooted less in a deductive logic of economic advantage and exploitation than in a loosely-conceived collection of values reflected in the patriotic literature of the day and the ritualized celebration of social unity in the Golden and Diamond Jubilees of Queen Victoria's reign in 1887 and 1897. One of the more active Liberal thinkers in the Unionist ranks, Albert Venn Dicey, went little further than this in accounting for new currents of opinion. 'The yearly crowning of Nelson's column,' he wrote in the centenary year of the Battle of Trafalgar, 'the influence exerted by the writings of Froude, of Seeley, and above all of [Admiral Alfred] Mahan, the tales and the verses of Rudyard Kipling, with their glorification of British imperial sway, and the echo which the teaching of all these writers finds in the hearts of the English people throughout the United Kingdom and our self-governing colonies, all tell their own

[30]J. H. Muirhead, 'What Imperialism Means', *Fortnightly Review*, 168 (August 1900), 187.
[31]Coventry Patmore, 'Thoughts on Knowledge, Opinion and Inequality', *Fortnightly Review*, 48/42 (August 1887), 264.

tale.'[32] Within mainstream Liberalism the tone rarely reached even this range of colour. The parliamentary group which after 1886 became known as the 'Liberal Imperialists' (or 'Limps') held views about the Empire but concentrated on domestic issues in the early years of their association, while they had no one, except possibly Haldane, who qualified as a major intellectual force on behalf of the imperialist cause. To the extent that they espoused imperialism at all, such Liberals tended to do so in an absence of mind: imperialism found favour so long as it felt comfortable alongside better-established and more habitual modes of thought.

We have seen that two such modes dominated Liberal theory in the 1890s. Idealism, the first of them, tugged against the pull of imperialism at least in the sense that it rejected as offensive to self-realization the subjection of one man's will to another's. But so long as imperialists could claim that they acted on behalf of annexation precisely in order to further the self-development of 'primitive' areas, then Idealists could only applaud. The British colonial power had tried, according to Caird, 'to make our government tend to the good of the governed' and had resisted the temptation to turn its colonies into thinly-disguised fronts for the extraction of mineral resources or the use of cheap labour. 'In this way commerce with us has generally gone hand in hand with civilisation.' Muirhead likewise offered qualified support to imperialists, providing that they stressed the 'organic' connexions between one country and another and guarded against turning the Empire into a collection of unrelated fragments.[33] Neither self-realization nor organicism seemed, however, the point of the foreign policy which culminated in the Boer War of 1899; and those events helped propel the Idealists, like so many other Liberals, away from their benedictions of imperialism and towards the adoption of a moralized democracy for all states as their ideal. This change of ground had an intriguing relationship with the second element in Liberal thought that requires comment – the new mood of Darwinism.

Competitive struggle supplied an obvious rationale for expansion, after all. Kidd may have doubted the appropriateness of imperial annexations in the 1890s, but many others who felt themselves sensitive to the racial implications of natural selection found no difficulty in evolving from it a language of destiny for the Western Aryan. Over the centuries the Teuton had supposedly evolved characteristics – energy, initiative, independence, imagination, creativity – that marked him off from the Celt (unstable, unreliable, unresourceful and Catholic) and the Negro (ignorant, infantile, deceitful and pagan). These distinctions were built into the heart of things as 'facts' and they were held to support a certain rough justice. One could lament the superiority of the Teuton: many good Liberals did. But doing so would not halt the inevitable consequences of that superiority any more than one could persuade the tide to stop rising. So for a Darwinist theorist such as Karl Pearson, the very definition of a modern nation referred to 'an organized whole' which was 'kept up to a pitch of external efficiency by contest, chiefly by way of war with inferior races, by the struggle for trade routes and for the sources of raw materials and of food supply.' Principles and moralities must serve rather than govern this process. 'What are all our ideals but hints which Nature gives us of the great purpose she is achieving in her own great way? . . . [The] necessary work of the

[32]Alfred Dicey, *Lectures on the Relation between Law and Public Opinion in England during the Nineteenth Century* (1905), 456–7.
[33]Edward Caird, 'Notes on an Ethical Ideal', in *Lay Sermons and Addresses delivered in the Hall of Balliol College, Oxford* (Glasgow, 1907), 114; Muirhead, 'What Imperialism Means', 183.

world [could not] be arrested. When war has done its rough, stimulating, disciplinary work it will cease, but not before.'[34] The most imperial of liberals tended, naturally, to shy away from language of that kind; and the liberal refusal to follow 'biological' thought along the road it had made for itself by the late nineties offers one insight into the diminution of imperial sentiment among the liberal intelligentsia. Conscience-ridden observers, for whom 'Empire' still embodied a variety of missions, philosophies and hopes felt uncomfortable in the company of men and women obsessed by the virtue of blood sacrifice and racial purity. From the turn of the century this style of imperialism struck deeper root among what historians have come misleadingly to call the 'Radical Right' and reached its high point of vigour during the First World War.

Various forms of radiation from the scientific community undoubtedly affected the liberal understanding of objectives and dangers. But they did not operate in isolation from other intellectual tendencies which also highlighted the unacceptable face of imperialism; and among these perhaps two played a specially significant role in conditioning liberal attitudes. The first derived from a conception of economic truth which, for all the developments in economic theory that had taken place since the death of mill, continued to find favour among Radicals until well into the twentieth century. Its key assumption suggested the importance of basing all intercourse between nations on the doctrine of free trade and avoiding the temptation – all too clear since the Bismarckian use of the *Zollverein* – to justify tariff systems on imperial grounds: a position that would throw almost all liberal thinkers into opposition against Joseph Chamberlain's campaign for imperial preference between 1903 and 1906. A second strand of criticism originated in the drive towards political democracy through the Reform Acts of 1867 and 1884. In this area of discussion a feeling mounted that imperial sympathy ran counter to ambitions for a democratic Liberalism that sought to liberate subject peoples, both domestic and foreign, from political impotence and reconstruct the political framework that through the nineteenth century had failed to divest Britain of its class system and the privileges that still attached themselves to birth, wealth and connexion. To holders of such ambitions the preoccupations of imperialists seemed at best a diversion and at worst another instrument by which an élite would consolidate its power. In the years of the Boer War, moreover, these two strands intertwined in a way that turned liberal imperialism within the intelligentsia into a minority enthusiasm.

Among the more ardent imperialists, regardless of party, signs already existed by 1900 that the rigid Cobdenism of the past would fade before the requirements of imperial success. John Neville Keynes (father of the theorist who would later transform economic thinking in Britain) had argued a decade earlier that the distinction drawn by German economists between political economy, which inquired into principles of wealth formation and distribution within a single state, and 'cosmopolitical' economy, which concerned itself with economic relations between states, implied that the advantages of free trade might vary with the type of state scrutinized and the sorts of questions asked about it. Little more than this was needed for the more critical liberals to announce the death of Manchesterism and the need for a new view of the links between economic structure and political action. 'Manchester . . . was all for peace', one might argue, 'because industrial peace meant undisturbed

[34]E. Wake Cook, 'The Organization of Mankind', *Contemporary Review*, LXXX (September 1901), 398. For Pearson, see Stephan Collini, *Liberalism and Sociology: political argument in England 1880–1914* (Cambridge, 1979), 177.

markets for the sale of its goods. Now that those markets are in danger of closing, the Industrial Spirit is Imperialist and even warlike, and demands that they be kept open. Even the Cobden Club is swinging round.' Once so far, the answer seems but a step away:

> A glance ahead will show that Western nations, in forcing their trade on yellow and black races, are educating the latter into formidable competitors. Like the Japs they will better their instructors, and, with their more favourable economic conditions, will flood the Western world with commodities at prices it cannot compete with. To avoid being dragged down to their own level of subsistence, the great world powers will be compelled to draw a ring fence of tariffs round their possessions. In our own case the British Empire contains nearly all climates and resources that will enable it to be entirely self-contained and self-supporting. The comparative free trade inside the fence will starve isolated countries to come in.[35]

The step nevertheless struck most Liberals as a step too far. The Cobden Club had not in fact come round. Both at the level of abstract argument and in its political application in Chamberlain's attempt to construct an alternative economics that might supplant an ever-rising scale of direct taxation to fund collectivist social policies and robust defence policies, the strengthening bond between imperialism and tariffs gave rise to suspicion rather than inspiration. For a Liberal Unionist like Dicey, irrevocably committed to the ideals of Empire, the tariff connexion disturbed his equanimity without making him change his mind. Quite simply, 'the maintenance of the Union seem[ed] a matter of more importance than even strict adherence to the doctrine of Free Trade.' But Dicey knew well enough that other 'imperial' minds took the opposing point of view; and the hoped-for drift towards protectionist economics among the liberal intellectuals never took place. Many years later, indeed, in the mind of Keynes *fils*, the centrality of free trade as a political axiom strengthened rather than diminished as the British economy drifted further into the shallows over the next half century.[36]

Democratic theory presented fewer certainties than free trade to those seeking to oppose the drift towards imperialist sentiment, but its importance developed in the period after the Boer War as an element in the Liberal critique of Conservative and Unionist politics. That some relationship subsisted between the internal political structure of a state and its potential for external aggrandizement had seemed plausible because the rise of imperialism and the advance of 'democracy' had run hand in hand. The association was an odd one. Logic suggested that the rise of democracy ought to mean the withering away of exploitation; and certainly a strand of liberal opinion tried hard to demonstrate that process as the lust for Empire grew more powerful. The former Liberal 'light' Goldwin Smith admired empire no less than democracy, but he came to believe that one would fall victim to the other. His experience of Canada and the United States gave him a vantage point very different from the British. 'To proclaim Democracy', he wrote in 1894, 'is to renounce Empire. This will before very long appear. America has no empire and the democracy

[35]Cooke, 'Organization', 402. Cf. J. N. Keynes, *The Scope and Method of Political Economy* (1891), 76n, and Walton, 'New Imperialism', 310.
[36]A. V. Dicey, 'To Unionists and Imperialists', *Contemporary Review*, LXXXIV (September 1903), 307. The dogged commitment of John Maynard Keynes to free trade as a party doctrine is skilfully explored in Peter Clarke, 'The Politics of Keynesian Economics, 1924–31', in Michael Bentley and John Stevenson (eds.), *High and Low Politics in Modern Britain: ten studies* (Oxford, 1983), 154–81.

knows its unfitness for Imperial sway. . . Great Britain has an immense empire . . . which is now given into the hands of electors who could hardly point out India on the map.'[37] The assertion – it hardly amounted to an argument – invited challenge on a number of grounds. The electors, in the first place, had not been given Britain in the 1890s (or since, for that matter). Their ignorance about the location of India proved no more damaging to 'Imperial sway' than Rosebery's trying to sail the fleet up mount Ararat through a geographical oversight. The 'fitness' of the democracy for empire was improving – to some extent through the education reforms of 1870 and beyond, but also by close contact: many electors would shortly know more than Goldwin Smith about the Sudan and the Transvaal because they tramped all over them under a rifle and pack. If the working classes had not been to Constantinople, their music-hall songs were no less confident that the Russians would not have it. The presupposition, in other words, that imperialism would atrophy with the burgeoning of democracy had no convincing foundation in experience; indeed Chamberlain hoped to make the Empire into a form of *Volk*-idiom so that further extensions of democracy would amplify the sense of imperial cohesion rather than undermine it. But liberal faith in democracy as an antidote to imperialism remained unshakeable. It provided an interesting wing of Liberal argument between the Boer War and the First World War. It virtually predicted that a figure like E. D. Morel would emerge from somewhere on the Liberal Left to challenge the morality of Empire. It implied the coming of a Norman Angell to press the ideals of rational internationalism. In the shorter term it took its force, however, from the writing of two liberals we have already encountered – John Hobson and L. T. Hobhouse – whose stringencies encouraged the economic and democratic critiques of imperialism to fuse into a single challenge.

Hobson's came first. For some years he had brooded, as a *soi-disant* renegade economist, over the perils of industrialism in a non-democratic state. Imperialism he took to figure among those dangers and, certainly by the time of the Boer War, he counted revolt, envy and stagnation among its blessings.[38] But the most coherent exposition of his views appeared at the end of the Boer War in *Imperialism: a study* (1902), a book to which Lenin would later add notoriety when he identified it as one of his more helpful sources when preparing his own critique of imperialism on the eve of the Russian Revolution. Ostensibly the book has an economic thrust: indeed the origins of imperialism are traced back, as we have seen, to an 'economic taproot' whose significance receives considerable stress. Yet the taproot makes more sense when seen as subordinate to a political understanding of what British society ought to be like. Together with all liberals of all kinds at all times, Hobson saw nothing wrong *in principle* with the capitalist mode of economic organization. He believed simply that the purpose of government in the economic sphere lay in making capitalism work in a wholesome way; and what emerges from *Imperialism* most directly is a view less of Hobson's conception of capitalism than his conception of wholesomeness.

The agenda seems fairly plain. He wanted a society characterized by a drastically reduced inequality of wealth and a weakening of class barriers; and he wanted, at this stage of his thinking, enhanced democratic control of government and of the nation's economic resources. These instincts penetrated Hobson's economic thought at a number of points and underlay his doctrine of underconsumption which ran broadly

[37]Goldwin Smith, 'The Impending Revolution', *Nineteenth Century*, XXXV (March, 1894), 360.
[38]See Clarke, *Liberals and Social Democrats*, esp., 90–9. Dr Clarke's examination of Hobson's understanding of imperialism is particularly lucid and the present writer is much indebted to it.

as follows. The Victorian ethic of thrift had not reinforced the nineteenth-century economy, as commonly supposed, but had instead sabotaged it. Britain's social structure predicted that saving would prove possible only for a tiny economic élite; and that élite naturally sought the most remunerative return on its savings by investing them rather than dispersing their wealth among others by buying commodities in the domestic market and thus helping to support British workers. Rather than consume what it produced, the industrial economy had developed a strangulated hernia at the point at which profits should have been flowing back into wage-packets, prompting more consumption and therefore more production and still higher wages. Rather than encourage industry, thrift had turned into its enemy: siphoning off resources into channels that could benefit only a small group of people – the savers – instead of returning money to the area in which its fertilizing powers might encourage the wealth of everyone to grow. Rather than remain in Britain, that money had gone abroad in a fever of overseas investment out of the mistaken belief that the result would be 'good business'. What it had in fact produced was a country starved of capital in the economic field and, in the political one, a series of dubious annexations and rivalries that held more promise of war than profit. It followed that in order to reverse the process one needed not so much an economic theory as a political strategy aimed at altering the structure that encouraged these damaging practices. A government equipped to act in the name of the people could enact programmes of taxation which would re-direct wasted savings from the vaults of the bourgeoisie and the rentier class and direct them into the pockets of the men and women who created the country's wealth but who currently lacked the spending power to lubricate the machine of production and consumption.

Hobhouse learned a good deal from this analysis and the journalism in which it had been couched before and during the South African war. But his rejection of imperialism in *Democracy and Reaction* (1904) rested on an ethical critique as much as an economic one and touched a nerve of sentiment running back to Sidgwick. He framed imperialism within a spacious distaste for reactionary thinking in all its manifestations. Certainly the familiar invigilation of 'new' imperialists with their 'operative principle' of supporting 'the forcible establishment and maintenance of racial ascendency' makes an early appearance in the book; and his evocation of their achievements does not lack warmth:

> Under the reign of Imperialism the temple of Janus is never closed. Blood never ceases to run. The voice of the mourner is never hushed. . . . The naked fact is that we are maintaining a distinct policy of aggressive warfare on a large scale and with great persistence, and the only result of attempting to blink the fact is to have introduced an atmosphere of self-sophistication, or in one syllable, of cant into our politics which is perhaps more corrupting than the unblushing denial of right.[39]

But imperialism served as a sub-theme in his mission for affirming 'right'. The tone, moreover, had changed. Idealism had never been a compulsive strain in Hobhouse but such dalliance as he had had with it had lapsed by 1904. His cheerfulness about the potential for good of the Labour movement had become much more guarded. The singular truth of the day – that this was a bad time in which to be a Liberal – did not escape him. So far, indeed, the thinking of Hobhouse would not have caused pain to Gladstone had he still been alive. The cutting edge came rather in the recommenda-

[39]L. T. Hobhouse, *Democracy and Reaction* (1904), 29, 49.

tions for the future. The collectivist tendencies of the 'new Liberalism' received a significant boost from Hobhouse and half-implied the need for a proto-socialist party that would pull the country's attention away from the sordid sparkle of annexations and tub-thumping and refocus it on a programme of statist social reform.

Both Hobson and Hobhouse had developed their views piecemeal in the higher journalism that offered an easy outlet for liberal thinkers – periodicals such as *The Speaker* and *The Nation*. Their writing took its form in a current of social-democratic reflection which they exemplified but by no means exhausted. Indeed what remains striking about these years is the sheer volume of political writing on the part of Liberals who bore some mark of post-Gladstonian opinion – Radicals, often, who wanted to see the Liberal party assume a different stance, transcend its long-standing intra-party feuds and prove its worth as a governing force as they believed the Gladstonians had done in the 1860s and 1880s. On the other hand, the years of opposition had given theorists, no less than cabinet ministers, an opportunity to display tantrums and design table-top models for the new society. As Balfour's Conservative government slid hopelessly towards its end in 1904 and 1905, it remained unclear whether the next Liberal government would find the time and energy to listen to its theorists or whether it would proceed like its predecessors in identifying problems only when it could not avoid doing so and facing them on its feet rather than with an archive of prepared briefs. Enough had appeared in print and from the platform, meanwhile, to validate at least one claim. If the Liberals won the next election they would resume control of government in a climate more pervasively charged with the exposition and criticism of political principles than any government had known since Earl Grey called his Whigs from the wilderness in 1830.

6

In The Trough: Party Moods 1886–1905

The resilience of doctrine

Individual members of the Liberal party knew something of the tidal movement in speculation familiar to a Green or a Hobhouse. Many politicians had received a university education and had usually concentrated on subjects in the humanities. MPs read periodicals; on occasion they wrote for them. Individual members of the intelligentsia sometimes became politicians for a while – James Bryce, for example, or an enduring editor of the *Manchester Guardian*, C. P. Scott. Some tried, none harder than Richard Burdon Haldane, to make a political career out of their association with the thinking classes. Yet the importance of these bridging points between the politicians and intelligentsia may blind us to a no less significant asymmetry in the relationship. This is, quite simply, that politicians became successful intellectuals far more readily than intellectuals became successful politicians. The reason for that asymmetry bears heavily on the argument here because historians often assume in their discussions of ideas and politics that they are considering a single continuum rather than divergent areas of practice, each with its own sub-language and defence mechanisms. In the case of Liberalism during these difficult years following the schism of 1886, the natural assumption is that ideas generated a new form of Liberal politics that succeeded brilliantly at the polls in 1906 and inaugurated new departures in party practice. The argument here will run in a different direction. It will suggest that the shifts of emphasis evident after 1886 in political rhetoric indicate a crisis not in political theory but in party doctrine; and that the need to rediscover doctrine followed from the collapse of a Gladstonian style of Liberal behaviour rather than preceded it. Doctrine resembled the cart more closely than the horse.

Party doctrines are understood here to mean an often-unspoken network of assumptions and associations that give political parties a sense of themselves as distinct identities.[1] They are what is left of 'ideas' and 'theories' when parties have assimilated the bits they can cope with and turned them into a slogan, a boxful of phrases, two

---

[1] I have developed the distinction between theory and doctrine more generally in an essay on 'Party, Doctrine and Thought': see Michael Bentley and John Stevenson (eds.), *High and Low Politics in Modern Britain: ten studies* (Oxford, 1983), 123–53.

paragraphs for the current 'speakers' guide'. They carry with them a recommendatory warmth proportionate to their age and their relevance to great disputes of the past or, no less important, to the great men who conducted them. Parties abandon their doctrines on pain of relinquishing their past: the thing that has made them what they are. For although 'Free Trade' or 'Peace, Retrenchment and Reform' or 'Home Rule for Ireland' may become husks with the passage of time, they retain their blood for the party faithful among whom they function as a relic. And the thought also brings with it some negative implications. Certain 'theories' will fail to be assimilated because they prove unable to surmount the defences that doctrine builds over the years. What worried the Liberals of the 1880s and 1890s, of course, was that certain new doctrines might *have* to be generated by the party if it were to survive at all.

Gladstone had presented Home Rule to the Liberal party very much in this light. Certainly, the idea of giving Ireland a parliament presented the electorate with a substantial dose of political theory during the first half of the 1880s and the proposal plainly contained far more than a party ploy. But it did not seep into the party framework in the way that, say, collectivist thought or anti-imperial argument had done. It by-passed all the filters. The leader of the Liberal party thrust it into the centre of party 'principle' following an internal struggle with his own conscience and an external confrontation with the few senior party members who still believed in him. This meant that in January 1886 Liberal doctrine had become radically different from what Liberals thought they believed in December 1885. But note how their response differed, and had to differ, from that of the intelligentsia reviewing these events in a cooler and more sceptical frame of mind. The university men who opposed the concession of Home Rule to Parnell's Irish – easily the most vociferous and powerful collection of the liberal 'lights' – simply relinquished the Liberal party and transferred their loyalties to the Conservative party or, more usually, to the Liberal Unionist party of Hartington and Chamberlain. Liberal politicians, on the other hand, felt their hands more securely tied by public statement, long-held connexion with a party organization, constituency association and family tradition. Many of them felt miserable over the turn of events; most of them stayed. Less than a third of Liberal MPs deserted in 1886.[2] For those who remained, however, the difficult years had only just begun. The resonances of Home Rule jarred painfully against other doctrines long defended as sacrosanct, especially those concerning property; and few Liberals had changed their minds about those. Conceivable in one sense as an extension of familiar doctrines, Home Rule left Liberals in other senses with some circles to square.

The squaring did not look very plausible. Several elements contributed to the failure, but Gladstone himself comes to mind first as the most obvious pressure in the direction of stagnation. Indeed for the Liberal leader (77 years' old in 1886) the entire problem inside the Liberal party had come about through its truckling to alien tendencies. Home Rule had done all the squaring that the situation required: it had 'riddled out' the 'weak-kneed' who could not take the pace.[3] True, an unforeseeable difficulty sprang up when Parnell became the object of a poison pen in 1887 and made it hard for Liberals to stress Ireland as much as Gladstone would have wished.

[2] See Michael Hurst, *Joseph Chamberlain and Liberal Reunion: the round table conference of 1887* (1967). Chamberlain had originally expected much of his proposals for reconciliation and looked to Harcourt, Herschell and Fowler for a sympathetic hearing.
[3] Gladstone to Brett, 2 January 1891, in Maurice V. Brett (ed.), *Journals and Letters of Reginald Viscount Esher* (4 vols., 1934–8), I, 148.

But his solution amounted to keeping the party's head down rather than going for fundamental redrawing of its brief. If we examine a speech from 1889 and compare it with those at Midlothian, it becomes at once apparent how little forward movement there had been in Gladstone's thinking about the state and its function in promoting social welfare. 'If the Government takes into its hand that which man ought to do for himself, it will inflict upon him greater mischiefs than all the benefits he will have received or all the advantages that would accrue from them.'[4] *Plus ça change. . . .* In thinking about Scotland, which Haldane claimed he, Gladstone, never understood, his mind went backwards rather than forwards and reverted to the idea of disestablishing the Church there – not a Scottish priority, incidentally, and indeed a proposal actively opposed in some Liberal circles worried about its possible electoral unpopularity.[5] Gladstone's mind had in fact become firmly grooved, not to say obsessed; his blinkered determination to make Ireland the centre of Liberal imagery told heavily against the idea of rethinking other ways of appealing to his audience. Age – nothing subtler – prevented him from seeing that Ireland had become a public yawn.

Senility hardly explains, on the other hand, why many other Liberals believed that the road they travelled after 1886 would bring them back to power without any doctrinal reassessment. To help make sense of that, one needs some appreciation of the distortion produced by a pressing, cluttered horizon and an immersion in short-term change. For an MP elected in 1886, a disappointing result at the general election had been followed by an encouraging performance in by-elections since then – suggesting that public opinion looked favourably on the material about Home Rule with which the Liberals had presented them. Between 1887 and 1890 the party made substantial inroads into the Marquess of Salisbury's Conservative and Unionist majority. Even after 1890, when the scandal of Parnell's citation in a divorce case probably accounted for some falling off in the Liberal performance, party strategists nevertheless continued to believe themselves to be doing well in the eyes of the British public: indeed, Gladstone himself thought a Liberal majority of 100 at the next election by no means unlikely. The disappointment of 1892 – a majority of only 40 – again lost some of its sting when the Liberals performed better than a government would normally expect to have done in the by-elections of 1892–4.[6] But, as we saw in chapter two, a longer-term perspective clearly reveals that, compared with the electoral effectiveness of the Liberal party before 1885, these encouraging polls merely reflected a marginal improvement during a period of sustained failure that would not end until the *annus mirabilis* of 1906. What happens in politics frequently matters much less than what seems to have happened; and so long as some kind of Liberal success continued to give encouragement to party activists, no great retuning of the message seemed necessary.

To discuss the requirements of a sound Liberal strategy from the vantage of retrospect in any case loses sight of a crucial third element that struck contemporaries all too forcibly: the *psychology* produced by the sudden changes of 1885–6. Possibly

[4] Gladstone at Saltney, 26 October 1889, quoted in D. R. Brooks, 'Gladstone's Fourth Ministry 1892–4: policies and personalities' (unpub. Ph.D. thesis, Cambridge, 1978), 154.
[5] Haldane reported in West diary, 30 June 1893: see H. G. Hutchinson (ed.), *Private Diaries of the Rt. Hon. Sir Algernon West, GCB* (1922), 171; cf. Eighth Duke of Argyll, *Autobiography and Memoirs* (ed. Dowager Duchess of Argyll, 2 vols., 1906), II, 450ff.
[6] For the by-elections, see J. P. D. Dunbabin, 'Parliamentary Elections in Great Britain, 1868–1900: a psephological note', *English Historical Review* (1966), 97–8.

for the first, definitely not for the last, time in Liberal history, doctrine had fused with a defence of public personalities and their capacity to embody great truths and right thinking. Neither the Gladstonians nor the Unionists could approach the question of party belief after 1886 in a mood of clinical analysis. Their clubs and drawing rooms and Lobby huddles were throbbing with recrimination. 'During the years 1886–90,' the Unionist Henry James recalled, 'party feeling in social circles was most bitter. Since 1831 . . . nothing like it had existed.'[7] Among the Liberal Unionists the mood of betrayal naturally ran strongest. Men like Harcourt and Spencer who had not followed their fellow Whig, Hartington, into the fight against Home Rule caught the edge of it almost as cuttingly as G. O. Trevelyan who deserted Gladstone in 1886 and rejoined him in 1887, thereby earning the loathing of everybody. The Gladstonians replied in kind, angling most of their attack against Chamberlain himself who picked up blackballs like marbles in any club where Liberals held some leverage.

In the public sphere a spiking of the Unionists would likewise suffice as a statement of policy and obviate any need to say anything positive. Notice how a young hopeful – Herbert Henry Asquith – dispatched Salisbury's government when it met parliament after losing the 1892 election. He directed his amendment to the Address at the Tories only to swipe sidewards at Chamberlain and his friends:

> you have gone in for a course of peddling and huckstering in what you call progressive legislation. You have done so in order that you might keep step with a small but dwindling band of deserters from the Liberal camp, an accidental and ephemeral combination, which was born the day before yesterday, which will be forgotten the day after tomorrow.[8]

Such a position contained a good deal of intelligence, granted the unquestionable confusion of the Gladstonians about what they wanted to say. But it demonstrated a characteristic of British Liberalism that would become a permanent accompaniment to its arguments: an inability to transcend the slights and abrasions of party existence in order to attempt a realistic overview of its situation. The Liberal tendency to feed on division as though God had put it there as a test of grace did nothing to loosen thinking about doctrine. It rather prompted Liberals to think what they thought before – only more so.

Of course, not all Liberals felt this way. Radicals did not and they comprised an important segment of the parliamentary party after 1886. Some of the Liberal parliamentarians connected with the intelligentsia took a more detached view also. Scott and Haldane have already entered this discussion. Scott remembered asking Hobhouse to join the *Manchester Guardian* and stressing 'that the relations of Liberalism and Labour must govern the future of politics, and that the problem was to find the lines on which Liberals could be brought to see that the old tradition must be expanded to yield a fuller measure of social justice, a more real equality, an industrial as well as a political liberty.' This certainly sounds like a clear-headed strategy with a far-seeing recommendation for Liberals to follow. Haldane made many similar sounds in the nineties: he talked about a 'language of the social good' coming into currency among 'a growing number of the younger Liberals'; he commented on the need to win 'the confidence of the workmen who will turn the next

[7] Lord Askwith, *Lord James of Hereford* (1930), 189–90.
[8] Asquith in Commons, 8 August 1892, printed in *Speeches of the Earl of Oxford and Asquith, KG* (n.d. [1927]), 20–1.

election.'⁹ But remarks of this kind demand a context and, when set in one, do little to clinch the case for a resurgent *party* doctrine before 1900. Scott's recommendations go to a theorist who requires no conversion in order to attract him to an organ of progressive journalism. Haldane's exhortations go to the readers of the *Progressive Review* who are no less converted than Hobhouse; and it becomes important for him to stress that younger Liberals believe what he is saying precisely because older ones evidently do not. Or appeals of this kind are aimed at the unregenerate leader, Rosebery, in the faint hope that he will take some notice and by doing so help reverse the disaster suffered by the party at the polls in 1895. The climate of expectation and pressure that such scraps of *obiter dicta* help produce has an importance of its own: it cannot be dismissed as an irrelevance to the Liberal party and its operations. The point is rather that doctrine and party practice conditioned one another at every point. To understand what took place in the air, we must also examine what took place on the ground.

Party practice and despair 1886–95

Liberals supplied the membership and policy for three distinct ministries in the decade following the crash of 1885: Gladstone's third and fourth governments of 1886 and 1892–4; and Rosebery's only government of 1894–5. Yet these separate experiences – all of them unprofitable and unhappy – merge in the memory both with each other and with the period of opposition between Gladstone's failure to impose Home Rule in 1886 and the beginning of his second failure to do so in 1892. The reason is soon stated. Gladstone's obsession with Home Rule had become, through the ruction of 1885, the beginning and end of Liberal politics. When Liberals spoke about an issue which by the end of the 1880s had become 'a weariness to all parties',⁹ they narrowed their public identity and left an impression of having forgotten the other pressing issues on which they ought to mount initiatives or responses. When they did not talk about Ireland, critics surmised that their talk would remain hot-air until they confronted and surmounted the Irish hurdle they had built for themselves. Throughout it all the presence of Gladstone had its effects whether he were present or not. Even Rosebery's government, formed after Gladstone's retirement, failed to become post-Gladstonian in any recognizable form except in its foreign policy where Rosebery's imperialism at last found an outlet. At his own downfall in 1895, Rosebery needed no reminding that the crushing of the Liberals at the general election that summer commented on far more than the events of his own disastrous period of office. 'Mr. G.'s general policy since 1880'¹⁰ struck him as the fundamental problem. And he was right.

Gladstone's five-month government in 1886 had confirmed that the premier had lost none of his single-mindedness. As before, he throve on evading, rather than refuting, criticism; and since he now walked on eggs because of his atrocious man-management during the Christmas revelations about his *volte-face* over Home Rule, he called the cabinet together less than once a week. Its most dangerous moment came when the first movement at cabinet level towards a Home Rule bill took place and both Hartington and Chamberlain resigned. The defeat of the bill, granted the power of

⁹ Derby diary, 27 May 1889, in John Vincent (ed.), *The Later Derby Diaries: home rule, Liberal Unionism and aristocratic life in late-Victorian England* (Bristol, 1981), 128.
¹⁰Rosebery to Ripon, 13 August 1895, quoted in Peter Stansky, *Ambitions and Strategies: the struggle for the leadership of the Liberal party in the 1890s* (Oxford, 1964), 180.

the Conservative party in the House of Lords, posed no problem; but it was not needed. Despite a memorable performance by Gladstone in the Commons, 93 Liberals voted against the second reading in June 1886 – enough to terminate the first Home Rule bill and drive Gladstone into an election that left him head of a mere fraction of the Liberal party while Salisbury dug in for what would obviously prove a long spell at the crease.

These events are well-known. So is the public sequel. Ireland dominated the agenda during the period after the spring of 1887 when the Conservative Chief Secretary earned his spurs as 'Bloody Balfour'. But the Liberal message suffered from the Irish Nationalists and swings in their fortune. Three events in particular shaped the Liberal calendar in the second half of the 1880s: the forged letter printed in *The Times* in April 1887 that made Parnell apparently condone the murder of Cavendish and Burke in Phoenix Park in 1882; the revelation that the letter had come from the pen of an imposter who subsequently committed suicide; and the collapse of Parnell's public standing – this time for good – when the divorce proceedings filed against Mrs O'Shea made plain the nature of her relationship with the Nationalist leader. For the Liberals this pattern of rise and fall implied a careful reading of the Irish commitment. It had to go into minor key when Parnell's integrity came under question. It deserved full pedal, on the other hand, when Parnell's exoneration brought a strength of public sympathy that it would have been foolish not to enlist. Yet that very enthusiasm only made the doom of Liberal–Nationalist relations the more inevitable when Parnell's alleged moral frailties became the property of every street-corner news-vendor. Dealers in Liberal optimism like the ever-faithful Earl Spencer kept up their whistling despite it all. 'We have got through the Parnell smash,' Spencer tried to persuade the not-a-bit optimistic Harcourt in 1891, 'with a success which shows our political constitution is stronger than anyone ever thought it was.'[11] Among those, like Harcourt, for whom Ireland had turned into an albatross, the success seemed hard to find.

Not least, one had to bear in mind the subterranean movements that had taken place away from public view since 1887. Conservative politics had found a firm footing that year, with Churchill's impetuous resignation at the end of 1886 and Hicks Beach's supersession by Balfour in Dublin. Unionist ranks also closed once it became clear during 1887 that the four Unionists who rejoined the Gladstonians over the toughened Irish coercion bill would not turn into a tidal wave and when the Gladstonians had made it obvious through their demeanour at the Round Table conferences intended to reunify the parties that they would not have Chamberlain back at any price short of sackcloth and ashes. Looking around themselves in the House of Commons, meanwhile, Liberal MPs recognized in one another a collection of 'Radicals' of various sorts – more of them, proportionately, than at any time before. But while the Irish mess of 1885–6 had boosted the stock of Radicals, it had also cut off their head. It had removed Birmingham and the men who had given Radical politics much of its direction since the second half of the 1870s. The relationship between this headless Radicalism and the party generally would obviously bear heavily on the ability of both to mobilize opinion and act effectively. Both needed, moreover, somehow to mobilize Gladstone.

The relationship with party personnel became strained at an early date because Radicalism chose to run in new channels. Chamberlainite Radicals had fought their

[11]Spencer to Harcourt, 30 September 1891, in A. G. Gardiner, *The Life of Sir William Harcourt* (2 vols., 1923), II, 159.

corner before 1885 as professional politicians using the familiar bases of support and theatres of activity. They developed the use of the 'caucus' as a means of strengthening their constituency organizations; but once at Westminster they played the game. The Gladstonian Radicals after 1887 looked to quieter forms of pressure and association. They lacked parliamentary performers of the stamp of Chamberlain. They still had Dilke, but his personal life had ruined him; they had Henry Labouchere but the Queen's disgust at his republicanism would keep him out of any likely Liberal government and left him looking very much a fringe figure. Instead, Radical hopes tended to focus on bodies such as the National Liberal Federation, the Liberal Central Association and the Liberal Publications Department. For the Radicals themselves, this style of involvement brought little reward, except in helping promote the range of catch-cries, from Welsh disestablishment to local veto over licensing arrangements, that found a reflection in the 'Newcastle Programme' of 1891, on the basis of which the party hoped to fight the next election. They lacked a commanding figure inside the Liberal organization to do what Bonham had done for the Peelite Tory party. Their central figure in both organizations was Francis Schnadhorst who lacked the ability to set the world on fire even discounting his deafness and developing insanity. They lacked, too, a Chamberlain or Lord Randolph Churchill who could *use* a slice of the party organization in order to build an energy-centre from which to make a mark in the places where decisions were made and priorities framed. The buildings in Parliament Street and Abingdon Street that housed these bases of Radicalism lay outside that geography.

By 1890 this dispersion of effort had produced a strange paradox: the 'Radical' section of the Liberal party, contentiously quantified by Henry James at 150 MPs out of 210 Gladstonians,[12] had never enjoyed so clear a predominance in Liberal parliamentary politics. Yet its power, understood in hard-nosed terms as its capacity to make senior Liberals do what it wanted, had never run so low in living memory. Certainly the party leadership had to listen: only a collection of fools would have ignored the basis of its parliamentary support. But it proved possible for the leadership to slide along without making any firm commitments and to wrap up a rag-bag policy like the Newcastle programme in an appropriate phraseology that stressed what needed stressing and carefully elided over what ought to be forgotten. Gladstone's favourite weapons became those of silence and prolonged absence – devastating responses to enthusiasts wanting to push and go. More *au fait* politicians like Harcourt expended endless temper on '*subs* who arrange everything according to their own second-rate ideas',[13] but they did not allow second-rate people to prescribe priorities or cloud their thinking about tactics. The Radical organizations had become irritations and bores rather than generators of a new form of Liberal politics. Only as we look forward does the significance of their development become apparent. These years had seen the beginning of the Liberal party's self-dissipation into a series of separate nodes. The fragmentation of the party during those desperate years after 1918, with their leagues and their councils and their schools and their inquiries, creeps backwards like a craze of fissures to the wider divisions of the 1890s and the turning of Liberal politics into a more diverse and public discourse than Gladstone had tolerated during his middle years.

[12]Chamberlain diary, 5 December 1890, in J. L. Garvin and J. Amery, *The Life of Joseph Chamberlain* (6 vols., 1932–69), II, 409.
[13]Harcourt in 1890, quoted in Michael Barker, *Gladstone and Radicalism: the reconstruction of Liberal policy in Britain 1885–94* (Hassocks, 1975), 159.

One fissure ran, of course, between Liberals who defined their party by its resistance to the patriotic fervour and lust for territory that everyone recognized from the mid 1880s, and those who saw Liberalism as that fervour's most enlightened and necessary corollary. Indeed, with the formation after 1886 of a group of self-conscious 'Liberal Imperialists' who wanted to develop the importance of the Empire within Liberal public argument, we come directly into contact with one of the strangest aspects of late-nineteenth-century Liberalism for a modern reader to assimilate. 'Imperialist' stands high among terms of twentieth-century political abuse, together with often meaningless allegations such as 'fascist' or 'sexist'. The conventional wisdom finds no problem in proclaiming that imperialists are nasty and their doctrines immoral. Their energies would be better spent in thinking of ways to improve their own society rather than subjugating others. Butter is better than guns, this argument says: we should build schools and hospitals instead of bombs and missiles. How very odd, then, that late-Victorians who wanted to carry out programmes of social improvement in Britain, on the one hand, and those who wanted to develop the Empire as a political and economic unit, on the other, were often the same people. More than that, they linked these two areas in their own minds as crucial ingredients of any rational approach to the problems they took to face Britain. The Liberal Imperialists concentrated on the domestic aspect of this approach in their early years; but, as the pace of international tension and aggrandizement heated through the 1890s, they turned quite as much as Conservatives to the opportunities presented by the Empire and the threats to it that demanded their opposition. Since this group included men of great talent and high rank within the Liberal party – Rosebery, Asquith, Grey and Haldane became pre-eminent among them – they presented the leadership with a clear purpose when Rosebery held office in 1894–5, and a no less clear challenge when he did not.[14]

The fissures in Liberal opinion ultimately reached Gladstone himself, of course, and created a pattern for much of the environment within which he had to work. How far he responded to their presence in any significant way remains controversial. His behaviour during these late years has given some historians an impression of strengthening radicalism (a view on which one can rest a coherent account) but it neglects the degree to which the radicalism served Gladstone's very narrow political intentions. 'When one philosophizes,' the great French cynic Fustel de Coulanges once observed, 'one says what one wants.' Gladstone knew what he wanted and philosophized to make it happen. He wanted a remoralized Liberal party, recommitted to individual liberation, Home Rule for Ireland, and the transcending of socialism by the Ten Commandments. He was prepared to put his name to the Newcastle Programme and his voice to selected items in it; he would happily give a Private Member's Eight Hours' Bill his vote but not the government's parliamentary time essential if it were to have a chance of becoming law; he would resist payment of MPs (a major Radical platform) even if it meant agreeing with Rosebery. When he disagreed with Rosebery he would steer around unpleasantness by not telling him what he was doing. To see in the last years of Gladstone's power the seed-bed of the new Liberalism that would supposedly bring the party its remarkable win at the polls in 1906 has its attractions in a reading of public evidence. It sits ill at ease with the private, however, and places in shadow the issues waiting to torture the Liberal party

[14]For a thorough treatment of this theme, see H. C. G. Matthew, *The Liberal Imperialists: the ideas and politics of a post-Gladstonian élite* (Oxford, 1973). Bernard Semmel's older book, *Imperialism and Social Reform: English social–imperial thought, 1895–1914* (1960), ties together these strands.

during the later part of the 1890s – defence, imperialism, socialism, above all the South African war – which did so much to turn the party and its thinking towards new positions and help force it, despite itself, into a dialogue with a version of reality very different from that depicted in Gladstone's fantasies.

Certainly the experience of the Liberal governments of 1892–5 did nothing to suggest their emergence from fantasy. 'Ludicrous' is a favourite adjective of Liberal observers through those dismal sessions whether they are speaking of the Home Rule Bill that Gladstone pushed through the Commons only to watch it sink to its inevitable grave in the Lords, or the cabal of Radicals on the Liberal Left who fancied that they held a stranglehold on policy or the behaviour of the imperialists on the Right who made Rosebery their imperfect god and Africa their target. That the Foreign Secretary of Gladstone's fourth ministry, Rosebery, and the Chancellor of the Exchequer, Harcourt, loathed and would not speak to one another said little by itself: Harcourt, after all, loathed everyone. But it symbolized the misery of Liberal relations just as Rosebery's insomnia reflected their disquiet. At only two points did a constructive response to policy emerge: with Asquith's Employers' Liability Bill in 1893, which the Lords destroyed in the following year by removing its elements of compulsion; and Harcourt's introduction of death duties in his 1894 budget which, for all the modesty of their level, gave Lloyd George a groundplan for some of the thinking behind the People's Budget of 1909.

From Rosebery's short term of power the central memory became Uganda and the premier's determination (one formed since his tenure of the Foreign Office under Gladstone) to annex it for the British Crown regardless of opposition. The effect on anti-imperialists needs no comment. Together with Grey's seeming eagerness to confront the French at the beginning of 1895 – again in the African theatre – it scotched any notion of the primacy of 'New Liberalism' in the higher reaches of the Liberal party. Even the occasion of the government's welcome death, following the loss of a vote to reduce the salary of Rosebery's Minister for War, Sir Henry Campbell-Bannerman, signalled that the Liberalism of the Rosebery regime had proved very old indeed. Nor would Rosebery readily forget the name of the minister – a Glaswegian draper and warehouseman – whose responsibility for supplying the army with cordite had been so indelibly associated with the government's collapse. For only when Campbell-Bannerman became leader of the Liberal party in 1898 would the doctrines of the New Liberalism stand any chance of recognition within the decision-making echelons of the party. That situation would in turn depend on the removal of Rosebery from Liberal politics and the conversion of his disciples to the politics of compromise.

Out of the shadows

Behind the future visible from 1895 lay the unrisen sun of 1906. That contemporaries could not see it perhaps helped magnify their sense of gloom. That we cannot avoid it probably contributes to our misapprehension of a decade during which the Liberal party turned itself from a bundle of politicians almost too contemptible for opposition into an organization seemingly capable of moving mountains. The mountains at least seemed clear enough: too many policies, too many Radicals, too many imperialists, no leader, no candidates, no money; a Conservative–Unionist coalition of interests on the Right, an independent and increasingly pushy Labour organization on the Left. Marienbad and Homburg, favourite retreats on the continent, had never looked so inviting. Those who stayed to think about the future had salvaged one luxury, without knowing it, from their recent calamities. They had acquired certainty. Since the days of Gladstone's elation about Ireland they had lived on the possible and the conceivable – a string of promises and delusions holding out the hope that the world would not do to them what it threatened to do. By removing that delusion, the *débâcle* of 1895 at least suggested the size of the problem if not the means of its solution. On the other hand, the sourness, hopelessness and negativity among Liberal correspondents of the mid nineties argue that, whether or not they had read Hobson and Hobhouse, Liberals saw no clear way forward beyond allowing the hours to pass and waiting for something to happen.

Their leaders had plainly contributed to the defeat in significant ways; and over the next eight years the question of who should present Liberal ideas to the public weighed heavily on the party. Little help looked likely from beyond its confines. Both Joseph Chamberlain and the Duke of Devonshire (as Hartington had now become) accepted office under Salisbury in 1895 and squashed any lingering expectation that they would one day return to the Liberal party to pull it out of the fire. In the case of Chamberlain that much had been clear for a number of years: the snub over the 'Round Table' in 1887, when the Gladstonians had made it clear that they did not want him back, had persuaded him to look elsewhere for a political career. The prospects for Hartington seemed less clear-cut. In 1886 he himself had seen the point of biding his time, as he explained to his confidante and mistress, the Duchess of Manchester:

> if I join the Government even as Prime Minister [a mooted possibility] I shall separate myself from the Liberals, and I shall lose all influence with them; and sooner or later the whole Liberal party would be committed to Home Rule which will not be the case if we can manage to maintain the present position until Mr. G. disappears from the scene.[15]

The Liberal Unionists did not maintain their position at the polls and Gladstone went without leaving an opportunity for the Unionist leadership to find its way back to the Liberal party. We know, in fact, that Gladstone had it in mind to recommend the Unionists' *bête noire*, Spencer, as his successor had the Queen bothered to ask him his opinion. Only after severe perturbations in the leadership after 1895 would attempts be made to recruit Devonshire back to the Liberal leadership and those petered out at the beginning of 1904. They had become plausible at all, one ought to add, because his Unionist colleague Chamberlain had by then given back to the Liberals their sense of identity as a doctrinal force.

Considerable importance attaches to the point that organized Liberalism proved capable of regrouping around common doctrine only when outside agencies supplied the pressure and smoothed the path. Haldane's young men may have begun to speak of a 'new Liberalism' as early as 1895 but the party as a whole did not move in the direction of social radicalism in the aftermath of the 1895 defeat. Certainly the Radicals, what was left of them, pressed their policies and found some room for manoeuvre in their 'capture' of the National Liberal Federation at the end of the decade. But historians talk about the capture more readily than they ask whether the NLF had been worth the siege. For beyond these commanding depths little sign emerged of a reshaping of the Liberal message or, indeed, any real appreciation of profitable lines of argument. The overwhelming sense conveyed by Liberal history after 1895 is one of shrinking horizons and a feeling of involution. What Liberals want to discuss is themselves: their leaders and their limitations, the poverty of their organization, the trouble caused by their own imperialists. A major opportunity for comment such as the engineering lockout of 1898 is lost in the compulsion to rehearse internal suspicions. Sir Henry Campbell-Bannerman and Herbert Gladstone, respectively the new leader and new chief whip, made some impact in reducing the level of bickering. But, as Sir James Kitson, the hard-headed MP for Colne Valley, told Gladstone at the outset, there was little point in discussing the principles of Liberal legislation until that job had been done. 'Then perhaps we may have the power to do useful work.'[16]

Imperialism supplied the foreground for much of the difficulty in the late 1890s. The South African war obviously brought public discussion to a head but long before then Liberal problems had displayed an imperial or foreign-policy dimension. Consider the leadership issue, for example. Rosebery's management came under immediate attack following the electoral disaster of 1895 but when he resigned in one of his tempers in 1896 the occasion of his resignation called up echoes of 1876 because the stimulus came from Gladstone's re-emergence from retirement to castigate another Turkish massacre – this time in Armenia. Rosebery's dyspeptic successor, Harcourt, lasted only two years; and *he* cut loose over the party's dislike of his supposedly weak attitude to the government's coming to the edge of war in the Fashoda incident of 1898 when British and French forces stood toe-to-toe for a time in the Sudan. On the imperial level, the great issue of these years concerned the (unsuccessful) effort to implicate Chamberlain in the secret dealings that led to Dr Jameson's raid on the Transvaal at the end of 1895 that had turned almost at once into a stunning fiasco. Yet inevitably the Liberal imperialists brought the party to its greatest test over the question of whether to support the government in its decision to enter on a war with the South African Boers in 1899.

This subject has comprised the centre of a growing body of work by recent historians of the period[17] and space allows only a brief pause where a longer one is merited. At least two types of significance have their roots in the South African imbroglio for an historian of Liberal doctrine: it provoked radicalism into something like a renaissance following a period of random focus; and it gave the imperialists the opportunity they had been seeking since 1894 to reshape the core of Liberal sentiment about the place of Britain in the world. The first of these made the greater noise and the lesser impact. Everyone knows the stories of the new Welsh hero, David Lloyd George, and his escape from Birmingham town hall disguised as a policeman in order to escape a 'jingo' audience vowing to kill him. Nor did he fight alone. An important section of the party and a powerful component of Liberal opinion in the country opposed the war as immoral and pointless. By so doing they helped lay the foundations for the anti-war element inside the party that would attract larger head-

---

[16]Kitson to Gladstone, 3 February 1899, quoted in R. E. Ellins, 'Aspects of the New Liberalism 1895–1914', (unpub. Ph.D. dissertation, Sheffield, 1980), 221. Dr Ellins throws considerable light on the party after 1895: see esp. 188–244.

[17]The Boer War has given rise to a considerable modern literature. For an authoritative analysis of its origins, see A. N. Porter, *The Origins of the South African War: Joseph Chamberlain and the diplomacy of imperialism* (Manchester, 1980). Other helpful accounts will be found in Richard Price, *An Imperial War and the British Working Class: working-class attitudes and reactions to the Boer War, 1899–1902* (1972); and Stephen Koss (ed.), *The Pro-Boers: the anatomy of an anti-war movement* (Chicago, 1973).

lines as the international situation deteriorated after 1906. But public opinion in general probably took on a moderately khaki colour – it is hard to be sure because the so-called 'Khaki' election of 1900 offers only weak evidence through its plethora of uncontested seats – and in so far as the Liberal party sought to make itself a party of government once again, much depended on the ability of its centre and right to frame a convincing position over the conduct of the war and its aftermath.

The men at the centre of imperialist politics inside the Liberal party make more sense to posterity as Liberals looking for a new party doctrine than as politicians acting from an assimilation of imperial thought and writing. Some of them doubtless had read Seeley's *The Expansion of England* (1883) and come into contact with imperial journalism or the personality of Milner, Harcourt's former adviser at the Exchequer. And their most prominent spokesman by 1899, Sir Edward Grey, had spent an emotional youth that perhaps still sought an outlet in mission. But the central problem presented itself as finding some way to overcome the 'nightmare of futility' that Grey discerned in the Liberal experience of the past few years. Transcending it would demand a doctrine that would genuinely stir the public and rebuild British Liberalism on ground more appropriate to current conditions than the scrub and thistle left it by Gladstone. It would also require inspired leadership to help the electorate realize that pride in the Empire and its possibilities for the future need not remain the monopoly of Salisbury's party. From the standpoint of the 1980s it is hard to judge which was the more implausible perception: the feeling that a terrible new beauty was about to be born, or the certainty – too widely held to allow dismissal at sight – that Rosebery best embodied it.

The marketing of Rosebery was the Liberals' most memorable contribution to the Boer War. Of course, the initiative came from a small group, the so-called Liberal Imperialists, and ran into powerful opposition from the 'official' Liberalism that Campbell-Bannerman had spent the previous year trying to control. It also failed. But the Rosebery programme showed clear symptoms of infection by theory and therefore deserves some notice. It picked up resonances from current journalism and the mood of scientific inquiry into the condition of the people voiced from Mayhew to Booth and the Webbs. It spoke about 'national efficiency' – the phrase of the moment. ('Efficiency' has shifted its meaning in recent years: one needs to think of it as a slogan appropriate to a health farm.) It promised a 'clean slate' on which the new politics could be drawn. There was the feeling of cross-party evangelism aimed at a pervasive but blurred collectivism and also directed, of course, at the Liberal Unionists whose detachment from the Conservative party might once again become practical politics. Had Rosebery's announcement of his new Liberalism in speeches culminating at Chesterfield in December 1901 begun a significant departure, and had the Liberal League, formed to promote it, grown any teeth, then the Liberal politics we now associate with the early twentieth century might have looked rather different. It would have been a welfare Liberalism, owing as much to Bismarck's as did Lloyd George's radical version; it would have been statist without the overtone of 'progressivism' that Liberals produced over the next decade. It would have given Labour politics (and after 1906 the new Labour party) more room to develop than progressive Liberalism could choose to give; but on the other hand it would have built firmer resistance on the centre-right than Asquith's later brand of Liberalism dare attempt – something closer, possibly, to the populist posture of Baldwin a generation beyond.

Pipe dreams: all of them. Even if Rosebery had proved a vehicle for any consistent message, and he never did, how would this politics have supported itself? How, in

1906 or 1907, would a Liberal Imperialist government have financed a big navy and a unilateralist foreign policy? Granted its basis of possible support, a lurch towards direct taxation would hardly commend itself. But the alternative, tariff reform and the re-imposition of economic protection, cut across the public commitment to free trade that all Liberals had made since leaving their cots. Then think of Ireland. How could a generation of Liberals renounce their public stance on Home Rule? It was highly significant for the party that when Campbell-Bannerman and Rosebery met after the Chesterfield speech, their sticking point remained Ireland just as Ireland provided the occasion of the final breach between Rosebery and the Liberal party in 1905. The intellectual currents whipped up by the South African war and its revelations of ineffectuality at the centre and mass deprivation in the country as a whole helped political thinkers to move to odd tables: Milner eating with Webb, Haldane with anyone who would listen. But political clubs and dining groups cut no ice with party management nor with the doctrinal legacy that no party could afford to jettison at a stroke. By translating itself as a form of radical doctrine, Liberal imperialism had become an apolitical force, one which custodians of established Liberal positions had no difficulty in resisting. Rosebery apart – he remained consistent at least in his intransigence – the imperialists relegated their great plan of 1901 to an embarrassing memory and followed Asquith back to the centre by 1906.

Until 1903 the centre of the party machine had concerned itself with electoral and financial matters more urgently than it had begun a revolution in policy. Campbell-Bannerman had brought his gift for quietude to bear both on the imperialists and on the Left of the party with its social reform ambitions. He had reflected the currency of social concern that no one could avoid after the Boer War and talked about the need to confront the reality of a population that ignored its substantial sectors of poverty and deprivation.[18] Such views caught the breeze but hardly felt its force or understood its direction. As one commercial employer speaking to others around him on the Liberal benches, the leader of the Liberal party showed little instinct for the working class and what it (or they) wanted. Sidney Webb and his kind mediated those wants: they translated them into language that governing classes and members of the established intelligentsia could understand. Bland Liberal statement seems arid, therefore, in contrast with Webb's language as he tells H. G. Wells that he, Wells, does not know whereof he speaks. 'The English wage-earning class . . . is rapidly putting on "bourgeois" characteristics, developing any number of markedly different classes and strata, segregating with great rapidity into streaks of bright colours, which are becoming more intense.'[19] Liberal thought on the working class did not have many bright colours. Even Lloyd George, whose notorious refusal to read anything leaves one unimpressed by his quotations from Rowntree's wartime study of York, saw a Welsh rural working class in his mind's eye rather than an English urban one.

The project endured, needless to say, of assimilating all classes into a common and interdependent organism. Were all reported speeches of Liberal politicians to pass through a computer programmed to recognize key phrases in organicist rhetoric, the count of instances might well prove impressive. But the impact of new thinking along

[18]'We used to hear of a submerged tenth in the population. We now know of a submergeable third.' In the House of Commons, 10 June 1903, quoted in A. M. Gollin, *Balfour's Burden: Arthur Balfour and imperial preference* (1965), 214.
[19]Webb to Wells, 8 December 1901, in Norman Mackenzie (ed.), *The Letters of Sidney and Beatrice Webb* (3 vols., Cambridge, 1978), II, 145. He was deriding the portrayal of the working class in Wells's *Anticipations* (1901).

these lines at the level of party management and high-political strategy remains elusive before 1906 and highly oblique thereafter. The Independent Labour party of 1893 and the Labour Representation Committee of 1900 presented a sharper threat in these areas; and here the Liberals made some modest moves. Herbert Gladstone's negotiation in 1903 of a secret pact with Ramsay MacDonald, on behalf of the LRC, to avoid enervating divisions in the progressive vote in selected constituencies has become the best-known example of that programme, together with a greater willing-ness than heretofore to take working-class men as parliamentary candidates in Liberal constituencies. This initiative can be over-worked, however, to underpin a case for Liberal panic and helplessness in face of a Labour challenge. In some localities Labour pressure at the municipal level had already become a problem by 1906: the case of the West Riding of Yorkshire comes especially to mind.[20] Other areas produced far less difficulty. Mining centres still displayed considerable loyalty to the old connexion, for example, even when their trade union leaders did not become, as one disgusted ILP member alleged 'of the South Wales miners' leaders, 'simply puppets of the Liberal Party.'[21] Confronting socialism mattered as a rhetorical task and formulaic responses to the presence of worrying alien forces appeared on most platforms. But it is noticeable how often they appear behind and below other formulae referring to the House of Lords and the need to tether it, or Ireland and the need to settle it, or the comity of nations and the need to enhance it, or – louder and louder – free trade and the need to defend it.

Which direction the Liberal party would have taken if Joseph Chamberlain had not made his spectacular speeches recommending a return to economic protection and the use of preferential tariffs to develop the colonies, invites questions that hinge on a number of imponderables. What seems certain is that May 1903 became, as a result of Chamberlain's *démarche*, a threshold in Liberal development – not simply for its effect on the Liberals' electoral recovery but also for its significance in determining the kind of party that the electorate would approve in 1906. Campbell-Bannerman's party would, without free trade, have faced its electorate from a stance somewhere to the left of the one it in fact assumed three years after Chamberlain began his campaign. For that campaign conferred the ultimate advantage on its opponents: it removed any need to think. The bottom drawer of every Liberal desk had its sheaf of material about the sanctity of free trade and the suicide that its abrogation would mean. Chamberlain's protectionism switched the priority from creating new forms of Liberal language to reinforcing hallowed ones from the past and making sure that Herbert Gladstone could raise enough cash to put up a Liberal in every constituency that looked vulnerable. It did what Campbell-Bannerman cursed his own inability to achieve, by making the Liberal party *passive*. And with a Conservative government languishing under Balfour and drifting into every kind of scrape and snare through its educational policy, its licensing policy, its Irish policy and its colonial policy – with only the Entente Cordiale of 1904 to redeem it – passivity had much to be said for it.

By the spring of 1905 the Liberal party needed not a thought between its ears to feel justifiably confident of forming the next government. Observers such as Sir Almeric FitzRoy who had remarked only a few years before on 'the bankruptcy of modern

[20]See Keith Laybourn and Jack Reynolds, *Liberalism and the Rise of Labour 1890–1918* (1984), which con-centrates on the West Riding experience.
[21]Quoted in David Howell, *British Workers and the Independent Labour Party 1888–1906* (Manchester, 1983), 28.

Liberalism as a guiding and illuminating force'[22] had to this extent missed the point. In the circumstances of 1905 it sufficed to be the Not-Conservative party. Indeed, an analysis of what Liberal candidates actually talked about during the campaign of January 1906, when the new prime minister, Campbell-Bannerman, tested the popularity of his party at a general election, confirms this image very clearly. The half-a-dozen issues to which 70 per cent or more Liberal candidates referred were those prompted by what the Conservatives had done (education, Ireland, licensing, the use of Chinese 'slave' labour in the Transvaal and blanket attacks on the invalidity of the Tory mandate of 1900). The leading issue, represented in 98 per cent of election addresses, naturally became free trade.[23] Only in the lower half of the list of topics, commented on by less than half of the candidates, does one encounter the areas in which the recommendations of a new Liberalism might tell: unemployment, housing, workers' compensation, the eight-hour day. This allows us a certain brutalism in assessing the impact of social theory on Liberal politics before 1906; but better, perhaps, to put the point minimally. If the atmosphere generated by new Liberals through their writing and speaking made a contribution to the way in which the Liberal party behaved, that contribution crystallized least in those areas that documentary evidence from the politicians themselves seems best suited to support. From the perspective that these survivals help posterity to create, it looks very much as though party Liberals invented their newness rather as a response to the embarrassments of success in 1906 than to the presentiments of failure in 1895.

[22]FitzRoy diary, 6 November 1902, in Sir Almeric FitzRoy, *Memoirs* (2 vols., 1925), I, 110.
[23]Tabulation in A. K. Russell, *Liberal Landslide: the general election of 1906* (Newton Abbot, 1973), 65.

7

High Tide: And Ebb

The theory and practice of power 1906–14

We have a maxim in the Liberal party, which was first used by the late Mr. Gladstone – (cheers), – and which was the central point in the doctrines of my father, Lord Randolph Churchill. I mean the maxim 'Trust the People'.

Winston Churchill at Cockermouth, 25 July 1906[1]

Churchill had an axe to grind in assimilating the party he had joined only two years before to the positions maintained by Gladstone's chief tormentor in the 1880s; but in grinding it he implied something significant about the Liberal party in its moment of absolute victory. His picture of Liberalism as a form of free-trade Tory Democracy misses many of the former's nuances but only sharpens the portrait in omitting inessential lines. Just as Randolph Churchill had manipulated a vague sense of continuity with the tradition of Tory populism, so Campbell-Bannerman's Liberal party offered itself to the public as an embodiment of the hopes of the masses. Quite what to say to the masses once the embodiment had been achieved posed questions that most Liberals preferred to think about rather in the long term than immediately. For the moment one could proceed as before: by reversing what the Conservatives had done. Government in the first year or so would demand 'no constructive ideas', as Haldane later complained, 'merely objections to other people's ideas'.[2]

Dwelling on the Liberal party's empiricists does not argue out of existence a climate of opinion that must have imposed itself on Liberals at all levels over the past few years. Academic treatises such as the young Herbert Samuel's exposition of *Liberalism* or Chiozza Money's *Riches and Poverty*, which appeared only months before the Campbell-Bannerman government came to power,[3] played some role in

---

[1] Printed in Robert Rhodes James (ed.), *Winston S. Churchill: his complete speeches 1897–1963* (8 vols., New York, 1974), I, 647.

[2] R. B. Haldane, quoted in D. A. Hamer, *Liberal Politics in the Age of Gladstone and Rosebery* (Oxford, 1972), 323.

[3] Herbert Samuel, *Liberalism* (1902) [introduction by Asquith]; L. Chiozza Money, *Riches and Poverty* (1905).

striking the mood; but the argument had gone further than the bookshops. Revelations of national disgrace in the living conditions of the working class, divulged by the recruitment campaign required by the South African war, led directly to the establishment of a Physical Deterioration Committee whose report proved influential: indeed its rather smug chairman saw its lessons all around Westminster in 1906.[4] By the end of that year, the Churchill who had presented himself as son-of-Randolph a few months before had moved towards a language of his own that digested parts of this developing social-democratic position. We look, perhaps, to the period after 1908 when he became Member for Dundee for the speeches that best reflect the sea-change in rhetoric; but the Glasgow speech of October 1906 contains so self-conscious a fusion of theory with party politics that it invites stress here as a rare instance of a politician catching contemporary currents of thought about so abstract a conception as the nature of 'collectivism' and then turning them into a party doctrine:

> It is not possible to draw a hard-and-fast line between individualism and collectivism. You cannot draw it either in theory or in practice. . . . Man is at once a unique being and a gregarious animal. For some purposes he must be collectivist, for others he is, and will for all time remain, an individualist. Collectively we have an Army and a Navy and a Civil Service; collectively we have a Post Office, and a police, and a Government; collectively we indulge increasingly in all the necessities of communication. But we do not make love collectively [an exuberant point which Churchill later dropped when rousing the puritans of Dundee], and the ladies do not marry us collectively, and we do not eat collectively, and we do not die collectively. . . . The whole tendency of civilisation is, however, towards the multiplication of the collective functions of society. The ever-growing complications of civilisation create for us new services which have to be undertaken by the State . . . I go farther; I should like to see the State embark on various novel and adventurous experiments . . . I look forward to the universal establishment of minimum standards of life and labour, and their progressive elevation as the increasing energies of production may permit. I do not think that Liberalism in any circumstances can cut itself off from this fertile field of social effort, and I would recommend you not to be scared in discussing any of these proposals, just because some old woman comes along and tells you that they are Socialistic.[5]

Whether the Churchill of June or the Churchill of October offers the better guide to Liberal party behaviour during the years of Liberal ascendency before 1914 prompts questions that have given rise to sustained discussion and disagreement among those who have studied the period and we must return to their arguments in the final chapter of this book. For the moment it will suffice to note the depth of theoretical presupposition that surrounded public discussion of politics in these years and the degree to which politicians sometimes aimed to persuade their public that they were borne along by it. Doubtless that posture often merely suggested a helpful pose; but in a sense the lack of conviction mattered little when politicians found themselves committing themselves and their party to propositions it would later feel awkward to renounce. In this period before the First World War party doctrine shows a clearer accommodation with general currents of political thought than seems evident for any other period we have been considering. Where caution floods into the argument is where climate is made the explanatory force for everything that the Liberal party did and where the sheer ballast of heavy, suspicious, intolerant, insensitive, incurious,

[4] FitzRoy diary, 21 July 1906, in Sir Almeric FitzRoy, *Memoirs* (2 vols., 1925), I, 297.
[5] Churchill at Glasgow, 11 October 1906, *Complete Speeches*, I, 675–6.

unadventurous whiggery becomes transformed into helium by the admiration of Liberal historians for Edwardian Radicals. Anyone conscious of the specificity of the period's Liberalism will want to hold Churchill in the mind as a cameo of new thinking in parliamentary politics; but the Churchill of 1910 who saw his Liberalism through the windows of the Admiralty building contributed just as much to the tone of Liberal politics as had the Churchill of Glasgow and Dundee. While recalling Churchill in 1910, recall also his leader, Asquith, and the prime minister's conviction that 'some of our colleagues write and talk too much'. When sharing the Radical Josiah Wedgwood's 'dissatisfaction with the Whiggery of our front bench',[6] recall too the obstinate fact that control and power in the British political system normally lie with those who sit at the front.

In this sense, at least, Campbell-Bannerman certainly kept most of his Radicals behind him. Morley, if he counted any longer as one, had to be brought into the cabinet but found himself placed at the India Office. Bryce came in, less obviously, as Chief Secretary for Ireland until Augustine Birrell replaced him in 1907. But the correspondence between Morley and Bryce hardly implied revolution; it expresses scepticism about radical demands, *a fortiori* in Morley's acute suggestion that there was no point trying to govern the country against the wishes of the middle class.[7] Only one fire-eater reached the cabinet and even he – David Lloyd George – had eaten less of it in recent years out of an attempt to turn himself from a provincial troublemaker into a national focus for democratic enthusiasm and hostility to privilege. Churchill, who shared Lloyd George's sense of strategy, lacked the Welshman's status. His under-secretaryship at the Colonies emphasized his subordination by placing him under the control of one of the party's redoubtable Whigs, the Earl of Elgin. In all the central offices of state, meanwhile, imperialist or whig personnel bulked large: Grey, Crewe, Ripon, Asquith, Haldane. Away from the ministerial benches Radicalism certainly had more purchase though no precision seems possible over its strength. Exactly how many Liberal MPs one ought to count 'Radical' in this parliament depends largely on the generosity of definition; but one historian's identification of at least 25 consistent 'social radicals' offers a basis for argument.[8] The argument remains, however, sharply double-edged. Those parliamentary Radicals would certainly throw a pinch of ginger into Liberal politics and reinforce the need for the leadership to frame intelligent responses to Radical initiatives. On the other hand, 40 out of 400 hardly argues predominance. Added to traditional Radicals in the House, this figure rather allows one to say that the 1906 parliament demonstrated the strength of Radical numbers more effectively than any previous one had done. It can also safely be said that other elements in the Liberal party's make-up continued to exercise a formidable influence and particularly so among the senior echelons whose sociology little reflected the trend.

Theory made, for all its appearance on the platform, little impact on priorities

[6] Asquith and Wedgwood, quoted in R. E. Ellins, 'Aspects of the New Liberalism 1895–1914' (unpub. Ph.D. dissertation, Sheffield, 1980), 325, 394.

[7] See Morley to Bryce, 6 January 1908, quoted in José Harris and Cameron Hazlehurst, 'Campbell-Bannerman as Prime Minister', *History* (1955), 376.

[8] 'The overall impression is of an advanced Social Radical section, rarely less than 25 strong in any division, and drawing on a further body of support which in itself (including the Lib–Labs), may well have exceeded 40. Behind this group ranged a somewhat larger number of Radicals who were prepared to lend support, in the manner of traditional Radicalism, to causes of which they approved. . .'. H. V. Emy, *Liberals, Radicals and Social Politics* (Cambridge, 1973), 187.

during Campbell-Bannerman's government. The divisive effects of imperial argument between 1900 and 1903 had left most Liberals clear that disaster lay along the road of reawakening them. Indeed, foreign affairs in general became Grey's domain and one that he controlled in near-secrecy – a lesson presumably learned from his tutor, Rosebery. But in so far as the attention of the cabinet turned inwards to domestic policy, it began by picking up pieces left by Balfour's government in the fields of trade-union reform and education. It succeeded in reversing the so-called Taff Vale judgement of 1901 that had left union funds liable to claims for damages in the event of the courts deeming a strike 'in restraint of trade' – a popular move and one that the Conservative party decided not seriously to oppose through its poodle in the House of Lords. Education caused more problems. That the Liberal bill, attempting to relieve some of the anxieties of nonconformists about the working of the Balfour Act of 1902, failed in the House of Lords was not a problem. Part of the point of making a fuss about education lay in proving to the electorate that the Lords would behave irresponsibly in throwing out the bill and by so doing contribute to that process of 'filling up the cup' of grievance against the second chamber in which the Liberal party had been engaged since 1892. What hurt was rather that few seemed to care when the bill died. Even Churchill, who plainly held his audience spellbound during his performances in 1906 and 1907, ran into rough weather when he turned to education; he comes across in print as feeling uncomfortable with the subject and anxious to talk about something else.[9]

Campbell-Bannerman himself probably had much to do with the decision to hold back from attacking the Lords at once. His friends knew he was weakening physically and had rather lost his zest. Granted the loss of credibility on the part of this immensely powerful administration by the beginning of 1907, the timidity nevertheless undermined the Liberals' image. 'They said just the same with infinitely more threatening emphasis when the Lords threw out the Home Rule Bill in 1895', Lady Monkswell recalled. 'We smile . . ., and don't feel very much frightened.'[10] If the Liberals had a doctrine with which to frighten the propertied, indeed, it consisted not in their constitutional theories so much as in their fiscal. Yet here too some caution about the role of the abstract makes sense. Asquith's budget of 1907 has rightly attracted the attention of historians interested in the development of fiscal radicalism; and his provision of a surplus in that budget for the later introduction of Old Age Pensions cannot be gainsaid. Yet the swing to direct taxation which the budget helps exemplify followed almost inevitably from the policy position taken on free trade over the past 10 years. Introducing his budget on 18 April 1907, Asquith argued that the resources of taxation '*within Free Trade*'[11] had not yet been exhausted; but the tendency of his provision marks clearly enough the need for the Liberal party to move strongly towards progressive taxation as a necessary development granted that the income from possible tariffs could not enter practical politics. Like Old Age Pensions, the idea presented little novelty to the generation of 1906 because both of these ideas had roots in the 1890s. They suggested, however, a line of attack that promised more room for the exhibition of reforming doctrine than tepid reproaches to the House of Lords.

The hypothesis is often advanced that the radicalization of Liberal theory, however

---

[9] 'Well, the harm is done. the bill is dead. ("Hear, hear," and laughter.)' Churchill at the Free Trade Hall, Manchester, 4 February 1907, *Complete Speeches*, I, 711–13.

[10] Diary, 12 February 1907, in Hon. E. C. F. Collier (ed.), *A Victorian Diarist: later extracts from the journals of Mary, Lady Monkswell 1895–1909* (1946), 171–2. I have reversed the order of the quotations.

[11] Asquith, *Speeches of the Earl of Oxford and Asquith, KG* (n.d. [1927]), 88.

tepid, comprised a reaction to socialism and to the threat of the new Labour party. We can return to the question when considering progressivism as a view of the period, but some cold water can do no harm at this point. The evidence that the governments of Campbell-Bannerman and Asquith worked with one eye on the Labour party is thin and always vulnerable to counter-example. When Asquith referred to unemployment, for instance, the occasion caught a colleague's attention because it was the first time he had heard Asquith mention it. Only by tilting the argument consistently in the direction of optimism, from the point of view of Labour's influence, is it possible to present a coherent account of Labour's growing power. Such accounts allow sceptical readers to play with italics to considerable effect:

> The pressure exerted by the Labour Party also succeeded in severely embarrassing the government *on at least two occasions*, and *one* Liberal minister confessed that the Labour campaign on behalf of the Right to Work Bill *could well* divide the Liberal left from its right. Although *the actual form of the programme which the Liberals introduced in 1909–11 owed little or nothing to the Labour Party's own Bill* . . . the actual fact of the programme was *a tacit recognition* of the success of the Labour propaganda campaign of 1907–8.[12]

Arithmetic offers a cruder guide than such intimations but it has some point in the discussion. A Labour party of about 30 MPs sat in an ocean of 400 Liberals between 1906 and 1910. The imperative to do the bidding of Labour rests on perceptions about the future which many Liberals demonstrably did not hold or on a retrospective reading of possibility from a post-war vantage point conditioned by an environment very different in all its variables from that familiar to an Edwardian administration.

Each of these themes deepened in its intensity during the premiership of Asquith after April 1908. The expected succession, following the collapse of Campbell-Bannerman's health, made a slight difference to the party's orientation: it brought a temporizing, cool-brained lawyer to the centre of Liberal politics but also pulled Lloyd George and Churchill into promotion behind him, since Lloyd George's highly-successful tenure of the Board of Trade landed him the Exchequer and thus made room for Churchill at the cabinet table for the first time. Taken together with 'Loulou' Harcourt's febrile support of pacificist lines of argument and the addition of Herbert Samuel to the cabinet in 1909, an entrenchment of radical Liberalism becomes arguable. The subtraction of 'C-B', on the other hand, often slips the memory when the sums are done; and the vastly-enhanced expectation of centre-right Liberals to a receptive ear demands acknowledgement. Nor should the 'wait and see' legend that found so many thermals in the turbulent atmosphere of the Great War mislead anyone thinking about the years of Asquith's prime. He was a strong man and a formidable enemy.

Doctrine and possibility clashed most manifestly in 1908–9 at the intersection of foreign policy, defence and taxation. That meant Germany, Dreadnoughts and the People's Budget. It meant Grey, Haldane and Lloyd George; it meant the Liberal Foreign Policy Committee, newspapers frothing with invasion rumour; it meant incandescent Admirals and the Committee of Imperial Defence murmuring betrayal, visits to Germany to learn about unemployment benefit, MPs in the smoking room asking who would pay for it all. True, the effervescence died down. Other, more attractive issues came – or were pushed – to centre-stage as the Liberal public had

[12]K. D. Brown, *Labour and Unemployment 1900–1914* (Newton Abbot, 1971), 170.

its attention occupied by the House of Lords and the constitutional crisis in 1910–11, the arson campaign of the Suffragettes, the threatening civil war in Ireland. But the crisis in doctrine had already occurred and perhaps those external attacks masked the tensions within British Liberalism that only the straightjacket of a total war would prevent its practitioners any longer from evading. And throughout the events leading to the Irish imbroglio in the summer of 1914, the essential framework within which policy matured consisted less of fears that the Labour party might rise to a dominating position than of an anxiety that the Conservative party would revive from its reversal of 1906, just as Salisbury had brought it back to life after Gladstone had knocked it down in 1880. A past that contemporaries knew about seems a better starting-point for assessing their ambitions than a future they did not.

Foreign affairs and defence brought with them a most unhelpful past from a Liberal point of view. The problem did not lie in a felt need to develop imperialist policies: indeed the ex-Limps approached their difficulties very flexibly. Saddled with the Naval Defence Act of 1889, that committed them to a sustained programme of capital ship-building, and with Grey's secret conversations with the French two years before, which had committed the government to sending a British army to France in the event of a German attack on her, the Liberal leadership simply sensed itself boxed in. German designs on North Africa and Berlin's determination to win an arms race hardly helped soothe those who worried about the country's ability to defend itself. And that anxiety affected extensive sectors of the public – perhaps for the first time on such a scale because the popular press, particularly Lord Northcliffe's papers, gave it much amplification. So when Radicals threatened to move an amendment to the Address at the beginning of the 1908 session of parliament on the need to reduce naval estimates, ministers took them seriously and took evasive action.

When they failed to escape from the issue for long, the pressure of ministers who wanted a reduction – Lloyd George, Crewe, Harcourt, McKenna, Burns[13] – turned the question by the spring of 1909 into a public debate. What might once have seemed appropriate to a sleepy committee (a technical discussion about whether to lay down four new keels or six) now became a mass jamboree – 'we want eight and we won't wait'[14] – with a more pointed expression by the electors of Croydon who had just made their feelings tell against the Liberal candidate in a by-election. But already one detects a feeling that more than sabre-rattling was at stake. Certainly Grey had come close enough to preparing the Fleet for action to see the issue as more than an exercise in public relations. But the crisis revealed the depth of division in the party. Sir John Brunner's Liberal Foreign Policy Committee had orchestrated resistance to the government's defence estimates in recent years and remained Germanophile in its tendencies. Nor was it at all clear that Asquith himself would go to the stake for more ships. He had written to McKenna during the previous session: 'As you know, I have for a long time been growingly sceptical (in the matter of shipbuilding) as to the whole "Dreadnought" policy. . . . There is much money in it – and more than money.'[15] One is speaking, of course, of a government in which most of the cabinet, not to mention party committees, knew little of Grey's activities until 1911. Meanwhile the Admiralty got its eight.

[13]These ministers at any rate filled the sights of Admiral Fisher: Esher journal, 7 February 1908, in M. V. Brett (ed.), *The Journals and Letters of Reginald Viscount Esher* (4 vols., 1934–8), II, 280–4.
[14]The public controversy is recaptured by A. J. P. Taylor in his short essay 'We Want Eight, and We Won't Wait': see Taylor, *Politics in Wartime* (1964), 53–6.
[15]Asquith to McKenna, 4 July 1908, quoted in S. E. Koss, *Sir John Brunner: radical plutocrat* (1970), 224.

A former Limp, H. H. Fowler, now Lord Wolverhampton, announced an interesting reaction to the naval controversy and at once made the right connexions. 'He rejoiced that the naval controversy had terminated in substantial acceptance of the Admiralty's programme, but took a very gloomy view of the financial situation. He regretted the large surrender of sugar duty in the last budget, which could hardly be made good by playing with tea or any other item of indirect taxation.'[16] The new Chancellor fully appreciated the problem; indeed he had spent part of the previous summer in Germany learning precisely how to finance an extension of the pension system envisaged by Asquith.[17] A combination of state compulsion of individuals to contribute to their own security and more rigorous direct taxation became the theme of Liberal fiscal policy from Lloyd George's radical budget of 1909 through to the introduction of national insurance in 1911, which occasioned another deputation to Germany. Lloyd George's dedication of his budget to The People hardly made the world tremble: most Chancellors make the people their inspiration. Rather, it *became* a people's affair when the Lords unexpectedly threw it out. The balance of current historical opinion falls heavily in favour of Lloyd George's surprise at that rejection and against its forming part of a carefully meditated plan of confrontation. But the greatest empiricist of the twentieth century lost no time in transforming the nature of the discussion to his own advantage. So involved did the electorate become in the politics of privilege that it quite lost sight of how bad a Chancellor Lloyd George was. His budgets raised the heart, certainly, but only into the mouth. Or so it seemed to old-school Liberals brought up on a muzzled state and good currency; they began to speak of 'bastard Liberalism', a left-wing deviation from the political economy etched in their collective mind by Gladstone.[18] Lloyd George continued unabashed, composing his speeches on the golf course and leaving the figures to his clerks. Luckily he saved his biggest financial disaster, the Marconi scandal apart, for the budget of 1914 from which the war, weeks away, rescued him.[19]

Doubtless he would have survived anyway because Lloyd George had an instinct to talk about whatever would win over his audience: friction he took as a warning to change the subject. Yet this translation of economic policy from a potential question-mark about the place of the state within Liberalism into a cap-and-muffler language about justice for those who toiled, is precisely the process that needs comment for it occurs at several other points in the junction of Liberal theory with practice between 1908 and 1914.

The constitutional crisis presents a case in point. Precursors of it had appeared in the Liberal experience for almost 20 years, so the squaring up to the House of Lords

---

[16]FitzRoy diary, 13 February 1909, in *Memoirs*, I, 374.

[17]See Bentley B. Gilbert, 'David Lloyd George: land, the budget, and social reform', *American Historical Review*, 81 (1976), 1060.

[18]For a good example of this sentiment, see the memoirs of Sir Alfred Pease, who had succeeded Gladstone's son Willy as MP for Whitby in 1880. 'It must be confessed that in Victorian times the Liberal Party was an *omnium gatherum* of the fast and the slow, of theorists and practical men, of aristocrats, plutocrats and democrats, but it was a mixture of talents. . . . It was broken up by Asquith, though Harcourt and Campbell-Bannerman ministered to its fall. As Gladstone sealed his fate by taking the Radical Chamberlain into his Cabinet to secure the support of the left, so Asquith sealed his by coalition with Lloyd George and "Limehouse".' *Elections and Recollections* (1932), 41. Pease never forgave Asquith for refusing to speak to him after he left the Liberal party.

[19]'L. G. has had a bad week. His stock stands low with the party. The Budget has been a fiasco.' Riddell diary, 12 July 1914, in Lord Riddell, *More Pages From My Diary* (1934), 218. Lloyd George's eccentricities at the Exchequer infuriated Charles Hobhouse: see Edward David (ed.), *Inside Asquith's Cabinet: from the diaries of Charles Hobhouse* (1977), esp. 73–6.

over its rejection of the 1909 budget came as a culmination of policy, for all the sense of crisis it engendered, as much as a surprising turn of events. By placing a 'safe' Liberal doctrine at the top of the agenda, moreover, it displaced to a lower priority the need to do other things to the constitution. The lack of any explicit *political* (as opposed to social) reform outside the curtailing of the power of the Lords stands, indeed, as one of the oddest absences in the programme of the most powerful Liberal government ever. Neither Campbell-Bannerman nor Asquith extended the franchise to the substantial section of the working class still beyond the pale of the constitution. Neither gave the vote to women. Admittedly, a mild reform bill of 1912 that would have brought the electorate to around the 9-million mark was ruled out by the Speaker of the House of Commons on the ground that an attempt to 'tack' a partial female-suffrage proposal to it altered the fundamental character of the bill. But its loss provoked comparatively few tears, just as the six-year delay in its introduction left behind questions better unasked. The militancy of the Suffragettes similarly helped rather than hindered inaction by making resistance to structural change more popular than risking concessions.

Socialism, another theme, required a rhetorical answer but little else. The Labour party contained many of the most violent opponents of socialism, after all, and would not formally commit itself to a socialist doctrine until the new constitution of 1918. For the moment one could patiently distinguish various species of socialist from one another and keep the discussion clinical. Balfour did not, it is true, keep cool when he lost his seat in 1906 but his acidulated remarks about corks floating on socialist tides lacked realism – a fault rarely found in his uncle. Salisbury had come to terms with socialism in a language that Churchill himself may have used as a model for his Scottish speeches. In 1894 the Conservative leader had announced on a public platform that he could see 'no harm whatever' in using 'the machinery of the State for the purpose of achieving objects in which the community is agreed.' 'There are some things which the State can do better than the individual', Salisbury had said: 'there are some things which the individual can do better than the State: and you must examine each case before you determine that, because it is socialistic, therefore, it is not to be entertained.'[20] An accommodation with socialistic recommendations had become common, that is to say, before the appearance of the Labour party in 1906 and it overstrains the latter's significance to see in Liberal approval of some socialistic ideas some fear of their finding themselves overrun. Not only do simple numbers suggest the unlikelihood of mass panic among the gigantic Liberal majority, but, as Campbell-Bannerman himself had warned Asquith, the Liberals needed specifically to guard against allowing the Labour party the privilege of claiming paternity for Liberal policies, and the best way of doing that lay in *not* paying too much heed to Labour demands.[21]

Extremism of the kind associated with Tom Mann and the syndicalists after 1910 posed no problem unless, as during the coal strike of 1912, the situation became objectively serious by threatening the distribution of a national resource. So far as imagery was concerned Liberals needed only to say that fundamental attacks on property itself (rather than on privilege, monopoly, etc.) struck at the heart of civilization and must meet robust resistance from all parties in the state. Moderation in their opponents presented Liberals with more dangers; but the gentle assumption of a

[20]Salisbury at Edinburgh, 30 October 1894, quoted in John France, 'Personalities and Politics in the formation of the Unionist alliance 1885–95' (unpub. Ph.D. dissertation, Cambridge, 1986), 402.
[21]Campbell-Bannerman to Asquith, 23 January 1906, quoted in Ellins, 'New Liberalism', 348.

centre–left position over welfare and direct taxation promised to leave Labour moderates without an identity except as sponsored spokesmen for the trade unions. For the unions and their representatives the business component of the parliamentary Liberal party doubtless maintained its instinctive dislike. But even beyond that interest-group, among the Liberal intelligentsia for example, there seems little evidence of warmth. Those who took their political economy from Mill found little room in their system for sectional organizations seeking to bend the laws of nature. When Beatrice Webb tried to stir Haldane against the Osborne judgement of 1909, which undermined the ability of the Labour party to draw revenue from individual unionists, she came away convinced that 'he [was] really in favour of it.'[22] The increase of Labour representation – helped by the renewal of the Lib–Lab pact – in 1910 certainly made Liberals take notice. But the Labour party cut a poor figure in by-elections, for all its better showing in some municipal contests; and while such data provides a shaky indication of the potential of Labour, it helps explain why it failed to dominate Liberal thinking. The problem that occupied pride of place among Liberal strategies after 1910 had in fact nothing whatever to do with the Labour party and had been invented partly by the Liberals themselves, partly by Redmond's Irish Nationalists and partly by Bonar Law's Conservatives who wanted to recast political discussion into a more acceptable form than that dominated by tariffs and the House of Lords.

The Liberals had kept Ireland at arm's length since the Parnell disaster. Much remained to be said for keeping it there after 1906. Asquith had made his most sensible remark about the subject in a letter to Herbert Gladstone just before the Liberals came to power. Any commitment to Home Rule, he had said, would bring with it 'incalculable and fatal mischief'.[23] By 1912, on the other hand, his own government had begun to head down that very road with a degree of profit or mischief that the coming of the War largely concealed. The explanation does not lie in doctrine: it begins with the odd logic of events since 1910 and feeds on the problems of the Conservative party. The Liberal party no more wanted Home Rule *per se* in 1912 than it had in 1906. Conditions had simply arisen that made it easier to contemplate it than to try to continue without it.

The two general elections of 1910 fought on the constitutional issue had left the Liberals with their parliamentary majority cut to nothing; they depended on Labour and Irish support. They became attentive for the first time to the wishes of their allies: Labour finally won the payment of MPs in 1911 and the reversal of the Osborne judgement in 1913; the Irish won a Home Rule bill in the aftermath of the constitutional crisis. The association of such a bill with the muzzling of the Lords through the Parliament Act commented on a history that had, since 1893, insisted on the pointlessness of attempting an Irish policy so long as the peers kept their teeth. It had also given the Liberals a plausible excuse for avoiding Ireland. With the electorate bored by the House of Lords and the Liberal party looking fragile once again because of its recent ructions over Grey's foreign policy in general and the Agadir crisis in particular, plus its internal dislocations over state welfare in general and the unpopularity of national insurance in particular, a regrouping around Ireland made more sense than at any point since 1886. A more unfortunate aspect of the Irish difficulty lay, however, in the opportunity it presented to the Conservative party

---

[22]Beatrice to Sidney Webb, 8 October 1910, in Norman Mackenzie (ed.), *The Letters of Sidney and Beatrice Webb* (3 vols., Cambridge, 1978), II, 349.
[23]Asquith to Gladstone, 22 October 1905, quoted in Ellins, 'New Liberalism', 339.

under its new leader, Andrew Bonar Law. For if the Liberals had little pleasant to talk about in 1912, the Conservatives had nothing at all. Impaled on their tariff-reform spike since 1903, they had reached a point of desperation in needing to pull attention elsewhere. They had the Big Navy idea which they had given some stress since the Dreadnoughts crisis of 1909. But the Home Rule bill brought back shades of Lord Randolph Churchill and 'Ulster will fight'. Better still, it did so at just the time when his renegade son sat in a Liberal cabinet.

The sequel forms one of the better-known episodes of twentieth-century history.[24] Conservative leaders used the opprobrium they had thrown on the Parliament Act to demonstrate the need for a Tory street politics in Ulster. They helped foment the newspaper language of 'civil war', 'gun-running', 'mutiny'. Within the Liberal party the Home Rule plan soon looked a botch and it seems likely that Asquith and his advisers underestimated the resistance to blanket Home Rule not only in Ulster or within the ranks of the Conservative party, but also within the Liberal party. The alternative hypothesis − that Asquith knew all along what the response would be and expected to ditch certain elements along the way − looks implausible when those who turned against the imposition of Home Rule included senior and congenial colleagues such as Grey, who told Morley in May 1914 that he would resign unless Ulster were excluded from the arrangement.[25] Pending a full-scale reconstruction of the high politics of 1913−14 in which Ireland could be made to figure as merely one facet in a wider texture of party considerations, we are likely to see more fog than light. But a provisional conclusion points towards Ireland's running out of control as a political instrument at some point in 1913 and assuming a life of its own as an issue − a development that it had been the point of policy to prevent for half a century.

Contemporaries had a fog of their own, not least about whether the Liberals could hope to survive for a third term. The level of optimism inside the Liberal party about that possibility warrants emphasis because historians frequently write the Liberals off long before the actors themselves felt persuaded of the decadence of their politics. Their by-election record since 1910 had, despite some Conservative advances, by no means disgraced them.[26] They had a more confident Labour party to face than in 1910, especially now that the reversal of the Osborne judgement would allow Labour to field more candidates at the next election. But then, the Conservative party was digging trenches for itself in Ulster − holes that could well become electoral graves. Liberal unpopularity over Lloyd George and Rufus Isaacs' involvement in the corruption scandal surrounding the Marconi company in 1913 promised to blow over. Lloyd George had supplied his own breeze for the purpose with a radical land campaign that he intended hawking round the rural constituencies as a sort of Authorized Programme. Welsh disestablishment (for some Liberals more fraught a question than Home Rule) looked set to harness nonconformity to Liberal politics with an adhesion not seen since the Balfour Education Act. None of these possibilities − Ireland, Wales, Land, the Labour party, the next election − held their place in the Liberal consciousness through July 1914 because, within the space of two incredulous weeks, everything changed and changed utterly.

---

[24]For a clear analysis, see A. T. Q. Stewart, *The Ulster Crisis* (1967).
[25]Esher to the King, 22 May 1914, in *Journals and Letters*, III, 167−8.
[26]See P. F. Clarke, 'The electoral position of the Liberal and Labour parties 1910−14', *English Historical Review* 90 (1975), 828−36.

The theory and practice of war 1914 – 18

The Liberals of 1914 had no direct experience of war against other major powers. They had not held office during the Boer War – the only war that most of them would have known – which in any case had taken the form of a mobile operation against guerillas in one of the colonies. They had no memory, unless now in their dotage, of the war in the Crimea against the Russians in 1854–6. Their party contained few military experts but a campful of anti-military philosophers. Their doctrines about war included recommendations about how to avoid one plus elevating thoughts about leaving the fighting, if it happened, to those who knew about such things. They hated conscription as an affront to individual liberty and the symptom of a bloated state. They mistrusted organization as a token of that very Prussianness that many of them had feared since Bismarck had made everyone aware of it. They disliked coalitions with more venom than Disraeli had read into the English character. They believed Norman Angell[27] when he told them that war in advanced capitalist countries would be unprofitable and therefore unthinkable. They shared the country's relief in 1914 that relations with much-abused Germany had never seemed better. They were about to fight the greatest war in the history of man.

Of course all intelligent observers had known since 1907 that the formation of rival diplomatic *blocs* among the powers of Europe had made war more likely. But the tensions and crises associated with that fear had made themselves felt more between 1908 and 1912 than in recent months when public attention had focussed on Ireland. Granted the acceleration of events following the assassination of the heir to the Austrian throne, Archduke Franz Ferdinand, at Sarajevo on 28 June, the Liberal party had no time in which to calm nervous backbenchers, reassure the electorate or negotiate comfortably with senior dissidents determined to keep Britain out of any war on the continent. In these circumstances Asquith did very well to avert a party collapse. He used Grey as a spokesman for high-mindedness in defending the record of the government in its relations with the Germans; but he also benefited from the Radical Pringle's surprising defence of the government's position and even more from Germany's attack on Belgium which could be represented as a great moral issue in a way that treaty obligations to France could not. Only two ministers – Morley and Burns – resigned after all the heart-searching. Armed with a so-called party truce, Asquith and his Liberal party went to war against the Central Powers without a coalition and with the addition of just one alien: General Kitchener, who found himself Minister for War, pointing his finger from walls and bill-boards at every pedestrian and bus.

What contemporaries called 'pacifism' had certainly troubled the Liberal leadership and left them unsure that they could persuade Liberals to take up arms. Yet Liberalism contained only a tiny proportion of true pacifists – understood as persons determined to resist waging war on any grounds whatsoever. Its destabilizing tendencies lay rather in the direction of 'pacificism'[28] with its stress on bringing the maintenance of peace to the top of the political agenda and the framing of proposals to place international relations on a more rational basis in order to render obsolete secretive manoeuvring between the chancelleries of Europe that seemed condemned

[27]Norman Angell, *The Great Illusion: a study of the relation of military power in nations to their economic and social advantage* (1910).
[28]For a working-out of this important distinction, see Martin Ceadel, *Pacifism in Britain 1914–45: the defining of a faith* (Oxford, 1980), *passim*.

out of its own mouth by the events of 1914. This was the sentiment that informed Asquith when, on the eve of the declaration of war, he believed that three-quarters of his own party opposed entry 'at any price'.[29] He exaggerated; but the undertow of feeling against Grey's handling of foreign affairs since 1906 remained a significant current inside the Liberal party and drove many of its younger and more talented members into E. D. Morel's anti-Grey organization, the Union of Democratic Control, which embodied pacificist priorities and acted as an important vehicle for conveying disgusted Liberals in the direction of the Labour party after the war.

The first year of the fighting brought radical changes to the environment which Liberals hoped to control. In order to carry out even minimal organization on the scale demanded by the size of the Western Front and the resources that it already had learned to gobble, Liberal ministers had no alternative to introducing illiberal policies. Censorship plainly came into play at once. The Defence of the Realm Act gave the government powers over the nation's raw materials, labour force and publication of matter related to the war. Most sensitive among possible desecrations of personal liberty remained the threat of conscription; it was first bruited seriously in the summer of 1915 and became the cause of a major ministerial crisis by the end of the year. In September, meanwhile, a new Chancellor of the Exchequer, Reginald McKenna, quietly expunged the commitment to free trade on which Liberal politics had been built for the past decade by introducing protective duties in his budget. All these initiatives hurt Liberals both in the House of Commons and outside. They troubled the intelligentsia who saw at once the implications for positions taken by serious liberal thinkers since the heyday of classical Liberal thought. Images of party Liberals doing what they had always criticized others for doing during the first few months of the war increased their discomfiture and contributed to the dislocation of British Liberalism.

To concentrate on the deeds, however, misses the point. None of these departures need have undermined the credibility of Liberalism, had the government been able, with discrimination and flexibility, to approach them from long range, prepare them, time them, above all talk about them in a carefully-modulated public language. The war's demands and pace gave Liberal politicians no space, no time, no air. Obviously they could speak the language of simple patriotism and call for support on behalf of the war effort, but that vocabulary belonged to the Conservative party whose members spoke it fluently and without effort. If the Liberals tried a language of their own, on the other hand, they sounded apologetic or irresponsible – out of touch with the pulse of the moment. They could not even, if all else failed, talk about something else: they were thus denied the safety net slung under British politicians that frequently protects them from disaster. When strikes had become embarrassing before the war, or the Suffragettes awkward, or Ireland had gone wrong, Liberal politicians could always face the other way and tell the public about the importance of land reform or the welfare state that the party had begun to build. In 1915 all the escape holes were blocked; one subject expunged all others; the government faced one test of success. Sketch maps of the current salient on the Western Front in Northcliffe's sour newspapers and the names of casualties piled in the columns of the local press became the reference points for popular estimation of political leaders and their promises. The Liberal party felt its grip weakening in this atmosphere just as surely as Lloyd George found himself shouted down for the first time in his life when

[29]Asquith to Venetia Stanley, 2 August 1914, quoted in Cameron Hazlehurst, *Politicians at War* (1971), 33.

he tried to quieten the workmen of the Clyde during that miserable spring of 1915.

Division and recrimination began to build within the party and its wider areas of support before the end of 1915. Interestingly, the trouble did not come principally from the Liberal intelligentsia and the party theorists: many of these remained loyal to Asquith's leadership and the prosecution of the war. A pacifistic group of Liberal intellectuals associated with the pre-war 'Bloomsbury group' centred on Leslie Stephen's daughters, their husbands and friends did set up an anti-government commune at Garsington Manor, the home of Lady Ottoline Morrell whose husband, Philip, was a Liberal MP. That society contained some distinguished names around its fringes – Bertrand Russell, D. H. Lawrence and, more incongruously, Maynard Keynes – but it did not typify the reaction of the Liberal intelligentsia seen more broadly. Most Liberal thinkers took an intense interest, certainly, in early moves to set up a post-war 'league of nations' in order to prevent a repetition of what had happened in 1914 – Bryce, Hobson, and Lowes Dickinson all played some part[30] – but only a minority held Grey responsible for the catastrophic turn of events. Some among them shared the impatience felt by other observers at Asquith's dithering, particularly after the formation of a coalition with the other parties in May 1915, but critics like C. P. Scott did not desert the Liberals because of their anxieties. One of the most signal and surprising developments of the inter-war period, indeed, lay precisely in the ability of the Liberal party still to rally impressive intellectual support for its policies long after the return of a Liberal government had ceased to appear a practical possibility.[31] If the Liberals met their death during the war, they did not do so at the hands of their thinkers.

The Conservative party seems a more plausible suspect, especially in the circumstances of coalition. In many ways the war had pulled it back from the edge of a serious blunder in its Irish ambitions. It had provided issues about which Conservatives looked persuasive and effective; it silhouetted the Conservative 'men of push and go' that Lloyd George had come to like. Their vigour hardly accounted for Asquith's mysterious decision to invite the Tory party to join the Liberals in a coalition in 1915. And since Asquith did not tell anyone why he did it, we have no way of knowing for certain what possessed him.[32] Three consequences certainly followed. The Conservative party moved back into government for the first time since 1905 with a determination to consolidate its bridgehead and enhance the position of 'win-the-war' politics at Westminster. Lloyd George, second, shifted from the Exchequer to a specially created Ministry of Munitions to deal with the revelations of scandalous shell shortages at the Front. Instead of proving a disaster there, as Asquith doubtless expected and hoped, he turned his stay at Munitions into a rhetorical triumph with no small material achievement to supplement it. Finally, a process of unsettlement among Liberals – one that the coming of the war had done most to set in motion – found confirmation and encouragement in the capitulation of May 1915. It reflected an awareness that the Liberal party had lost its way in compromises with

[30]See Henry R. Winkler, *The League of Nations Movement in Great Britain 1914–19* (Metuchen, N.J., 1967).
[31]Michael Bentley, *The Liberal Mind 1914–29* (Cambridge, 1977), 160–206, comments on this phenomenon. Cf. Michael Freeden, *Liberalism Divided* (Oxford, 1986), *passim*.
[32]Conspiracy, the need to avoid a general election, and personal crisis connected with the break-up of Asquith's relationship with Venetia Stanley have all figured in the story at various points. See Stephen Koss, 'The Destruction of Britain's Last Liberal Government', *Journal of Modern History* 40 (1968), 257–77; Martin Pugh, 'Asquith, Bonar Law and the First Coalition', *Historical Journal* XVII (1974), 813; Hazlehurst, *Politicians at War*, 235–60.

the evils thrust upon it by the exigencies of total war. It marked the arrival of a frame of mind within Liberalism that its friends and enemies would come to know all too well over the next 20 years: one dominated by the thought that Liberalism must purge itself of the dirtiness of a debased world. Liberalism tore its heart out between 1914 and 1918 in a private agony about true and false Liberals, right and wrong Liberalism; about being staunch and straight, or being like Lloyd George.

Responsibility for so many-faceted a happening as the disintegration of Liberalism in the twentieth century cannot plausibly fall on one pair of shoulders. How often, none the less, survivors of the post-war Liberal generation continue to blame Lloyd George for all the despair of the 1920s. Their allegation has point as well as facility. It implies the degree to which visions of Lloyd George as a personality had become overlain with images of him as embodiment of a certain understanding of Liberalism itself. His switch to a war persona, abandoning in an instant all the language about New Liberalism, began the association. His support for conscription, aided by the Tory Trojan horse after May 1915, strengthened it. The successful introduction and later extension of conscription seemed very much Lloyd George's achievement – or crime. His failure to die with Kitchener on HMS *Hampshire* in June 1916 (Asquith had asked him to stay in England to deal with the aftermath of the Easter Rising in Dublin) had made him unavoidable as Kitchener's successor at the War Office where, over the next six months as the Somme campaign made its sordid comment on the nature of modern warfare, he became unquestioned master of the political situation. Nerves already tautened by the events of the past year tightened still further in the recognition that Lloyd George seemed as unstoppable as he was unpredictable. 'Whatever friendly feelings I may have towards L1.G.,' one Liberal observer wrote on 6 June 1916, the day after Kitchener's death, 'I cannot pretend to be in sympathy with his methods, as I have seen them during the past six months & I am frankly afraid of what he is going to do next.'[33]

What he did next was to place increasing pressure on the leadership of Asquith by insisting on the need to transcend peace-time methods and give the running of war more immediate and frequent direction through a small war cabinet. That proposal remained at the centre of public argument between Lloyd George and his Conservative allies, on the one hand, and the prime minister on the other, until Asquith's ill-conceived resignation in December. The support for Lloyd George inside the Liberal party had little 'new Liberalism' in it: Churchill had left politics temporarily for the Front during the previous year after blame for the Dardanelles campaign in the spring had fallen (inaccurately) on him;[34] and Asquith had appeased Conservative loathing for Churchill by leaving him out of executive office. Radicals who once idolized Lloyd George now saw him as part of the threat to their view of the civilized world. Hard-nosed Liberals on the back-benches, those impatient with metaphysics at a time when the country's youth was suffering the onslaught on the Somme, comprised the main pressure-group thrusting forward the claims of Lloyd George to the premiership. For himself, the trappings of power probably did not much matter. When Lloyd George later said that he had not wanted to become prime minister but only to run the war, he reflected either the rhetorical fog through which he tended to see all events, or a genuine failure to understand that the one would mean the other.

---

[33]Spender to Murray, 6 June 1916, Elibank MSS, Nat. Lib. of Scotland, 8804 f. 26.
[34]Martin Gilbert has demonstrated the degree to which Churchill was made the scapegoat for cabinet decisions: see R. Churchill and M. Gilbert, *Winston S. Churchill* (1966–), III (1977), 188–447.

Those last months of 1916 have left in the historical record too crowded a texture to permit a simple précis.[35] Within the broader conspectus of Liberal history, however, one point at least seems insistent: that when Asquith – tired and bitter over the death of his son at the Front – resigned office in December, mistakenly believing that Lloyd George could not form a government, he made overt the division of British Liberalism into two opposed styles of political practice behind each of which distinct habits of mind and outlook had formed over the past two years. How much significance one wishes in retrospect to invest in this division depends on reactions to a broader interpretative matrix that the final chapter of this book will review. But the fissure never healed. It widened in 1918 when Lloyd George's 'coupon' election convinced 'true' Liberals that the debasement of the world could hardly go further. It closed between clamps when party leaders joined for a few weeks of intolerable togetherness to fight the general election of 1923 as a 'united' party. Thereafter the two factions sprang apart again into a natural, comfortable and secure revulsion from one another. Trivial or fundamental, the separation of parliamentary Liberalism into two irreconcilable poles of argument and leadership left the Liberal mind after 1916 with a split personality whose politics bewildered and amused an inter-war public preoccupied with other things.[36]

For the 'Asquithians' in their wilderness during the latter stages of the war, the Lloyd George coalition government with the Conservatives and Labour had no theory, and made its way without ideas or principles. In fact it had many ideas and enough principle to remain coherent. Intellectual support for Lloyd George's abrasive and decisive style of war leadership appeared in the 'garden suburb' that housed his new secretariat, and thoughtful Liberals such as Lionel Curtis and W. G. S. Adams played a part in presenting his case. Their central principle consisted quite simply of winning the war as fast and completely as possible. When inherited notions from the Liberal past conflicted with that objective they went onto the shelf rather than into the bin: the argument did not say that Liberal principles were bad ones, merely that they lacked appropriateness in these entirely novel conditions where the situation demanded more flexible approaches. Strands of the 'national efficiency' discussion reappeared in a climate that made the perils of 1901 look tame by comparison. Lloyd George's instinctive dislike of 'theology' in politics (despite the Welsh non-conformists' adoration for him) on occasion ran, admittedly, a little further than flexibility; his lying to the House of Commons about starving the Western Front of reinforcements during the critical spring of 1918 when the German offensive had been predicted brooks no denial in face of surviving documentation.[37] But the tenor of his government between 1916 and 1918 depended more on uplifting rhetoric about national purpose than on deception or dirty deals. Within limits, moreover, it achieved its objectives and looked set, indeed, for a long period of peace-time power after the prime minister and Bonar Law collaborated on a 'khaki' election that annihilated the Asquithians as a significant force in British politics and filled the House of Commons with MPs who owed their election to the support of voters convinced that the coalition should continue.

How individual Liberal supporters in the country felt about the political events of

---

[35]Lord Beaverbrook's colourful (and coloured) account in *Politicians and the War 1914–16* (1928), 287–501, should be supplemented by J. M. McEwan, 'The Struggle for Mastery in Britain: Lloyd George versus Asquith, December 1916', *Journal of British Studies* XVIII (1978), 131–56, and McEwan, 'The Press and the Fall of Asquith', *Historical Journal* XXI (1978), 863–83.

[36]For a development of this argument, see my *Liberal Mind, passim.*

[37]Nancy Maurice, *The Maurice Case* (1972) mounts a formidable indictment.

the war defies precise reconstruction. Newspapers remained muted unless, as with Northcliffe's papers, they had the power to act as participants in the news they reported. The party truce squashed open confrontation between the major parties and drove their discussions underground. For all their worries about conscription, the formative agencies in Liberal public opinion retained a strong pro-Asquith bias that may have carried substantial sectors of opinion into the Asquithian camp after 1916. Lloyd George's men did a considerable amount of work after the war in trying to reverse that bias, not least through the *Daily Chronicle*, which he bought, and the *Lloyd George Liberal Magazine*, which often came the closest that Lloyd George had to a party machine. But the impression remains strong that local constituency associations would have clung with some tenacity to Liberal commitments from the pre-war period and strongly mistrusted Lloyd George's behaviour. If they escaped the nausea felt among Asquith's close colleagues at the events of December 1916 – 'the smell of bilewater strikes up through everything'[38] – it seems likely that the image of Lloyd George's takeover in the minds of ordinary Liberals frequently did him harm.

A cross-current of great importance in Liberal thinking had meanwhile gathered strength. Not only had the war thrust the Conservative party back towards the centre of power at Westminster but it had also pulled the Labour party closer than ever before to the inner workings of high politics. Whether the Labour party would have cut a compelling figure in a 1915 election we cannot say. What cannot be gainsaid is that the first coalition of May 1915 brought Labour into minor office when Arthur Henderson became Paymaster-General without a cabinet seat. In 1916, moreover, Lloyd George's peculiar position as a renegade from the majority persuasion of his own party made the support of the Labour party crucial to his success in forming a government. And although the introduction of Henderson into the war cabinet ended in the embarrassment of Henderson's humiliating dismissal in 1917, Labour had had its first taste of office and an introduction to its traumas. The trauma surrounding Henderson's removal had, moreover, a still darker side for the other parties. The first Russian Revolution of Kerensky comprised its essential context and the second of Lenin lay weeks away. With the coming of the Bolshevik state, a new framework imposed itself at once on the nature of political language in Britain – one which would prove deeply unfavourable to the promulgation of a Liberal message that did not sound like a diluted version of Conservatism or a dangerous dalliance with Communism. The thought that Lenin killed British Liberalism is to this extent less flamboyant than it may appear. The Left suddenly found itself, and independently of the Labour party of Henderson and Snowden, a leading preoccupation and difficulty for Liberals.

It appears clear that Liberalism in Britain underwent major alteration during the war. Practice and theory went lame simultaneously: they always do. But thereafter the time-scales, seen in a long-term perspective, lose their synchronology. Liberal practice barely survived the war. Its practitioners fell at the first post-war hurdle, the coupon election of 1918. 'It then received a blow', Asquith wrote of his party just before his death in 1928, 'from which it has never since recovered.'[39] Perhaps it could not have recovered anyway. Most of the remarks left in the letters and diaries of Liberals after 1916 suggest that line of thought. Whatever the future might have held, the Liberal party never held office again, unless one counts the Coalition Liberals who tied themselves to Lloyd George's coalition between 1918 and 1922 or the few

[38]Vaughan Nash to Runciman, 22 December 1916, Univ. of Newcastle, Runciman MSS.
[39]H. H. Asquith, *Memories and Reflections* (2 vols., 1928), II, 172.

individuals who found places in the National Government of 1931 or Churchill's wartime Coalition. Theory, on the other hand, did not die; it attenuated and corrupted its own nature like an isotope. Liberal theorists irradiated the political discussions of the 1920s and 30s with their preaching over free trade, internationalism, state planning, unemployment, deficit finance and all the petty incidents and occasions where doctrine could find a hook. They claimed paternity for the new Liberal politics of the 1940s and drew lines of continuity between the Second World War and the First. Nor has the work stopped. Since 1945 the Liberal intelligentsia have become the custodians of conventional wisdom in Britain for all their lack of political power. The complicated process through which this happened has not been the subject of this book. Yet it remains the case that Liberal historians, long after the nineteenth-century Liberal party had gone to ashes, have helped perpetuate its mythologies and presuppositions. They have also stimulated intense opposition from commentators who see different images in the Liberal experience. We should not conclude this brief survey of Liberal theory and practice without acknowledging the presence of these moods and the interpretative frame in which the Liberal past has undergone revision and transformation.

8

Arguments

Fifty years of radical change have produced more than three arguments among their historians. In discussing so small a sample from among a wide selection of contemporary discussions, the intention lies not at all in narrowing the scope of interesting problems worth the attention of readers drawn to the period. Rather, the purpose consists in sketching three intertwined strands of historical writing that seem to find their way into most treatments of Liberal politics. Interpretative problems posed by Gladstone, by the status of progressive Liberalism before 1914, and by the ultimate collapse of the Liberal party, provide no more than a point of departure for thinking about the many issues and themes that have figured in this book. But no over-arching sense of Liberal politics is likely to present itself to a student of the period until highly-contentious sectors of the discussion come under review. Positions taken about these three elements together supply a posture which comes close to predetermining how one will respond to everything else.

Gladstone

Argument about Gladstone turns on a number of key episodes in a political career of numbing length. But those arguments, whatever their thrust, rest ultimately on images of him as a human or spiritual being; and the images have their own history, rather like a series of fading photographs. Gladstone himself began the portraiture. He wrote a *Chapter of Autobiography* in mid-career, but the grand autobiography intended to cover his entire working life never happened: he ran out of years. Following his resignation in 1894, however, Gladstone jotted down a few fragments about his later political activities[1] and commented in particular on the obsession of his later life – his 'conversion' to the Irish cause. Inevitably, these recollections pulled the past into the present in a very direct way and implied a level of consistency and direction in Gladstone's career that a reading of his earlier material has led some

---

[1] These fragments were used by successive scholars working on the Gladstone MSS but were brought together only as late as 1971. See Historical Manuscripts Commission, *The Prime Minister's Papers: W. E. Gladstone* (4 vols., 1971–81), esp. I, 96–139.

historians to judge implausible. There is that cloud in the west, that coming storm; then there is his mission to pacify Ireland; then there grows from the 1870s a conviction that the wrongs of Ireland have to be righted; and eventually Home Rule appears as the painful but inevitable logical conclusion. Gladstone's image of himself during the 1870s and 1880s obviously deserves attention and respect. Yet it seems reasonable to remind oneself that a man in his eighties was arranging his affairs: recomposing the past as a personal testimony in face of death and fear of God. The process invites self-deception as surely as it banishes lies.

During those last years, quiet except for Gladstone's hurtling out of retirement to abuse the Turks again for their crimes against the Armenians in 1896, John Morley stood among the old man's closest allies. He had supported the Home Rule idea against the more imperial Liberals in cabinet and within the party. He had a history of intellectual involvement and political engagement that rivalled Gladstone's in its breadth. That the family should have asked him to write the predictable 'official' biography when Gladstone died in 1898 nevertheless struck many people as more than strange. Certainly he held immediate memories of the period spent working with Gladstone since the early 1880s, 'the recollections of our unbroken sympathy in great tasks, the well-remembered voice, his gestures, traits of manner, the flash from his falcon eye'.[2] But Morley also possessed the greatest possible disqualification for a biographer of Gladstone. He was a self-confessed atheist. The family, indeed, tried to keep from him any knowledge of the diary that Gladstone had written virtually every day of his mature life; they then, having failed in that, left Morley in no doubt that they did not wish him to write about the religious element at all except when it came into the political story.[3] Most biographers would perhaps have disengaged themselves at this point. But Morley's vision of the book he wanted to write had more to do with political evangelism than theology. His two researchers – Francis Hirst and W. T. Stead – had cut their teeth in Liberal journalism and doubtless they also approached the mass of material at Hawarden with mental priorities rather different from their subject's.

The work began in 1899 and took four years. When the three volumes appeared in October 1903 (within weeks of G. E. Moore's highly influential *Principia Ethica*), they sold sensationally: 30,000 in the first year, 130,000 in the first decade. And, for all its sense of *parti pris*, Morley's thousand-page tribute amounted to more than 'an extended political pamphlet'[4] because it helped form the consciousness of an entire generation in its image of Gladstone. That image placed personal character at the centre of explanation of Gladstone's politics; and the character can be guessed from among the attributes in Morley's index: considerateness, co-operation, deference to colleagues, disregard of appearances, idealism, imagination, missionary temper, modesty, reserve, scrupulosity, self-control, self-distrust, simplicity, sincerity, tenacity of purpose. At the outset one feels that Gladstone is not merely on the side of the angels but occasionally flies with them. During the writing of the *Life*, indeed, Morley unveiled a statue of Gladstone at Manchester and allowed himself a moment of explicit valediction:

He had in his soul a vision high in the heavens of the flash of an uplifted sword and the

[2] John Morley, *Recollections* (2 vols., 1917), II, 92.
[3] See M. R. D. Foot, 'The Gladstone Diaries', in Peter J. Jagger (ed.), *Gladstone, Politics and Religion: a collection of Founder's Day lectures delivered at St. Deiniol's Library, Hawarden, 1967–83* (1985), 28. Gladstone himself had actually shown Morley one of the volumes of his diary.
[4] Foot, 'The Gladstone Diaries', 29.

gleam of the arm of the avenging angel. The thought with which he rose in the morning and went to rest at night was of the universe as a sublime moral theatre, in which an omnipotent Dramaturgist uses kingdoms and rulers, laws and policies, to exhibit sovereign purposes for good. This was the thought that lighted up the prose of politics with a ray from the diviner mind, and exalted his ephemeral discourse into a sort of visible relation with the counsels of all time.[5]

In the *Life* Gladstone spends more time on the ground as the letters and diary-entries gently pass by, substantiating the great man's thoughts on issues and crises of the moment. But the larger perspective suffuses the whole for the Dramaturgist is, of course, Morley himself. He breaks occasionally for soliloquy, deepening the character of his hero to prepare the reader for the next paradox in his behaviour.

It is curious that some of the things that made men suspicious, were in fact the liveliest tokens of his sincerity and simplicity. With all his power of political imagination, yet his mind was an intensely literal mind. He did not look at an act or a decision from the point of view at which it might be regarded by other people. . . . Is the given end right, he seemed to ask; what are the surest means; are the means as right as the end, as right as they are sure? But right − on strict and literal construction.[6]

Or there might be an anecdote to underpin scepticism for any suggestion of a political nature in Gladstone. Prime Minister four times he may have been; but Morley found in Gladstone no ambition. Neither did Gladstone.

Once in a conversation with Mr. Gladstone, some fifty years from the epoch of the present chapter, we fell upon the topic of ambition. 'Well,' he said, 'I do not think that I can tax myself in my own life with ever having been moved much by ambition.' The remark so astonished me that, as he afterwards playfully reported to a friend, I almost jumped up from my chair. We shall soon reach a stage in his career when both remark and surprise may explain themselves. We shall see that if ambition means love of power or fame for the sake of glitter, decoration, external renown, or even dominion and authority on their own account . . . then his view of himself was just. I think he had none of it. Ambition in a better sense, the motion of resolute and potent genius to use strength for the purposes of strength, to clear the path, dash obstacles aside, force good causes forward − such a quality as that is the very law of the being of a personality so vigorous, intrepid, confident, and capable as his.[7]

This is Gladstone as Great Liberal and the image dominated Gladstonian historiography until at least the beginning of the Second World War. Ensor's volume in the Oxford History of England (still often to be found on the shelves of school libraries) retained in the 1930s much of the flavour of Morley's approach to Gladstone, though it criticized Morley's documentation of the Irish crisis. J. L. Hammond, male partner in the famous marriage of historians that produced books on *The Town Labourer* and *The Village Labourer*, wrote a long study of Gladstone and the Irish Nation (1938) that again preserved much of the same imprimatur, conceiving Gladstone as 'the largest-minded man of his age'[8] and presenting the emergence of Gladstone's concern with Irish liberation in a rather linear and unproblematic way as

---

[5] Morley at Manchester in 1901, *Recollections*, II, 93–4.
[6] John Morley, *Life of Gladstone* (3 vols., 1903, 1907 edn), II, 780.
[7] Morley, *Gladstone*, I, 217–18.
[8] Hammond, *Gladstone and the Irish Nation* (1938), 724.

Morley had done. A change of emphasis among Gladstonian historians became evident, however, over the next 20 years or so. None of the early historians of the late nineteenth century knew anything of totalitarianism and the power of ideology. Nor were any of them especially interested in the history of Germany. The next generation had no way of avoiding the first and became understandably obsessed with the second. Hammond was, it is true, already 66 years' old when his book appeared in the year of Munich. But parallels and contrasts must have occurred to him between the age of his hero and that of Neville Chamberlain. 'I remember Herbert Paul saying at a very foul moment in the Boer War "I wd rather be a Hottentot than an Englishman at this moment" ', Hammond wrote privately in March 1939. 'N. C. is driving all decent minded people to feel like that.'[9] Hitler had already helped Gladstone enlarge into a Buddha for the decent-minded.

The German dimension became something of a theme among Gladstonian scholars. Erich Eyck's life of Gladstone[10] appeared in English in the same year as Hammond's book and a recent analyst of Gladstone's politics, E. J. Feuchtwanger,[11] continues the tradition whereby a historian of Germany turns to Gladstone. Agatha Ramm,[12] a brilliant editor of Gladstone's correspondence with Granville, made her historical reputation in the field of German history. Two of the most influential Gladstonian interpreters of the post-war period – M. R. D. Foot[13] and Philip Magnus (Sir Philip Magnus-Allcroft)[14] – carried out their early work against a background of distinguished war careers. Foot had won the *Croix de Guerre* for his war service and later became the historian of the Special Operations Executive. Magnus served with the Royal Artillery and in Intelligence. His life of Gladstone that appeared in 1954, and which is still often the basis of school and university essays, was completed in the atmosphere created by Alan Bullock's widely read study of Hitler and actually comments on the *liaison dangereuse* between charisma of the kind created by Gladstone and the form manufactured by Hitler. What breaks the connexion is Gladstone's religion and the ultimate rule of the divine:

> Behind the luxury and pride which capitalist industry had generated, behind Bismarck's ruthless concentration and use of force, behind the growing and almost universal demand for increased material satisfactions, Gladstone glimpsed monstrous shadow-shapes which convulsed his imagination. The full measure of the twentieth century's shame was concealed from him. He did not foresee extermination camps; he did not foresee the enslavement of a vast portion of the human race to a non-Christian creed which denies integrity to the individual conscience and personality; but he fought to the

---

[9] Hammond to Murray, 4 March 1939, quoted in Peter Clarke, *Liberals and Social Democrats* (Cambridge, 1978), 280.

[10] Erich Eyck, *Gladstone* (Zurich, 1938); *Bismarck after Fifty Years* (1948); *Bismarck and the German Empire* (1950); *A History of the Weimar Republic* (1962); *The Frankfurt Parliament 1848–9* (1968); etc.

[11] E. J. Feuchtwanger, *Disraeli, Democracy and the Tory Party* (Oxford, 1969); *Prussia: myth and reality* (1970); (ed.), *Upheaval and Continuity: a century of German history* (1973); *Gladstone* (1975); *Democracy and Empire: Britain 1865–1914* (1985); etc.

[12] Agatha Ramm, *Europe in the Nineteenth and Twentieth Centuries* (1952); *Germany 1789–1919: a political history* (1967); *Sir Robert Morier: envoy and ambassador in the age of imperialism 1876–93* (Oxford, 1973); etc.

[13] M. R. D. Foot and J. L. Le B. Hammond, *Gladstone and Liberalism* (1952); *British Foreign Policy since 1898* (1956); *Men in Uniform* (1961); intro. to Hammond, *Gladstone and the Irish Nation* (new edn, 1964); *SOE in France* (1966); (ed.), *War and Society* (1973); *Resistance: an analysis of European resistance to Nazism 1940–45* (1976); etc.

[14] Philip Magnus, *Edmund Burke* (1939); *Sir Walter Raleigh* (1952); *Kitchener: portrait of an imperialist* (1958); *King Edward the Seventh* (1964); etc.

last against the tendency to replace the worship of God by that of Caesar or any species of idolatry.[15]

Post-war Gladstones have a good deal of this X-ray vision. His groans over the degeneracy of the present soon become intimations of terrible things to come. He also becomes less Liberal in the sense that the party has a diminished status in these books beyond that of instrument.[16] Those writing about him become less Liberal too, though the uniting of the names of Foot and the now-dead Hammond in their study of *Liberalism* (1952) offered a link with the previous generation. But a more important distinction can be drawn about the source-materials used in the newer historiography. The post-war generation became singularly interested in the diary as a key to Gladstone's politics.

The editing and publication of Gladstone's diary has proved an enormous task. A first volume appeared in 1968 and by time of writing another eight have followed, bringing the story down to 1880.[17] Obvious claims can be made for this vast document as a primary source: its immediacy and authenticity carry a power that make it irresistible in certain areas, especially those concerned with Gladstone's family and with his spiritual searching. The most recent biography closely reflects this modern attention to the diary[18] and no serious student of Gladstone's politics can escape a confrontation with the exercise books that Gladstone usually had in his pocket and which he wrote up every night. What comes out of them? First, the overwhelming presence of tangible religion is startling. It begins virtually each entry: 'Ch. $8\frac{1}{2}$.' – Church at 8.30 or 8.45, for Holy Communion. It informs the devotional and sophisticated theological reading in French, German and Italian. It dominates the treatment of his family – a frequent recurrence in the diary's preoccupations. When the two enthusiasms ran together, as when Gladstone's sister Helen became a Roman Catholic, passion reached its peak.[19] The diary also reveals fascinating details of how its author spent, measured, accounted for every moment of his day, retrieved in the evening as though he were recalling a railway timetable. And because every political crisis of Gladstone's career finds some reflection in this busy document, the temptation becomes omnipresent to use the diary in order to *legislate* for historical interpretation by making every retrospective view pass a test of congruence with its text.

Just as the mood of post-war commentators can be reformulated in retrospect, so a more contemporary climate of criticism plainly shows the impact of the post-war world in which popular expectation of politicians has undergone significant shifts. By 1970 the insistence on the predominance of 'mission' in Gladstone had come under considerable scrutiny, not least in the work of John Vincent and Maurice Cowling.[20]

---

[15] Magnus, *Gladstone: a biography* (1954; paperback edn, 1963), 444–5.
[16] Both Foot and Feuchtwanger, for example, have stressed the Tory persona behind Gladstone's Liberalism.
[17] M. R. D. Foot and H. C. G. Matthew (eds.), *The Gladstone Diaries* (Oxford, 1968–).
[18] Richard Shannon, *Gladstone* (vol. I, 1982).
[19] For Helen, see *Diaries*, 31 May and 11 June 1842, III, 202, 205–6. The concern Gladstone felt over the business prospects of his son Harry sent his mind back to the family's financial collapse for an event of equal proportions; see esp. entry for 25 November 1875, IX, 83.
[20] John Vincent, *The Formation of the Liberal Party 1857–68* (1966); *Pollbooks: how Victorians voted* (1967); A. B. Cooke and J. Vincent, *The Governing Passion: cabinet government and party politics 1885–6* (Brighton, 1974); (ed.), *Derby, Disraeli and the Conservative Party* (Hassocks, 1978); (ed.), *The Crawford Papers* (Manchester, 1984); etc. For Maurice Cowling, see his *1867: Disraeli, Gladstone and Revolution*

Two aspects of that work are relevant here: its scepticism in face of the claim that politics comprise a direct outcome of belief and conviction; and a method of treating archival documents as the deposit of a group awareness among politicians rather than as the record of individual minds. Politics became seen, that is to say, as a collective mode of behaviour in which the activities of individuals became a response to those of others working inside a common system. This view places the diary under an interesting and unusual light. It silhouettes the degree to which it is silent, for example, about people other than Gladstone and his immediate family. 'Saw' is the operative verb for all of them: 'Saw Ld Northbrook'; 'Saw Russell'; 'Saw Duke of Argyll'. The substance of all this seeing lies in remote archives and other diaries which are therefore no less relevant to the Gladstonian story. Awarding Gladstone's diary the accolade of prime testimony leaves the history of Gladstone to Gladstone. It cuts out of consciousness the ways in which others viewed and dealt with him and thus shaped events. It also assumes that Gladstone's conversation with his inner essence (for such is the function of the diary) comprises the central material for a history of Liberalism – at best a dubious claim and at worst a serious distortion.

Modern readers face, then, an encounter with at least three Gladstones. The early creation renders Liberalism the reflection of a single great personality committed to the cause of freedom. The second makes Gladstonian politics merely the instrument – sometimes a rejected one – of an all-encompassing religiosity for which the diary supplies irrefutable evidence. The third emphasizes that Gladstone was a highly-successful Victorian politician who attained his objectives inside a complicated world of relationships that he could not control by himself and from whose members he differed more in the sublimities of his soul than the springs of his action.[21]

Beyond informing the general impression of Gladstonian Liberalism that historians compose, these images also come into play in sharpening argument over particular moments and events. Gladstone's mid-career and later years supply a number of such instances but perhaps they may be grouped into three categories: the nature of Gladstonian radicalism; the character of Gladstone's Irish commitment; and the legacy he bequeathed to the party at his final retirement in 1894.

That Gladstone set off down a radical path in 1868 seems clear enough: he was no longer the unreconstructed Peelite of the 1840s nor the mild reformer who had protruded at various times since then from beneath an impeccable Tory façade. When and why that transformation took place comprises the core of one recent argument. By seeing his politics and theology as a unified world it is possible to argue for the 1840s as a plausible threshold for the emergence of a new Gladstone – one seared by the catastrophe of his sister Helen's defection to Rome, one enlightened by God's manifest interference in human affairs through the horror of the Irish famine. Politics becomes the place where God's will is worked out and where Gladstone's role

---

(Cambridge, 1967); *The Impact of Labour 1920–24* (Cambridge, 1971); *The Impact of Hitler* (1975); *Religion and Public Doctrine in Modern England* (Cambridge, 1980–); etc.

[21] Cf. the view of Cooke and Vincent about Gladstone's view on Ireland in 1885–6. 'What has tended to escape notice about Gladstone, because he was an obviously charismatic figure, is how similar his views were to those of other people . . . . He was not a holder of extreme and unusual opinions, but above all a participant in an unusually wide consensus that there was no alternative between home rule and coercion. . . . There was nothing peculiar in Gladstone's behaviour except the long uncertainty about whether he would adopt home rule as a *sine qua non*, an uncertainty which suggests that, rather than be guided by any very strong personal views, he left his policies to be formed by the political situation as it developed.' Cooke and Vincent, *The Governing Passion*, 51–2.

as amanuensis has to undergo radical reconstruction.[22] But one can also situate the change in a less private setting. In 1867 Gladstone received his greatest political setback of the decade after his tepid and weak conduct of the Liberal reform bill in 1866 had led to the ousting of Russell's Liberal government and the decline of Gladstone's parliamentary reputation to its lowest point ever. Disraeli used the opportunity, as everyone knows, to push through his own reform bill which turned out more radical in its provisions than anyone in the government had intended. Is it accidental that Gladstone's most radical phase followed immediately after this object-lesson in parliamentary management? It seems to the present writer that the shift from Mr Gladstone to the People's William has much to do with the immediate impact of the events of 1866–7 as well as reflecting broader sea-changes in personal belief.[23]

In one sense that radicalism stands in marked contrast to the ambitions of dull Whigs and Adullamites who wanted the party to remain in a Palmerstonian mould. But we have seen that stringent limits circumscribed its willingness to subvert previous forms of Liberalism. An important segment of argument over radicalism thus becomes concerned with the status of radical politics within the wider Gladstonian party through the 1870s and the first half of the 1880s. Numbers affect the argument to no small degree: it is consequential that historians nowadays come up with a figure for the parliamentary Radicals that considerably exceeds, and on occasion doubles, those current in contemporary estimates. They do so on the basis of computer analyses of Houses of Commons division lists – defining 'Radicals' by the composition of particular voting blocs in the House.[24] How persuasive one finds this approach depends only partly on assumptions about computation and far more heavily on positions taken about what can be learned from division lists. So far as Gladstone's own perceptions are concerned, it seems clear that he gave one form of radicalism – the sort of moralizing protest against Iniquity embodied in John Bright – disproportionate attention and failed to assimilate the Birmingham variant of aggressive populism associated with Chamberlain and Collings. That failure (more properly, that decision) comments on the kind of 'Radical' that Gladstone intended to be and the formula for advance that he wanted to compose for the post-Whig politics of the 1870s.

Historical argument about Gladstone through that decade centres on the nature and relevance of his formula. One reading of him draws a straight line from the disestablishment of the Irish Church to Home Rule, running through the Irish Land Act of 1870, the liberating legislation of 1871–2, the Bulgarian crusade and Midlothian. The diary in particular allows a reading of this kind. Gladstone's radicalism becomes wider still and wider as the years pass and patience thins. An alternative perspective reveals more reticence than rampancy and a more ragged itinerary among Gladstone's wanderings through the 1870s. His natural inclinations over Irish land had to be stifled; he stifled them. His private hopes for the role of the Church in education had to go; they went. When Bright became too openly demotic in his speeches, he had to be squashed; Gladstone squashed him. His priority, on this

[22] Boyd Hilton, 'Gladstone's Theological Politics', in Michael Bentley and John Stevenson (eds.), *High and Low Politics in Modern Britain* (Oxford, 1983), 28–57; cf. Perry Butler, *Gladstone: Church, State and Tractarianism: a study of his religious ideas and attitudes, 1809–59* (Oxford, 1982).
[23] See Michael Bentley, *Politics Without Democracy: perception and preoccupation in British government* (1984), 203–19.
[24] For one quantitative procedure, see Thomas W. Heyck, *The Dimensions of British Radicalism: the case of Ireland, 1874–95* (Urbana, Ill., 1974).

reading, lay not in pressing forward radical solutions to great issues but rather in finding acceptable ways of achieving a sense of purpose and moral uplift without damaging the fabric that he had spent his mature life helping to knit. It was a radicalism of language, a platform revolution. Bulgaria fits that bill as well as simpler ones. The diary has Gladstone propped up in bed, 'called away' from his studies by lumbago and the crisis in the Balkans, scribbling at *The Bulgarian Horrors* which would once again infuse life into the Liberal castigation of Beaconsfieldism.[25] But the diary cannot say what Gladstone was *not* doing. It offers little clue to the lateness of his entry into a campaign that others had initiated.[26] Neither does it comment on the strategy for the Liberal party that presumably played some part in Gladstone's involvement.

That Gladstone continued his involvement with the Liberal party brooks no argument. He did not resign his seat; he still played a role, albeit a more distant one, in party strategy. Not that the resignation of 1875 appears in retrospect as a tactical ploy. It does not create the interpretative difficulty that (say) Harold Wilson's sudden departure was to raise a century later. More important, one cannot situate it in the same *milieu*. The sense of remove between then and now raises instead special problems of its own and 'highlights', according to the diary's editor, 'the danger of trying to extrapolate from a fundamentally religious mind those features of Gladstone's opinions, writngs, and actions which fit the categories of twentieth-century secularism.'[27] Yet the reality of the danger and the validity of the comment do not make Gladstone's success as a political operator go away. (One sometimes thinks that historical life would have become less demanding if Gladstone had proved as much a party failure as Peel, or at least had fallen off his horse while young.) As it is, we are left with the return over Bulgaria, the acclaim at Midlothian and the significance of this renewed trajectory for the future of Liberal politics. And all of this provokes further argument.

Ireland naturally supplies the location for no small part of it. Every student of Gladstone knows that his mission was to pacify Ireland. But few of them know where and when the Liberal leader made this famous remark. It was said in private to Evelyn Ashley on 1 December 1868 in the park at Hawarden, half-way through chopping down a tree, 'resting on the handle of his axe, . . . with deep earnestness in his voice and with great intensity in his face.'[28] So there is authenticity. But the words were said with blood tingling, partly from his summons by the Queen to form his first government, partly from hacking at the tree. They were uttered as a passionate prophecy rather than as a statement of policy or even of any clear intention. The ambiguity of Gladstone's *public* performance over the next 15 years helps the argument to bifurcate. One view sees disestablishment (1869), Irish land (1870 and 1881) and Home Rule (1885–6) as the natural progression from this private

---

[25] 'Kept my bed till four & made tolerable play in writing on Bugarian Horrors: the back is less strained in bed, where I write against the legs.' *Diary*, 31 August 1876, IX, 151. He had begun writing the pamphlet on 28 August.

[26] For this aspect of the situation, see R. T. Shannon *Gladstone and the Bulgarian Agitation, 1876* (1963).

[27] Colin Matthew in his introduction to *The Gladstone Diaries*, IX, xxxii–xxxiii.

[28] Hammond, *Gladstone and the Irish Nation*, 81. Hammond's account follows Morley's which in turn rests on Ashley's recollection of the incident published in the *National Review* 30 years later. Curiously, the diary makes no mention of either the tree or the affirmation. Evelyn Ashley is mentioned in the entry for the previous day; but 1 December has only the unhelpful 'Saw divers'. Ashley's memory may conceivably have fused together separate incidents: certainly the diary makes space for a tree during the previous day. 'Overwhelmed with letters. Not much possible. An hour out in aftn.' *Diaries*, VI, 640–1.

commitment, reinforced by diary entries in the interim.[29] Where Gladstone shrinks from radicalism, in this light, he does so out of necessary compromise in order to do limited good rather than none. An alternative persuasion has churned the field of study in recent years, however, and presented Gladstone-on-Ireland from a very different angle. Here the argument starts from action rather than private intention. It reports that Gladstone, for all his self-appointed mission, only went to Ireland once, in the autumn of 1877, to see conditions for himself. It dwells on the degree to which Gladstone, rather than impose a policy, constructed one out of the sentiments of those around him. It emphasizes, not so much a sense of crusade in 1885, as a groping forward towards a policy that would both quieten the Irish and resurrect a sense of Liberal identity at home:

> Gladstone did not in fact enter upon home rule in a state of incandescence. He did not have Parnellites to dinner: indeed, with one or two possible secret exceptions, he refused point blank to meet them socially or politically. His recorded conversation at the time shows no trace of good feeling toward them, and suspicion of their motives which readily turned to disparagement. He barely preferred them, politically or personally, to Chamberlain. His entry towards home rule had no happy or generous note about it. He was not buoyed up and in high spirits, as Peel had been in December 1845, by the knowledge that there was great work to be shaped. There was, in 1886, no union of hearts. From Gladstone's own point of view, the home rule fiasco is to be seen not as a tragic failure to achieve a potentially excellent settlement in Ireland, but as a not at all ineffective means of preventing that dire worsening of the situation over there which he had half convinced himself was imminent in January 1886. . . . Conventional accounts written in the shadow of party warfare entirely fail to convey how much Gladstone in 1886 was a sane, balanced, good-humoured but old-fashioned gentleman whose life contained much more private pleasure than public anguish.[30]

The mention of Joseph Chamberlain takes us close to the core of this argument. Gladstone wanted to retire: every source and school of thought concurs that withdrawal to private life constituted a prime objective for him. But he wanted to leave the party in safe hands. Hartington had been groomed for that task. True, he was a Whig and a very rich one. Yet once his interest had been roused – always a challenging task – he behaved in a level-headed way and could be relied on to steer a line marked by non-reactionary common sense, a commitment to party unity and a stolid hostility to hotheads. Chamberlain was a hothead; or so Gladstone thought. Worse, he displayed ambition of a worrying kind. The last outcome wanted by Gladstone was a Liberal party fallen into the hands of Chamberlain and his Birmingham cronies with a public commitment to social reform that would need, by its very nature, to make illegitimate use of the state – a sort of creeping municipal socialism carrying out on behalf of Liberalism proposals so far recommended only by the Fabian Society, the Social Democratic Federation and a collection of disreputable German intellectuals. Ireland can be bracketed within this situation as both a problem and an opportunity. Leading the party back to 1868 and the politics of moral effervescence would reassert the Liberalism in which Gladstone believed; it would

---

[29] For defences of the role of radical ideology in Gladstone's behaviour, see E. D. Steele, *Irish Land and British politics: tenant-right and nationality 1865–70* (Cambridge, 1974); and Michael Barker, *Gladstone and Radicalism: the reconstruction of the Liberal Party in Britain 1885–94* (Brighton, 1975).
[30] Cooke and Vincent, *The Governing Passion*, 53–4. Since its publication this book has provoked a discussion marked by considerable violence and occasional derangement. Its contentions and evidence remain crucial reading for any serious student of the period.

crush the unpleasant and 'unauthorized' Liberalism of Chamberlain in which he, Gladstone, emphatically did not believe; it would enable him to be piped ashore while the cabin boys remained in the cabin where they belonged.

These arguments interfere seriously with the question of Liberalism's health when Gladstone finally resigned in 1894. What kind of party did he bequeath? From one point of view it appears rejuvenated by the commitment to Irish liberty. Certainly the fissure of 1886 had given rise to great pain and difficulty; it had meant losing old friends and valuable supporters in the remnant of the Whig faction, apart from a few families; more significantly, it had led to the loss of much social-reform radicalism. On the other hand, the number of parliamentary defections remained comparatively small, as we have seen. Looking forward, moreover, it does not seem fanciful to see in the departure of Chamberlain one of the more promising incidents in the history of recent Liberal politics. Consider his later career. Having helped tear the Liberal party apart in 1886 he went on to shatter the Conservative party with his tariff reform programme in 1903. Perhaps his remaining inside the Liberal party would have placed intolerable strains on a party that had begun only slowly to adjust to the demands of a collectivist society. It may be that by reformulating policy along lines more congruent with Liberal experience, Gladstone created short-term problems through his immersion in the Irish difficulty, while, on a longer time-scale, setting in motion the necessary regrouping of forces that would ultimately bear fruit in 1906.[31] Far from having killed the Victorian Liberal party, Gladstone may inadvertently have provided the preconditions for its survival as an Edwardian presence.

Yet many historians, including the present writer, find this view implausible. Possibly it overstates the counter-case to see 1876 as the crucial fork in the road – the moment when, by coming out of retirement, Gladstone implicitly announced that the 'natural' line of progression for the Liberal party towards a policy of social reform and collectivist legislation would run into the blockage of Gladstone's obsessions.[32] But the loss of its most forward-facing style of radicalism, whatever date one puts on the development, seems important in deciding the degree to which the Liberal party would prove capable of coming to terms with a post-Gladstonian world. Rather than understand Gladstone's last years as the prolegomenon to Liberal recovery, it makes no less sense to read into them the death-throes of an individualist politics based on the language of mission and prophecy. In 1894 the Liberal party looked into a chasm. On the back of Rosebery, it then fell down it. The nineties proved to be less a consummation of the passions of 1886 than a dark night of the soul from which the party did not emerge until some point after the turn of the century. Resolving the Edwardian period into a sharp image partially depends, therefore, on the view of Gladstonian politics one chooses to adopt. And since 'progressivism' draws on that resolution for its effectiveness as an explanatory notion, the argument surrounding its use often implies a recollection of Gladstone, his intense face and earnest voice.

[31] See, for example, Michael Barker's argument that 'the Gladstonian epoch drew to a close upon a note of high expectancy; the retiring premier had indeed helped to sow the seeds of a new Liberalism which Campbell-Bannerman and Asquith ultimately harvested after the great electoral triumph of 1906.' *Gladstone and Radicalism*, 256.
[32] Richard Shannon offered this view of the Liberal future in his study of 1876: see *Bulgarian Agitation*, esp. 273–4. The image of Home Rule as an obstacle or blockage is endemic in contemporary material. See D. A. Hamer, *Liberal Politics in The Age of Gladstone and Rosebery* (Oxford, 1972), 99–184.

Progressivism

The doctrines of 'progressivism', or what came to be called 'New Liberalism', played an obvious if ambivalent role in political argument after 1895. Earlier chapters of this book have shown that the style of politics associated in the mind of the public with Lloyd George and Churchill became an explicit part of Edwardian Liberalism about which contemporaries frequently commented and which some of them took to be critical to the success of Liberal policy in the future. 'Liberalism', as one local newspaper put it in 1905, 'is not a stagnant opinion, but a flowing stream – the expression of the Progressive idea. . . . It will cease to be Liberalism when it ceases to be progressive and becomes fixed .' [33] That progressives comprised an important element in the House of the Commons and among journalists or publicists therefore goes without saying. But as well as operating as a contemporary focus for discussion, progressivism has more recently acquired an historical function; and that usage has in turn given rise to sustained argument about the health of Liberal politics before 1914 and the potential of Liberalism for surviving the coming of a mass industrial society. More prosaically, historians carrying in their minds an image of Edwardian Liberalism – sympathethic or hostile – have sought to protect their sense of the period by using progressivism as an explanatory device. And in order to understand their procedures, we have to clarify how and why progressivism became part of their arguments.

An impediment stood in the way of any serious consideration of progressivism so long as the assumption remained current that the Liberal party had little life left in it before the First World War dealt its death blow. Treatments of the subject before the 1960s strongly reflected that assumption, often in the shadow of George Dangerfield's entrancing historical novel (it is hardly less) that had explored *The Strange Death of Liberal England* 30 years before and placed the critical years of Liberal decline in the period 1910–14.

The arguments and significance of Dangerfield's book we shall approach more squarely in the next section of this chapter. Important here is the dating of an interest in the strange *Life* of the Liberal party; and the first announcement of such an interest came with Trevor Wilson's monograph on *The Downfall of the Liberal Party* (1966) which, by pushing forward the period of Liberal collapse, implied a persistent Liberal vitality before a chain of events after August 1914 decimated the party. The implication did not create progressivism; it generated Labourism. For among historians concerned with party politics before the First World War, the most convinced advocates of Liberal senescence had long been labour historians. The presence of a Labour party after 1906 in the context of an industrial society equipped with a powerful trade-union movement, and a late-nineteenth-century reorientation of political allegiance along the lines of class, convinced historians of (and on) the Left that the Liberal landslide of 1906 had to be understood as a flash in the pan – a moment of surface excitement that should not be allowed to conceal deeper, countervailing trends whose undermining of the Liberal position could only prove a matter of time.

Faced by the assertion of Liberal survival, labour historians responded in a batch of books in the late 1960s and by so doing began the dialogue between optimism and pessimism that has coloured argument about Edwardian Liberalism ever since.

---

[33] *Eastern Weekly Press*, 10 June 1905, quoted in George L. Bernstein, *Liberalism and Liberal Politics in Edwardian England* (Winchester, Mass., 1986), 78.

Henry Pelling's work on regional electoral patterns had already been in train for some years and when it appeared in 1967 it provided a good deal of evidence for the pessimistic case while remaining cautious in its conclusions. In later essays on the Liberal party, however, Pelling's stress on fundamental social change as the explanation of Liberal demise sharpened the argument and left those with a more hopeful view of Liberal prospects in considerable difficulty.[34] Paul Thompson's analysis of London politics meanwhile deepened it.[35] The picture drawn by Thompson of the desperate state of Liberal constituency politics in the capital and of a party withering from its roots upwards gave additional zest to the attack on Liberal plausibility. Of course, the thrust of labour historians varied from writer to writer and by no means amounted to an unambiguous case for pessimism. Roy Gregory's history of the miners, for example, argued the longevity of Liberalism in many mining constituencies, even after the defection of the Miners' Federation of Great Britain to the Labour party in 1909, and stressed the significance of the post-war period as the decisive theatre in the transition of miners *en masse* to their modern adherence.[36] Yet the sentiment had none the less strengthened by 1970 that offering a retrospective future to Edwardian Liberals, even assuming that a war would not come along and kill all that they valued, rested on a superficial reading of the nature of Edwardian society and a denial of its essentially class-oriented behaviour.

It was to this deficiency that 'progressivism' came to minister. While labour historians made their regional histories speak with one voice, a young research student at Cambridge had already made his region speak differently. Peter Clarke's doctoral thesis concerned itself with Lancashire and asked questions about the surprising strength of Liberalism there in the pre-war years.[37] Rather than discovering senescence in his study of constituencies, he found vitality. Instead of a process of rotting away, he found a process of adaptation among Liberals to the new social climate and a willingness to present, through the doctrines of progressivism, a series of arguments and recommendations designed not only to retain a particular social constituency for the party but also to extend it. More important, Clarke played against labour historians on their own pitch. He did not deny their premise that, by the end of the first decade of the twentieth century, a major shift towards class-based politics had taken place. But having accepted the change in environment, he demonstrated that in Lancashire (outside Liverpool) the Liberals had survived the transition and indeed begun to thrive in the new situation. The explanation for that survival lay, moreover, not in the resilience of traditional free-trade sentiment among the mills, but in the new appeal embodied in progressive ideas:

> It is very odd that historians should have neglected the term 'progressive' which has virtually been consigned to a not dissimilar period of American history. It is a classical instance of 'whig' usage. After the War, progressivism guttered on and flickered out. It was forgotten. Yet the term is hardly strange in the 1890s, and by 1910 it starts out from every newspaper page. Its use is important because it relates to changes in the nature of politics: changes which dispose of some of the triter judgements on the Liberal revival. This is not to say that labels should be taken at their face value. All those who glibly appropriated the progressive label in 1910 were not new Liberals. . . . But, with its

[34] Henry Pelling, *Social Geography of British Elections 1885–1910* (1967), 434–5: 'before the First World War, the question of whether the Labour Party could or would displace the Liberal Party . . . hardly seemed to arise.' Cf. Pelling, *Popular Politics and Society in Late-Victorian Britain* (1968), 101–20.
[35] Paul Thompson, *Socialists, Liberals and Labour: the struggle for London 1885–1914* (1967).
[36] Roy Gregory, *The Miners and British Politics 1906–14* (1968).
[37] P. F. Clarke, *Lancashire and the New Liberalism* (Cambridge, 1971).

connotations of social justice, state intervention and alliance with Labour, it aptly describes the basis of Liberal policy after 1906.[38]

It was 'a world in which the Grand Old Man would not have been at home';[39] but it was also a world in which Liberals had learned to fight and win.

This view of Liberal renaissance has since undergone shifts of emphasis, though the fundamental shape of the argument remains the same. Clarke developed his position in articles about progressivism, Liberal – Labour relations after 1910 and in a second book that portrayed in semi-biographical fashion some significant social-democratic intellectuals who spanned the rift between Liberal and Labour politics and thus exemplify the hinterland inhabited by progressive thinkers.[40] A move towards considering Liberal theorists in their own right also found a reflection after the mid 1970s in accounts of Liberal thought in its post-individualist incarnation:[41] an interesting wing of the discussion that raised rather different problems from those connected with the working out of parliamentary politics. Each development of the 'optimistic' position brought, needless to say, a rip tide of criticism and renewal of grounds for weakening the usefulness of progressivism as a rejuvenating doctrine. The straightforward reiteration of class reality offered one path.[42] A more recent survey of Edwardian Liberalism has chosen instead to allow class politics its venom but deny it teeth before the War.[43] To document and describe each of these bounces of the ball as historians pat it from one to the other over more than a decade would leave the most determined reader reeling; it would also prove rather tedious. Perhaps it will do more to assist clarity if we identify three themes that have recurred in these various disputations and the range of evidence that seems relevant in addressing them.

Most obvious among the possible responses to a regional analysis is a denial of the region's typicality; and Lancashire certainly seems vulnerable to that line of attack. It contains Liverpool – a vortex of unique political forces that will provide counter-evidence for virtually any proposition about the nature of national politics. It contains Manchester and therefore, in the Edwardian period, it contains the *Manchester Guardian* and C. P. Scott with his commitment to national progressivism and the personal links with its major figures that he possessed in an unusual degree. He knew and revered Lloyd George. Churchill, the other progressive 'twin', actually represented a Manchester constituency during the formative years of Campbell-Bannerman's government. To speak of the power of progressive publicists and their fertilization of the ground of party politics in Lancashire perhaps says nothing controversial about the situation there. But doing so might tend towards presenting a

[38] Clarke, *Lancashire*, 397 – 8.

[39] Clarke, *Lancashire*, 407.

[40] Peter Clarke, *Liberals and Social Democrats* (Cambridge, 1978).

[41] Michael Freeden, *The New Liberalism: an ideology of social reform* (Oxford, 1977); Peter Weiler, *The New Liberalism: liberal social theory in Great Britain 1889–1914* (1982); Stefan Collini, *Liberalism and Sociology: L. T. Hobhouse and Political Argument in England 1880–1914* (Cambridge, 1979); Collini, 'Hobhouse, Bosanquet and the State: philosophical Idealism and political argument in England 1880–1918', *Past and Present*, 72 (1976), 86–111; Andrew Vincent and Raymond Plant, *Philosophy, Politics and Citizenship: the life and thought of the British Idealists* (Oxford, 1984).

[42] See, for example, Alun Howkins, 'Edwardian Liberalism and Industrial Unrest: a class view of the decline of Liberalism', *History Workshop* (autumn 1977), 143–62.

[43] 'Neither the new liberalism nor Liberal policies of social reform represented fundamental reorientation of the Liberal party so that it could represent the interest of the working class rather than those of middle-class Nonconformists. . . . If class politics were coming, so was the decline of the Liberal Party – not imminently, perhaps, but eventually and inevitably.' Bernstein, *Liberalism and Liberal Politics*, 201.

special and unrepresentative political formation as a model of how national Liberal politics operated; it may therefore seriously overestimate the impact of progressive doctrines on the Edwardian Liberal party as a whole. Such was the thrust of Laybourn and Reynolds's consideration of Liberalism across the Pennines in the West Riding of Yorkshire.[44] They found that Liberalism there resembled old Gladstonianism more than the new model described by Clarke. They believed also that beneath the surface of parliamentary election results, a different story was emerging at the level of municipal elections – a history that predicted the growth of Labour rather than the renaissance of Liberalism.

Now these two lines of argument do not function independently and it is worth a moment's pause to consider their interrelation. At a parliamentary level, the opportunity to demonstrate a serious Labour challenge to Liberalism on either side of the Pennines before 1914 comes rarely and implausibly. Take the Yorkshire case. Of the constituencies in the West Riding, only three offer sympathetic evidence to those seeking Labour strength in national elections. Normanton kept out the Liberals for six of the eight elections between 1885 and 1910; but then Ben Pickard's personal stamp as a Lib – Lab explains much of that resistance until Pickard's death in 1904, after which the Lib – Lab tradition continued until its candidate defected to Labour in 1910. The other two instances both come from Bradford, the city on which much of Laybourn and Reynolds's analysis turns. Bradford West shows a strong Labour presence from Ben Tillett's unsuccessful but impressive showing in 1892 and 1895, to Fred Jowett's near-miss in 1900 and winning of the seat in 1906. Bradford East reveals no Labour wins but a persistent undercurrent of notable Labour support for the candidatures of Keir Hardie, at a by-election in 1896, and more especially for the Social Democratic Federation's candidate in 1906. Placed in a broader perspective of Yorkshire politics as a whole, however, these examples lose some of their lustre.

The glaring fact is that Liberals in Yorkshire were doing well in parliamentary elections in the years before 1914.[45] Among the 23 borough constituencies one can count six instances of places that remained consistently Liberal between 1885 and 1914. This is not interesting. Far more curiosity attaches to places which did not demonstrate a consistent affiliation. Of the 17 constituencies in this bracket, 9 were won by Liberals *in the three elections after 1900*. Liberal losses, that is to say, are not concentrated at the more modern end of the chronology in the way that a model of Liberal withering would imply. The curve of Liberal success seems to swing upwards, if it swings anywhere, as the War approaches. Most of these constituencies lie in the geographical West Riding though they do not comprise the parliamentary county constituency covered by the term 'Yorkshire (West Riding)'. Turning to the 19 seats that fall under this rubric occasions no embarrassment, however, since the case merely strengthens. Nine of those seats remained uniformly Liberal. Of the 10 that did not, five were won by the Liberals in 1906 and 1910. In the five that were not won, the central threat came more often from urban Conservatism than from the Labour party.

None of the problems facing the Labour party as a national electoral force gainsays the significance of its activities at local level; nor do they invalidate the claim that

[44] Keith Laybourn and Jack Reynolds, *Liberalism and the Rise of Labour 1890–1918* (1984).
[45] The brief analysis that follows is my own, drawn principally from material in F. W. S. Craig, *British Parliamentary Election Results 1885–1918* (1974). It excludes Cleveland (which was a Liberal fief of the Pease family) and takes no account of double-member seats. Liberal Unionists, Lib – Labs and Independents have not been counted as Liberals.

New Liberalism may well have been a region-specific phenomenon. The point is rather that Labour historians, regional or not, find unquestionable difficulty in substantiating the case for a powerful electoral threat before 1914. Instead they have moved, since the mid 1970s, in the direction of discriminating between electoral performance, reflected in general election results, and electoral potential implicit in other categories of evidence from the political history of the period. Three of these have enjoyed moments of prominence. Laybourn and Reynolds exemplify one such approach by addressing themselves less to the parliamentary dimension than the municipal one. Their picture of a mounting Labour strength in the localities becomes the basis for the suggestion that Labour posed an important threat to the future of Liberal politics, especially in an area where progressivism seems not to have operated with the vigour observed in Manchester. Nor is the device limited to regional studies. In treatments of Liberal–Labour relations at a country-wide level, considerable attention has been paid to the municipal theatre, with indeterminate results.[46] How convincing one finds this research plainly depends on the role accorded to data from local elections as predictors of anything else. The present writer tends to place on them the weight placed by most political scientists on modern local elections as indicators of electoral behaviour – very little. The spectre of Labour councils springing up all over Edwardian Britain does not of itself, even if it had taken place, seem overwhelming evidence in favour of a crisis in Liberal affiliation reflected in the quite distinct anthropology that seems to operate at general elections.

But a more sensitive line of defence against the allegation of Labour's ineffectuality emerged in the 1970s and deserves mention here. Several historians of Liberalism have made hay with Labour's by-election failure between 1910 and 1914. The party's candidates fared badly in three-cornered elections; indeed, their total national presence in parliament *decreased* by half a dozen over just the period when the Liberals were supposedly dying their strange death. The Liberal performance, meanwhile, has been portrayed as at worst variable and in many ways respectable.[47] In 1974 Ross McKibbin challenged the usefulness of electoral data in forming conclusions of this kind.[48] Rather than turn towards local elections, McKibbin directed attention at the Labour party as a national infrastructure with a base in a variety of labour organizations and analysed changes in the potential of both to construct a fighting machine. Much of the thrust of McKibbin's treatment concerned the period after 1914; but he cogently attacked the view that Labour had failed to make ground against Liberalism before the War by citing major developments in the broader history of Labour (not least a significant rise in trade-union membership between 1910 and 1914, which no election statistics would register) and by instancing the acceleration in Labour organization during those years and advances made in the systematic deployment of party *cadre*. Even this defence, however, invested Labour with no more than a certain futurity. It predicted that Labour would strengthen regardless of progressive Liberalism or the effects of a war. This shift in the argument from the situation before 1914 to that after 1918 marked a decisive turn in how labour

[46] Laybourn and Reynolds, *Liberalism and the Rise of Labour*, 154. See also Chris Cook, 'Labour and the Downfall of the Liberal Party', in A. Sked and C. Cook (eds.), *Crisis and Controversy: an essays in honour of A. J. P. Taylor* (1976), 38–65; but cf. Walter Arnstein's balanced survey, 'Edwardian Politics: turbulent spring or Indian summer?', in Alan O'Day (ed.), *The Edwardian Age: conflict and stability 1900–1914*, 60–78.
[47] See in particular Peter Clarke, 'The electoral position of the Liberal and Labour parties 1910–14', *English Historical Review*, XC (1975), 828–36.
[48] Ross McKibbin, *The Evolution of the Labour Party 1910–24* (Oxford, 1974).

historians approached the electoral politics of Edwardian Britain. It also quickened interest in a third domain that has since become central to the consideration of progressivism's role as a saviour of the Liberal party: the franchise question.

That the complexities of deciding who exactly could vote in Edwardian England bore implications for argument about the nature of electoral behaviour had not escaped the historians who wrote about electoral sociology at the beginning of the 1970s. At that stage the thrust of discussion undermined Labour optimism by demonstrating the implausibility of a 'whig' view of Labour's rise that assumed the presence of a 'democratic' framework after 1885. A change of mood appeared in 1976 with the publications of a joint study of 'the franchise factor' as a determinant of Labour's fortunes before and after the First World War.[49] Here the argument accepted the frailty of Labour's power as a pre-war force but placed both Labour fragility and Liberal robustness in an explanatory frame that highlighted the peculiar nature of the limited electorate on which Liberal success rested and the difficult future that awaited the party of Campbell-Bannerman and Asquith once Labour's potential electorate obtained the vote:

> ... there was in the pre-war electorate no large pool of voters uncommitted to the existing major parties: nor was the subsequent weakening of those commitments a factor which gave net advantage to the Labour party. It follows that the substantial post-war growth in Labour's relative strength must in large measure be attributable to the franchise extension and registration reform of 1918. It is difficult to say how large that measure is. ... We cannot say how many votes the introduction of universal franchise was worth to Labour, but we can say that it was a critical element in the emergence of the party as a major political force.[50]

'Class politics' the Liberals may have survived. But they had done so within the false (and temporary) security that the survival of a limited electorate, defined by the possession of property, promised them. The Liberals, if they did not die their strange death before 1914, deceived themselves none the less by living a charmed life – one that would lose its charm when, as it surely must, universal suffrage finally arrived.

Against that vision of the Edwardian present and future one might place another. It remains unclear for the moment, as we saw earlier, whether those against whom the electoral system discriminated before 1918 consisted entirely or even principally of working-class men. If residence qualifications are brought into play, then an argument becomes available to suggest that middle-class, mobile individuals – electors whose preferences may well have been Liberal – suffered disfranchisement. Within that electorate, moreover, it may be that the proportion of trade unionists bulked larger even than after the war[51] – a thought to bring renewed discomfort to those reprieved from the need to explain the 'failure' of Labour before 1914. But the Edwardian future allows even more openness of argument; and one of the more depressing features of current historiography lies in its dour denial of previous generations' freedom to have a future different from the one now frozen in our past. Why should it be assumed that the 'inevitability' of universal suffrage would of necessity guarantee the future of the Labour party? Perhaps it did so in the particular

[49] H. C. G. Matthew, R. McKibbin and J. Kay, 'The franchise factor in the rise of the Labour party', *English Historical Review*, XCI (1976), 723–52.
[50] Matthew, McKibbin and Kay, 'Franchise factor', 740.
[51] Duncan Tanner, 'The parliamentary electoral system, the "fourth" reform act and the rise of Labour in England and Wales', *Bulletin of the Institute of Historical Research*, 56 (1983), 205–19; Peter Clarke, 'The Edwardians and the Constitution', in Donald Read (ed.), *Edwardian England* (1982), 40–55.

configuration of political forces that led, against Liberal judgement for the most part, to its granting in 1918. Without the war's sudden explosion in a clear sky, however, a different configuration might have produced rather different results. The Liberal government's abortive attempt to extend the franchise in a controlled way in 1912 suggests the direction of its mind: towards a gradual evolution in the suffrage arrangements so that Liberal interests could be maximized. Had that road remained available – and it was the war, not the Labour party, that blocked it – we would now need to discuss the fourth, the fifth, possibly the sixth reform act. The time-scale of effective democratization might occupy the period, not from 1885 to 1918, but from 1885 to 1930 or 1935. The parties directing and responding to the operation might meanwhile have come to look markedly different by the 1920s from those familiar to Baldwin and his friends: no longer Conservative, Liberal and Labour but Constitutionalist, Social Democratic and Socialist. Fantasy has its perils; but so does wooden-headed determinism.

While this discussion about the electoral status of Labour politics ran its course, a parallel one about the party status of New Liberal ideology also became evident in the late 1970s. For in this issue the critics of progressivism found a more promising territory in which to decry fantasy. How convincing, for example, is the view that 'progressives' within the party succeeded in imposing on it a new 'ideology of social reform'? Michael Freeden's formulation of that case in 1977 presented an impressive analysis of the roots of 'organicist' reasoning in Liberal politics, just as H. V. Emy's older book about *Liberals, Radicals and Social Politics* had persuasively argued for the dispersion of a new current of thought among Liberal publicists and Radical MPs.[52] But problems about the model of party behaviour implied in these and other contributions showed no signs of going away. More than accident lay behind the strength of these approaches in analysing intellectuals and their periodicals as contrasted with their weakness in presenting a picture of how the Edwardian Liberal party actually worked, especially in its upper reaches. Now of course one can deny the reality of the upper reaches and contend that politics has its driving force in lower ones. But those observers who are struck by the importance of the cabinet, for example, in British party politics cannot help recalling the degree to which Lloyd George and Churchill lived lonely lives as apostles of the New Liberalism in that rarified atmosphere after 1906. Unless one try to call Asquith a New Liberal (and some have done so[53]), the feeling endures that a pragmatic imperialist with a revulsion from philosophy of all kinds held the premiership during just the period when progressivism is meant to have flowered; and that his closest collaborators – men such as the Marquess of Crewe, Sir Edward Grey, Richard Haldane, John Morley, Viscount Wolverhampton and Reginald McKenna – injected prominent offices of state with the Oldest of Liberalism and treated progressivism with a mixture of suspicion and contempt. The suggestion that such people 'must' have been influenced by the climate of New Liberalism created by their party activists has some plausibility, but then so does the thought that an influence of that kind ought to be evidenced among the relics left to us by those individuals.

It is now clear that such evidence does not exist in any compelling form; indeed for the most part it does not exist at all.[54] The men who ran the Edwardian party show in

[52] Freeden, *The New Liberalism*; H. V. Emy (Cambridge, 1973).
[53] Vincent and Plant, for example: *Philosophy, Politics and Citizenship*, 41.
[54] This is persuasively shown in R. E. Ellins, 'Aspects of the New Liberalism' (unpub. Ph.D. dissertation, Univ. of Sheffield, 1980).

their private archives virtually no sign of progressive motivation. Their letters and diaries speak the language of past generations: they bemoan immediate crises in party management; they comment on the interaction between personality and business; they organize the next fortnight, consult over the coming set-piece debate, fume over yesterday's speech reported in *The Times*, spread still further the latest scandal and gossip. But of course that very absence of material capable of warming the hearts of progressive historians brings with it another argument – one about appropriate source-materials for the study of party history. Does the seeming inability of Liberal politicians to write about or even mention Hobson, Hobhouse, Masterman and the rest of the progressive *alumni* mean that they never read such writers or never came across them at meetings or sat across from them at table in the London house of a Liberal patron, or shared a train journey with someone who had? Plainly not. What this silence may better argue, from the point of view of the progressive case, is the need to scrutinize public discussion in speeches and newspapers for a style of advocacy which the private letter never attracts, regardless of its author's intellectual commitments.

The position goes some way towards defending progressivism from a paucity of evidence in high places but, taken together with its thinness of representation at ministerial level, it seems more than a little forced. Besides, it is simply not the case that personal achieves fail to register reflective comment, though one sometimes has to read between the lines for it. The period of the First World War provoked many Liberals, as we shall see, into a form of soul-searching that frequently preoccupied their letters and seeped into their diaries. Granted that war produces specially-heightened sentiment, we may allow Asquith's peacetime cabinet a lower level of incandescence. It none the less comes hard to lend immunity to a near-total silence. Perhaps a more natural line of argument about the impact of progressivism on high politics would therefore concede that party management took its character from the constraints and stimuli that we associate with traditional Liberal politics. Certainly it faced a new difficulty in the need to swing fiscal policy towards direct taxation in order to keep control of an urbanized state; and this in turn demanded its own language of justification. An envelope of intellectual concern about various forms of social deprivation no less certainly surrounded politicians in their daily work. But what the evidence so far suggests is that 'progressivism' won more converts among backbench enthusiasts and constituency activists than among the élite charged with running the Liberal party and deciding its future course. And what that suggestion in turn implies is that New Liberalism might ultimately have turned into a disruptive force within Liberal politics instead of the framework within which the Liberal party would learn a new cohesion and sense of purpose. Rather than rejuvenate the old party, progressivism promised the eventual foundation of a new politics quite as distant from Asquith's world as his had proved from the one proclaimed at Midlothian.

Decline and fall

Gladstonians and New Liberals populate many images of pre-war Liberalism and together imply a view about the vitality of the Liberal party and its chances of survival in twentieth-century conditions. They also help fix one of the two axes along which argument about the ultimate collapse of British Liberalism has tended to run. They suggest that 1914 should appear in retrospect as a threshold of major importance in the story; and the question whether one sees the theatre of Liberal difficulty standing preponderantly in the pre-1914 or post-1914 period has lain behind much of the curiosity surrounding the downfall of historic Liberalism. But a second axis also figures in the discussion. This one veers from the position that Liberals became victim to an external assault of some kind – the Labour party, say, or the First World War – towards an interpretation of Liberal history dominated by various forms of internal collapse, as though for some reason Liberalism came to find its own gravity too oppressive to resist. Like all axes, these notional dimensions do not function independently but are instead brought into relationship by the patterns that historians draw between them. Any argument about the crushing or withering of Liberalism will allude to both the Edwardian and post-war periods. In commenting on forces without, it will of necessity remark on pressures within. Yet in the variations of stress placed and lines drawn there lies an interesting range of possibility to fuddle and fox the imagination.

Possibility found little rein at the hands of George Dangerfield with whom this argument properly begins. When he wrote *The Strange Death of Liberal England* in the early 1930s, the strangeness of his subject did not prompt him to look for uncertainty or ambiguity: the answers seemed as sharp as (a memorable image) the lines of Mr McKenna's face. They had to be so. The climate in which the *Strange Death* had its origins imposed itself on Dangerfield's creation as plainly as the economic depression impinged on the writing of Priestley or Auden. The moving finger in Dangerfield's case, of course, was not the economy but the background of the Great War, the knowledge that the Liberals did not survive it, the recollections of the pre-war Golden Age that had percolated through the biographies and memoirs published ever since – source-materials, incidentally, on which history had to rest in the absence of anything else. The *singularity* of that last moment before the submersion of civilization weighed heavily with Dangerfield because it seemed at once the most prominent and most dramatic feature of Edwardian England in the 1930s' consciousness. It felt natural to rekindle that warmth while surrounded by the chill of a modernity whose remove from the stifling summer of 1911 seemed only magnified by its cooling embers: Margot Asquith, looking for all the world like an aged rooster dressed in widow's weeds; Lloyd George, whose shiny-blue serge suit and dashes up the stairs two-at-a-time now looked more moving than impressive against the snow-white hair and lack of breath.

Out of that generation's recollection of itself, Dangerfield made a great historical story, a book that will be sold in the bookshops long after its countless volumes of correction lie dead in their libraries. There are times when Dry-as-dust has his way, none the less, and it should be said that enquiries *à la recherche du temps perdu* always wind up by writing the history backwards. In his own way Dangerfield saw socialism – indeed Communism – as an inescapable environment; he knew the civil war into which Ireland had fallen; he sensed the mood of emancipation that had given women the vote and extended it only a few years before he wrote. All of these things he shouldered backwards to preoccupy Asquith's government after 1910; so we find the Ulster crisis, the industrial difficulties posed by syndicalist strikes, and the suffragette question coming to centre stage and creating the frame for a final curtain. For the Victorians he feels what Lytton Strachey had felt in *Eminent Victorians*: some of his best passages identify contradictions within the sensibility that thinking Edwardians had inherited, particularly in their dialogue between smugness and radicalism, the simultaneous defence of property and need to alter it. Herein lies the inwardness of the situation depicted by Dangerfield, leaving Liberals confused and bifocal. Then from without came the striking trade unionists, the women and the Ulstermen to strike down a form of politics already stricken. By the time the Great War erupted, there was little left to kill.

Archival material made available since Dangerfield's time has underlined his exaggeration of these problems in the minds of those confronting them. Each caused a difficulty; none brought the government to its knees or led its ministers to feel themselves doomed.[55] But the weakness of Dangerfield's prognosis appears in other senses too. He lent little stress to progressivism and therefore gave the party no hope of a serum. His ascription of a fundamental cleavage in Liberalism between the interests of capital and labour could with equal accuracy be described as a tension long evident but also long withstood. To see it ripping apart the fabric of the Liberal party between 1910 and 1914 awards an arbitrary significance to years that one can see as simply part of a gradual evolution towards meeting the needs of a social-democratic party. His Labour party has large teeth; but we have already seen that progressivism may have pulled some of them and that Labour in any case had far fewer teeth than Dangerfield imagined. Not all of these considerations had matured before the publication of Trevor Wilson's account of *The Downfall of the Liberal Party* in 1966. Enough had become evident, however, to cast considerable doubt on the wisdom of Dangerfield's monopoly in this part of Liberal historiography and to suggest that a fresh look might suggest a different perspective.

Wilson's account lacked Dangerfield's drama: it presented the internal Liberal history of 1914 to 1935 in a clear narrative. By doing this for the first time the book nevertheless helped make sense of modern Liberal history as a whole by refusing to treat the post-1914 period as a vague epilogue. It also contained a phrase that stuck. Wilson wrote about the First World War as a 'rampant omnibus' that ran down the ailing senior citizen represented by the Liberal party in 1914.

> After lingering painfully, he expired. A controversy has persisted ever since as to what killed him. One medical school argues that even without the bus he would soon have died; the intimations of illness were symptoms of a grave disease which would shortly have ended his life. Another school goes further and says that the encounter with the bus would not have proved fatal had not the victim's health already been seriously impaired. . . . How long, apart from the accident, the victim would have survived, what future (if any) he possessed, cannot be said. All that is known is that at one moment he was up and walking and that at the next he was flat on his back, never to rise again; and in the interval he had been run over by a bus.[56]

The focus of the book clarified the politics of the First World War and the damage it wrought, not least in thrusting to the centre of affairs David Lloyd George. Ultimately the harm done seems personal rather than intellectual. The Liberal party goes into the war healthier, but not much more so, than Dangerfield had left it; it comes out as a traditional party that has undergone the misfortune of a split brought about by the exigencies of war and the use that the other parties intended making of them. Asquith is hard to cast as a hero but receives at least some sympathy. Lloyd George is the *bête noire* on whom a major responsibility falls for the state of the party. The story of the 1920s appears as a long coda of recrimination and ineffectiveness in a party system with which the Liberals, fixated on old issues and rhetoric, never come satisfactorily to terms.

[55] See Bentley, *Politics Without Democracy*, 346–70.
[56] Trevor Wilson *The Downfall of the Liberal Party 1914–35* (1966), 18.

The assertion of this polarity between an Edwardian theatre of Liberal decline, on the one hand, and a wartime crisis on the other, widened the nature of argument about the last days of Liberalism and provoked new inquiries into a period still regarded by many historians as somehow too contemporary to consider respectable as history. Once grant the Liberals a possible lease of life after 1914 and new dates for their demise come into focus: 1916, 1918, 1924, 1929, 1935. And through the 1970s these speculations won some attention, especially with the opening of the Beaverbrook library at the end of the 1960s and the coming into general availability of the vast Lloyd George archive and the papers of Andrew Bonar Law, not to mention those of Beaverbrook himself. Young historians produced new research papers about the later career of Lloyd George;[57] indeed new full-length biographical studies complemented the 50 or so biographies already published and a barrage of diaries and correspondence fed the growing public interest that television also encouraged.[58] Liberal electoral politics during and after the war seemed suddenly more convincing than earlier generations had assumed and research activity aimed at scrutinizing the performance of the Liberals at local and national level underlined the point.[59] All of this brought a response that we have already noted from Labour historians: a revulsion against treating so major a transformation as the death of Liberalism as the product of clashes between personalities during the First World War[60] and a strengthening of the arguments in favour of Liberal debility before the war came along.

It brought something else, enclosed in the same package. The argument that the war had proved fatal had rested on propositions about party difficulties that the war threw up; they had not argued the case that the war *in itself* and by its very nature had instigated the disaster.[61] This emphasis helped the 'Labour' case by allowing the period 1906–24 to be seen as a continuum and opening the possibility of comparing pre- and post-war conditions (general elections, for example) without the feeling gaining ground that an exercise in which the war had been 'removed' must rest on absurdity. The present writer resisted this position, among others, in 1977 by arguing that the war did not function negatively by challenging Liberals' sense of principle but rather had a positive role in helping them decide what those principles were and in providing unique conditions in which the traditional broad-church understanding of Liberalism could no longer find living-space among the constricted reference-points of total war. From this perspective, 1916 became a very important year: not merely as the occasion of a party fissure but rather as the moment when two versions of true Liberalism parted company. That those two versions never reunited, apart from a few weeks' rather farcical togetherness for the purposes of the 1923 election campaign, therefore became less of a surprise, as did the failure of Lloyd George ever to recapture the loyalty of traditional Liberals. Dangerfield's attractive

[57] These obviously became scattered in the journals and among compilations of essays, but for an important collection, brought together by the then-director of the Beaverbrook Library, A. J. P. Taylor, see Taylor (ed.), *Lloyd George: twelve essays* (1971).

[58] The interest in the later career was best illustrated in John Campbell's doctoral thesis, published under the title *Lloyd George: the goat in the wilderness 1922–31* (1977). The process continued in a mass of material relating to Lloyd George's family and private life: see below, note 69.

[59] Eg. Michael Kinnear, *The British Voter: an atlas and survey since 1885* (1968); Chris Cook, *The Age of Alignment: electoral politics in Britain 1922–9* (1975).

[60] See, for example, Henry Pelling's remarks in his essays on 'Labour and the Downfall of Liberalism', in Pelling, *Popular Politics and Society*, esp. 119–20.

[61] 'the "war" argument, though frequently embraced, has never been properly demonstrated, and in some cases not demonstrated at all.' Matthew, McKibin and Kay, 'The franchise factor', 736.

picture retained some of its textures in this discussion. But they suffered a time-shift into the middle of the very special environment created by the most impressive period of transformation present in the awareness of that generation of Liberals.[62] Needless to say, the argument has taken a number of other turns, moving away, for example, from a concentration on the 'high politics' of the question towards investigations of the effect of the war on back-bench and constituency politics.[63] It has also addressed the domain of doctrines and ideas. One of the most obvious facets of post-war Liberalism, after all, concerns the degree to which it retained the support of a significant intelligentsia. Numerous studies have directed attention at this survival and commented on the significance of small-'l' liberalism in the politics of the inter-war years.[64]

To analyse these individual contributions would perhaps pull the discussion away from the issues and concerns at the heart of this book. Better, therefore, to review the perspectives which these and the foregoing studies have highlighted for students looking for an understanding of the decades after 1914 in the history of modern Liberalism as a whole.

One of them emerges in a familiar dialogue within Liberal experience between 'high' and 'low' politics and the responsibility of each for the failure of the party to survive the 1920s as an effective fighting unit. A concentration on high politics makes available, for example, not merely a stress on 1916 as a significant threshold (the split of that year took place at a very high level and left even MPs bemused) but also an alternative picture of challenge to Liberalism from the one made current by those who emphasize the role of the Labour party. Many accounts of the decline of Liberalism treat the Conservative party, when they mention it at all, as part of a distant landscape and its strategists as passive spectators. But from a high-political level it seems obvious enough that the Liberal party suffered greatly from intelligent Conservative politicians who self-consciously sought to drain what Leo Amery called 'the ditchwater of Liberalism' and reduce to an arid plain the territory lying between the English party, on the one hand, and the un-English conspiracy of Labour, on the other.[65] To its critics, this mode of reasoning gives rise to the same sense of intellectual – and probably moral – rejection as did Cooke and Vincent's analysis of Home Rule. The evidence seems to them less a body of authentic diaries and letters than a collection of gossipy trivia that fails to depict the structural weaknesses of the Liberal party within the new political framework of the post-war years and in particular the challenges that near-universal suffrage and soviet-style socialism would bring to all its participants.[66]

A second argument reflects interests shown in historians' discussion of New

[62] Michael Bentley, *The Liberal Mind 1914–29* (Cambridge, 1977), *passim*. Michael Hart also later responded to the disposable-war position, arguing that '[a]fter the war . . . the Liberals became (and were perceived as) a party of the right, and [that] comparisons between pre-1914 and post-1918 voting figures in an attempt to detect a "progressive" electorate are therefore of limited usefulness.' 'The Liberals, the war and the franchise', *English Historical Review* XCII (1982), 820–32.
[63] See Edward David, 'The Liberal Party Divided', *Historical Journal* 13 (1970), 509–32.
[64] Most recent among these is Michael Freeden, *Liberalism Divided: a study in British political thought 1914–39* (Oxford, 1986). Cf. Bentley, *Liberal Mind*, chapter 5, and Clarke, *Liberals and Social Democrats*, chapters 7 and 8.
[65] This case forms some of the argument in Maurice Cowling, *The Impact of Labour 1920–24: the beginning of modern British politics* (Cambridge, 1971) esp. 341–411.
[66] For an example of that critique see McKibbin, *Evolution of the Labour Party*. I summarized some of these feelings in an article, 'What is Political History?', in 1977: *Durham University Journal*, XXXIX (1977), 133–9.

Liberalism before the war. Of course, the context has changed beyond recognition. No question after 1918 of showing how the Liberal party might rescue itself through the propagation of doctrines about collectivism and welfare: the Liberals no longer have a massive governing majority but a tiny parliamentary presence plus the hangers-on associated with Lloyd George. Yet the contention endures that the heirs of New Liberalism continued in their enthusiasms and, by so doing, ensured the survival of a very important tradition within British politics – one that fed directly, not into the Liberal party that plainly now struggled to retain its relevance in the new environment, but in the direction that the Labour party would take and the policies that it would later espouse.

> . . . this is no simple tale of ideological regression . . . [L]iberalism was not dormant between the wars, nor was its path one of unmitigated failure. In the long run, it succeeded in one important mission – to keep alive the hopes and aims of British progressives; to pass them on, in slightly different form, to different bodies, perhaps for a future time. . . . The liberal heritage could not be contained in a single demonstrative act [such as the Beveridge Report]; the success of that heritage was a generalized one. By the end of the [inter-war] period . . . most progressive intellectuals, political activists, and reformers no longer recognized their principles as explicitly liberal. Liberalism had transcended its distinct institutional and ideological shape and thus, paradoxically, ensured its survival.[67]

Like all such arguments, the view has its negative facets. An assumption that Liberalism split into two varieties – one central, one left of centre – is hard to deny. To see in the leftward-looking one the future of liberal ideology begs a number of questions, none the less, and ignores the degree to which Asquithian Liberalism retained a hold over party politics. Indeed, as with arguments about progressivism, the thesis becomes least persuasive when the nature of the party (as opposed to a vague ideology) occupies the centre of attention. Perhaps Liberalism made a significant contribution, less to the Labour party of G. D. H. Cole and Harold Laski, than to the internationalism and mild propensity towards planning that found its way into Tory thinking by the mid 1930s. Perhaps the process amounts not so much to transcendence on the Left, in other words, than to dissolution and spillage just about everywhere.

   Both themes in these days of decline found a reflection in the career of Lloyd George; and the weight placed on his significance in precipitating the downfall of British Liberalism recalls a final area of interpretation that requires comment. Seven decades after the division of the party brought about by Lloyd George's rise to power, many people continue to believe that, almost single-handed, one man unleashed the forces that brought down an historic political institution and inaugurated the period when politics became what Roseberry called 'an evil-smelling bog'. Part of the bitterness surrounding Lloyd George's historical reputation derived from its Asquithian origins: a collection of writers from the 1930s to the 1950s wrote indictments of Lloyd George's betrayal of everything that Liberalism had represented in the time of Campbell-Bannerman and Asquith.[68] Only gradually has a

---

[67] Freeden, *Liberalism Divided*, 11, 371.
[68] *The Autobiography of Margot Asquith* (2 vols., 1920) began a persistent tradition reinforced by the later, official Life of her husband: J. A. Spender and Cyril Asquith, *Life of Herbert Henry Asquith, Lord Oxford and Asquith* (2 vols., 1932). For greater inventiveness, see Centurion, *The Man Who Didn't Win the War: an exposure of Lloyd Georgism* (1923); J. M. Robertson, *Mr. Lloyd George and Liberalism* (1923); Charles

more informed historiography made inroads into the catalogue of contempt. The publication of Lloyd George's letters to his wife and to Frances Stevenson, the mistress whom he was to marry at the end of his life, together with the appearance of editions of Stevenson's diary and the journal of Lloyd George's amanuensis in the 1930s, A. J. Sylvester, have injected new vigour into the defence.[69] More than documents have played their part. Doubtless the shift of political expectation in the train of 'Suez' and 'Profumo' prepared the ground for a more sympathetic understanding and placed Lloyd George among those bad men of history – Charles James Fox and Disraeli shared the same cell – who gradually became rather more acceptable among readers of history than the great and the good.

The pendulum has swung a long way, possibly too far for credibility. Lloyd George underwent a transformation into a formidable world statesman: his lies whitened, his corruptions extenuated, his malice denied. Rather than appear the architect of Liberal catastrophe, he emerged as the only leading Liberal with a clear grasp of reality and sufficient flexibility to react quickly enough to changed conditions. The abandonment of New Liberalism after 1914 changed colour and became a mere postponement; its failure to dominate the post-war coalition came to seem an enforced capitulation to economic circumstance and party pressure more than a betrayal of personal values.[70] The later career likewise underwent a revival of interest. The wilderness years after 1922 attracted a major study. Even the more geriatric period of the 1930s, portrayed in Sylvester's diary, reawakened academic concern in the importance of Lloyd George's New Deal proposals and the possibility of his return to government.[71] But although these studies may have exaggerated Lloyd George's importance as an agent in party politics and the depth of doctrine that he brought to them, they focussed attention on the symbolic significance of one of the twentieth century's great political careers and underlined the stress that historians of Liberalism need to place on perceptions and images among those who were charged with finding a future of some kind for Liberal politics.

That future is now past. Some believe that a new one can still be made; but, even if they are correct, the Liberal politics of the future will not revive the years of Gladstone, Asquith and Lloyd George but attempt a different project altogether. Yet enough threads of continuity remain in the situation to entice a disappointed posterity into creating a worrying view of late-nineteenth- and early-twentieth-century politics that transforms the subject into what Michel Foucault used to call a history of the present. More than ever has this been the case since disappointment among the British liberal intelligentsia changed gear in 1979; and the time may now

Mallet, *Mr. Lloyd George: a study* (1930); Donald McCormick, *The Mask of Merlin: a critical study of David Lloyd George* (1963).

[69] A. J. P. Taylor (ed.), *Lloyd George: a diary by Frances Stevenson* (1971); Taylor (ed.), *My Darling Pussy: the letters of Lloyd George and Frances Stevenson 1913–41* (1975); Kenneth O. Morgan (ed.), *Lloyd George Family Letters* (Cardiff, 1973); Colin Cross (ed.), *Life with Lloyd George: the diary of A. J. Sylvester 1931–45* (1975).

[70] For an impressive evocation of Lloyd George as a great Liberal caught in an impasse, see Kenneth O. Morgan, *Consensus and Disunity: the Lloyd George coalition government 1918–22* (Oxford, 1979) Cf. the same author's previous studies, *David Lloyd George: Welsh radical as world statesman* (Cardiff, 1963) and *Lloyd George* (1964).

[71] See Stephen Koss, 'Lloyd George and Nonconformity: the last rally', *English Historical Review*, LXXXIX (1974), 77–108.

be right to remember the sheer specificity of Liberal politics in their classical period and the unique pattern of constraints and stimuli that guided their development. British Liberalism as it defined itself in the eyes of Mill and Green and Hobhouse, or in the policy documents and private letters of two generations of politicians, responded to what fashion now calls a 'culture'. The culture was not a clone of a European process; nor did it exist, as a convincing political environment, for more than half a century. It none the less sustained, for that golden moment, a version of politics that seemed serious and relevant to those who argued and practised it. It might have won a future for itself, moreover, had not engagement with a new sort of war brought with it the ultimate weapon of destruction: not military defeat but cultural pessimism. By crushing the values of certainty and optimism – a complete universe encoded in the single word 'decency' – the First World War not only buried the Liberal future but rendered hopeless the past by which Liberals had chartered the course that took them there. It ill-serves history when more modern observers evade their own disappointments by picking up the dropped compass.

Further Reading

Since the final chapter of this book has taken the form of a critical review of key areas in Liberal historiography, it seems unnecessary to dwell again on the material discussed there. But perhaps it would be helpful to mention in a separate note some obvious sources by which a student of Liberal politics might deepen an understanding of the period after reading an introductory study of this kind. The reader should be warned none the less that the selection appended here has been angled away from books considered in chapter eight. It has also been confined to comparatively recent books and a few contemporary sources.

No single volume complements this one, though Richard Shannon's *The Crisis of Imperialism 1865–1915* (1974) is reliable on the general politics of the period, as are two more recent surveys, E.J. Feuchtwanger, *Democracy and Empire: Britain 1865–1914* (1985) and the earlier sections of Keith Robbins, *The Eclipse of a Great Power: modern Britain 1870–1975* (1983). The second half of my own survey of high politics, *Politics Without Democracy 1815–1914: perception and preoccupation in British government* (1984) may also come into play in clarifying the strategic discussion of Liberal politicians after 1868. For a more intensive treatment of specific Liberal party issues and policies, D.A. Hamer, *Liberal Politics in the Age of Gladstone and Rosebery: a study in leadership and policy* (Oxford, 1972) offers a clear and accessible account, though it perhaps overstresses the 'sectional' understanding of Liberalism. Galdstone himself is difficult at the moment because we do not yet have the second volume of Professor Shannon's major biography which will cover the years after 1865. For a stimulating essay, see Boyd Hilton, 'Gladstone's Theological Politics', in Michael Bentley and John Stevenson (eds.), *High and Low Politics in Modern Britain* (Oxford, 1983), 28–57. Gladstone's diary becomes particularly important in this context and Colin Matthew's introduction to volume seven is especially recommended as a masterly evaluation of Gladstone in the years after 1868 (M.R.D. Foot and H.C.G. Matthew [eds.], The *Gladstone Diaries* [Oxford, 1968–]). For some recent papers see Bruce L. Kinzer (ed.), *The Gladstonian Turn of Mind*: *essays presented to J.B. Conacher* (Toronto, 1985). Other Liberals present an easier quarry through the excellent biographies available. Richard Jay's, *Joseph Chamberlain* (Oxford, 1981) filled an important gap, for example. Robert Rhodes James's older book on *Rosebery* (1963) is still enjoyable; the late Stephen Koss wrote a good short life of *Asquith* (1976), John Wilson a longer one of Campbell-Bannerman (*C-B: a life of Sir Henry Campbell-Bannerman* [1973]); Keith Robbins's study of *Sir Edward Grey* (1971) is an impressive book based on considerable archival research. Among longer studies, John Grigg's continuing life of *Lloyd George* promises much (3 vols., 1973–), while Martin Gilbert's massive series on Churchill has now reached the end of the Second World War (Randolph Churchill and Martin Gilbert, *Winston S. Churchill* [7 vols., 1966–]). Hartington, Morley, Campbell-Bannerman, Harcourt and Haldane continue to elude first-rate biography though there have been a number of helpful studies. An excellent recent analysis of Liberal policy is contained, on the other hand, in Bruce K. Murray, *The People's Budget 1909/10: Lloyd George and Liberal politics* (Oxford, 1980), one of many monographs on the Asquith government.

On the more theoretical side of the subject, the political thought of the later Utilitarians and the Idealists continues to attract interest. Christopher Harvie's *The Lights of Liberalism: university liberals and the challenge of democracy 1860–86* (1976) is a good starting-point. Among more recent publications, Bernard Semmel's *John Stuart Mill and the Pursuit of Virtue* (New Haven, 1984) picks up the Utilitarian thread and, for the Idealists, Andrew Vincent and Raymond Plant, *Philosophy, Politics and Citizenship: the life and thought of the British Idealists* (Oxford, 1984) provides a useful analysis, though the present writer retains an affection for Melvin Richter's earlier portrait, *The Politics of Conscience: T.H. Green and his age* (1964). W.H. Greenleaf's extended study of *The British Political Tradition* (3 vols., 1983–) naturally contributes to this wing of the discussion, as does the vast conspectus that Maurice Cowling presents in his series of volumes discussing *Religion and Public Doctrine in Modern England* (3 vols., Cambridge, 1980–). If one were to select from numerous individual studies, Stephan Collini's examination of Hobhouse has perhaps proved the most fertile (*Liberalism and Sociology: L.T. Hobhouse and political argument in England 1880–1914* [Cambridge, 1979]), though José Harris's study of *William Beveridge* (Oxford, 1977) is helpful on social policy. The serious student of Liberal philosophy might want to turn to J.B. Schneewind, *Sidgwick's Ethics and Victorian Moral Philosophy* (Oxford, 1977) or to some of the later pieces collected in Stephan Collini, Donald Winch and John Burrow (eds.), *That Noble Science of Politics: a study in nineteenth-century intellectual history* (Cambridge, 1983). For an attempt to bridge the gap between thought and policy see Geraint Williams and Robert Pearson, *Political Thought and Public Policy in the Nineteenth Century* (1984).

Primary sources – those contemporary to the period – often frighten away readers for no good reason; and the timidity seems especially unfortunate in a period so rich in printed diaries and correspondence. Not everyone will want to cope with the Gladstone–Granville correspondence edited with such distinction by Agatha Ramm some years ago, though their four volumes remain essential reading for students of foreign policy and high politics: see Agatha Ramm (ed.), *The Political Correspondence of Mr. Gladstone and Lord Granville 1868–76* (Royal Historical Society, Camden series, 3s, LXXXI-II, 2 vols., 1952); and *1876–86* (2 vols., Oxford, 1962). *The Amberley Papers* (ed., Bertrand and Patricia Russell, 2 vols., 1937) hold no such terrors. Nor does the Carlingford diary, with its unique invigilation of Gladstone's behaviour (A.B. Cooke and John Vincent [eds.], *Lord Carlingford's Journal: reflections of a cabinet minister, 1885* [Oxford, 1971]). And if the calendar of extracts from contemporary diaries and letters printed in A.B. Cooke and John Vincent's *The Governing Passion: cabinet government and party politics in Britain 1885–6* (Brighton, 1974) seems a little overwhelming, it also presents an unrivalled flavour of what it must have been *like* to be a senior politician when Liberal politics was falling apart in the 1880s. In the days before and during the First World War when Liberalism was supposed to be strangely dying (again), the diaries of Lord Riddell (*More Pages From my Diary* [1934]) and the correspondence of Asquith with his confidante (Michael and Eleanor Brock [eds.], *Asquith: letters to Venetia Stanley* [Oxford, 1982]) likewise give the image a certain three-dimensionality. For the twilight years when all was long lost, go first to Liberals' autobiographies where they all think themselves young again and refight the old battles from the winning side, or sometimes the side that ought to have won. What passion there is in Viscount Grey's refusal to put any passion at all into his *Twenty Five Years 1892–1916* (2 vols., 1925). What sense of commission and allegation lies behind Margot Asquith's ommission and expiation in her notorious *Autobiography* (2 vols., 1920).

Index